D1546300

THE GENERAL WILL BEFORE ROUSSEAU

STUDIES IN MORAL, POLITICAL,
AND LEGAL PHILOSOPHY

General Editor: Marshall Cohen

THE GENERAL WILL
BEFORE ROUSSEAU

The Transformation of the Divine into the Civic

Patrick Riley

JC
328.2
.R55
1986

PRINCETON UNIVERSITY PRESS
PRINCETON, NEW JERSEY

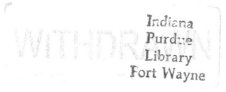

Indiana
Purdue
Library
Fort Wayne

Copyright © 1986 by Princeton University Press
Published by Princeton University Press,
41 William Street,
Princeton, New Jersey 08540
In the United Kingdom:
Princeton University Press, Guildford, Surrey

All Rights Reserved

Library of Congress Cataloging in Publication Data
will be found on the last printed page of this book
ISBN 0-691-07720-7

Publication of this book has been aided by a grant
from The Andrew W. Mellon Foundation

This book has been composed in Linotron Palatino

Clothbound editions of Princeton University Press books
are printed on acid-free paper, and binding materials
are chosen for strength and durability

Printed in the United States of America
by Princeton University Press
Princeton, New Jersey

For Judith N. Shklar
Non est auctoritas super terram qui comparetur ei.

CONTENTS

PREFACE

This is a study of the transformation of a theological idea, the general will of God to save all men, into a political one, the general will of the citizen to place the common good of the city above his particular will as a private self, and thereby to "save" the polity. It is a transformation that took place, in French moral and political thought, between the death of Pascal—the first great writer on general will—in 1662, and the publication, precisely a century later of the work that gave general will a permanently secular and political meaning, Rousseau's *Du contrat social* (1762).[1] Perhaps, however, "transformation" is too strong a term, for a careful reading of Pascal's *Ecrits sur la Grâce* and *Pensées* shows that he recommended generality of will to human beings as readily as he found it in God, and Rousseau's theology is as devoted to generality, to nonparticularity, as is his politics. Perhaps one should say, more carefully, that between 1662 and 1762 the general will of the citizen waxes a bit, the general will of God wanes a little, but that Pascal and Rousseau (and between them Malebranche, Bayle, and

---

[1] The best studies of the historical development of the general will are Judith N. Shklar's "General Will," in *Dictionary of the History of Ideas*, ed. Philip P. Wiener (New York: Charles Scribner's Sons, 1973), vol. 2, pp. 275ff., and Alberto Postigliola's "De Malebranche à Rousseau: Les Apories de la volonté générale et la revanche du 'raisonneur violent,' " in *Annales de la Société Jean-Jacques Rousseau* (Geneva: Chez A. Jullien, 1980), vol. 39, pp. 134ff. (The author is greatly indebted to M. André Robinet, general editor of the *Oeuvres complètes de Malebranche* [Paris: Vrin, 1958—], for having called his attention—during the 1980 Leibniz Congress at Ferrara—to the studies of Sig. Postigliola. The latter, in turn, generously invited the author to present a much-shortened version of what are now chapters 1, 3, and 5 of the present work as a lecture at the Istituto Universitario Orientale, Naples, in December 1982. The comments of Sig. Postigliola, and of

Montesquieu) looked at everything—God, nature, human nature—in the light of general lawfulness. One tends to think of Pascal as "theologian," Rousseau as "political theorist"; but both had a universal range and cherished *généralité* throughout that range. This is not surprising, for Pascal and Rousseau worried about the justice of God, the rightfulness of the divine operation, just as they worried about the justice of men. For both thinkers, justice was intimately linked to generality, general lawfulness, the absence of "particular" exceptions and favors.

When one is looking for something—influence, for example—one fails to find it only if one is lacking in ingenuity. But that same ingenuity is ingenious enough to construct the object of its search, and to take that construction for a discovery. Thus, it is well to be aware that, when one seeks the antecedents of Rousseauean general will in Pascal, Malebranche, Bayle, and others, one will inevitably, if not construct, at least bring out and heighten the "forward-looking" elements that "foreshadow" Rousseau; this is even necessary, if one's aim is not to offer a perfectly rounded portrait of those earlier figures, but to throw into relief the "occasional causes" of general will in its greatest advocate, Jean-Jacques Rousseau. All of this will make Pascal, Malebranche, and Bayle seem even more "pre-Rousseauean" or "proto-Rousseauean" than they are; the only antidote is to mention (at least *en passant*) the things that

his colleagues and students in Naples, have been very valuable.) To be treated with some reservations is the history of general will offered by C. W. Hendel in his generally very fine *Jean-Jacques Rousseau, Moralist* (Oxford: Clarendon Press, 1934), vol. 1, pp. 100ff., for reasons stated in chapter 4 of the present work. One should also consult the short but excellent history of *volonté générale* in Bertrand de Jouvenel's "Essai sur la politique de Rousseau," which introduces his edition of *Du contrat social* (Geneva, 1947); de Jouvenel brings out in particular the *rapports* between Pascal and Rousseau. There are brief but helpful comments in Robert Wokler's fine essay, "The Influence of Diderot on Rousseau," in *Studies on Voltaire and the 18th Century* (Banbury: Voltaire Foundation, 1975), vol. 132, pp. 68ff., and in André Robinet's exhaustive *Système et existence dans l'oeuvre de Malebranche* (Paris: Vrin, 1965), pp. 83ff.

make Pascal Pascal and that keep him from turning into Rousseau *avant la lettre*.

Standing between Pascal and Rousseau, the poles between whom general will worked itself out over a century's time, the great figure is the Oratorian Father Nicolas Malebranche (1638-1715). One may reasonably doubt whether general will would have caught on as a general idea had not Malebranche made it the heart of his most controversial work, the *Traité de la nature et de la grâce* (1680), the final edition of which appeared in 1712, precisely fifty years after the death of Pascal and fifty years before the publication of *Du contrat social*.[2] For it was Malebranche's *Traité*, more than Pascal's writings, that made general will the center of a philosophical controversy that finally drew in Arnauld, Leibniz, Fénelon, Bossuet, Fontenelle, Bayle, Montesquieu, and dozens of lesser figures; and it was other Malebranchian ideas—those of "order," "occasionalism," and moral "relations of perfection"—that shaped those parts of later French thought that were not primarily colored by "general will."[3] Since Malebranche's practical thought is as little known outside France as it is inherently interesting and historically influential, the middle part of this study will be taken up with the Oratorian Father, without whom "general will" might have died out with the death of Pascal.[4]

[2] The best general study of Malebranche's influence on later French philosophy is certainly Ferdinand Alquié's *Le Cartésianisme de Malebranche* (Paris: Vrin, 1974); see particularly the four Appendices entitled "Malebranche et Kant."

[3] For a good account of the Malebranche-criticisms of Arnauld, Bossuet, Fénelon, Leibniz et al., see Ginette Dreyfus's Introduction to her edition of Malebranche's *Traité de la nature et de la grâce*, 1680 ed. (Paris: Vrin, 1958), passim. A splendid account of Bayle's views on Malebranche is to be found in Elisabeth Labrousse, *Pierre Bayle* (The Hague: Martinus Nijhoff, 1964), vol. 2, pp. 187ff.

[4] Malebranche's philosophy seems to be enjoying a kind of renaissance in the English-speaking world; the last few years have seen the publication of Charles J. McCracken's *Malebranche and British Philosophy* (Oxford: Clarendon Press, 1983), which contains a reliable eighty-page essay on Malebranche's thought followed by excellent chapters discussing the relation of

PREFACE

In the end—to say it at the beginning—the "generality" cherished by Pascal, Malebranche, Bayle, Montesquieu, and Rousseau turns out to occupy a place midway between *particularity* and *universality*, and that *généralité* is something distinctively French. This becomes visible if one contrasts French moral-political thought with that of Kant, viewed as the perfect representative of German rationalistic universalism ("I am never to act otherwise than so that I could also will that my maxim should become a universal law . . . reason extorts from me immediate respect for such [universal] legislation"),[5] and with that of William Blake, seen as a typical representative of English ethical "empiricism":

> He who would do good to another
> must do it in Minute Particulars,
> General Good is the plea
> of the scoundrel, hypocrite and flatterer.[6]

The discovery of an *ethos* that rises above "minute particulars," that moves toward universality but has its reasons for not building *on* reason, and for drawing up short at a more modest "generality"—the advocacy of a kind of willing that is more than egoistic and self-loving and *particulière* but less than a Kantian, universal, "higher" will[7]—that is the distinctively French contribution to practical thought

Malebranche to Locke, Berkeley, and Hume (as well as to English *malebranchistes* such as Norris), and of a new translation—the first in three centuries—of Malebranche's *De la recherche de la vérité* (*The Search after Truth*, trans. T. M. Lennon and P. J. Olskamp [Columbus: Ohio State University Press, 1980]), which has as an appendix a valuable "philosophical commentary" on Malebranchism by Lennon.

[5] Immanuel Kant, *Fundamental Principles of the Metaphysic of Morals*, trans. T. K. Abbott (Indianapolis: Library of Liberal Arts, 1949), pp. 19-21. For a full commentary on this passage, see the author's *Kant's Political Philosophy* (Totowa, N.J.: Rowman and Littlefield, 1983), pp. 38ff.

[6] Blake's lines are quoted by A. J. Ayer in *Part of My Life* (New York: Oxford University Press, 1977), p. 176. Cf. Blake's remarks on Sir Joshua Reynolds's *Discourses*: "To Generalise is to be an Idiot. To Particularise is the Alone Distinction of Merit. All Sublimity is founded on Minute Discrimination." Cited by Kenneth Clark in *Moments of Vision* (New York: Harper and Row, 1981), p. 9.

[7] Shklar's phrase in "General Will," p. 279.

worked out by Rousseau, who socialized the "general will" bequeathed to him by his greatest French predecessors. The genesis of "general will" is in God; the creation of the political concept—yielding a covenant and law that is a mosaic of the Mosaic, the Spartan, the Roman, and the Lockean—is the testament of Rousseau.

ACKNOWLEDGMENTS

The General Will before Rousseau, which aims to uncover the hidden seventeenth-century theological roots of Rousseau's most famous political concept, stands to Rousseau himself as art-history stands to art or music-history to music: as something secondary but not inconsequential. It is helpful to know that Raphael's Peruginesque sweetness was transformed by the sight of Michelangelo's Sistine power; but what finally matters is the *School of Athens* or the *Disputà.* It is useful to learn that Mozart drew together the Italian *buffo,* French *galant,* and German contrapuntal styles; but what finally matters is the *Jupiter Symphony* or *Don Giovanni.* It is interesting to find out that Rousseau inherited "general will" from a long line of distinguished French theologians; but what finally matters is *Émile* or *Du contrat social, en soi.* The history of ideas is no substitute for ideas, just as musicology is no substitute for musicianship—as we have learned through some unmusical "authentic" performances; but a little extra second-order light thrown on great works is always welcome. At the opening of *De l'esprit des lois* Montesquieu quotes Correggio's *ed io anche son pittore;* if one cannot be a painter, one can at least remove time-yellowed varnish and restore original colors.

The greatest satisfaction a scholar can know is to have his work intelligently appreciated by the most qualified judges. And if those judges—when the veil of anonymity is finally lifted—turn out to be one's friends, then the satisfaction is multiplied. There are no greater experts on "the general will" than Judith Shklar and George Armstrong Kelly; their praise of what was sound in my manuscript encouraged Princeton to publish it, and their criticism of what was defective led me to try to improve it. (Need I add that while the better things in the manuscript are often traceable to Shklar and Kelly, the remaining defects are wholly my fault?)

To Judith Shklar, who first roused my interest in Rousseau, and whose *Men and Citizens* (just re-issued by Cambridge University Press) is the finest study of Rousseau in English, I dedicate this book. Her definitive article, "The General Will" (*Dictionary of the History of Ideas*), has served me as a model and inspiration, and in a sense the present book is just a filling-in of the interstices of that article. For twenty years I have been the beneficiary of her generosity and knowledge, and it is a pleasure to acknowledge that by making *The General Will before Rousseau* a kind of *hommage à Shklar.*

My debt to George Armstrong Kelly—that charming and generous scholar—is scarcely much smaller. He provided a thorough, searching "Reader's Report" on my manuscript for Princeton; and it is due to his suggestions that I added a substantial, much-needed passage on Rousseau's "Letter to Voltaire on Providence"—one of Rousseau's most important defenses of *généralité.* To have so learned a friend is a constant joy.

If I owe most to two old friends, I have also received invaluable aid from others. Pride of place must go to Sig. Alberto Postigliola, Secretary of the Italian Society for 18th Century Studies and Professor at the Istituto Universitario Orientale, Naples. His splendid essay, "De Malebranche à Rousseau" (*Annales Jean-Jacques Rousseau*), provided me with many ideas, and his kind invitation brought me to Naples in December 1982 to present much of my work in the form of a (lengthy!) lecture.

My acquaintance with Sig. Postigliola I owe to Professor André Robinet (Paris and Brussels), general editor of the critical edition of the *Oeuvres complètes* of Malebranche (Paris: Vrin, 1958—). A thoughtful letter from him (1980) both introduced me to Sig. Postigliola and encouraged me to finish my work. (It is to my old friend Dr. Gerda Utermöhlen of the Leibniz-Archiv, Hannover, that I owe in turn my introduction to Professor Robinet: the chain of one's debts, Marley-like, is long! And thanks to Dr. Utermöhlen I was able to hold and touch the letters exchanged by Malebranche and Leibniz; that physical contact strengthens one's conviction that these men are dead only in the most trivial sense.)

I am also indebted to a number of libraries and archives in both Europe and America. The Bibliothèque Nationale, Paris, permitted me to examine and copy several extremely rare works; the Bibliothèque d'Honfleur, Calvados, let me work with the manuscript of Malebranche's last work, the *Réflexions sur la Prémotion Physique*, while overlooking a view often painted by Monet; the Bibliothèque du Musée Calvet, Avignon, supplied a copy of a rare edition of Pascal's *Pensées*. I was enabled to work with various Leibniz-manuscripts not just by the Leibniz-Archiv, Hannover, but also through the kindness of the British Museum, London, the Bodleian Library, Oxford, the Biblioteca Nazionale, Florence, and the Österreichische Staatsbibliothek, Vienna.

In the United States I have received valuable help from the rare book department of the Library of the University of Wisconsin, Madison, which let me work uninterruptedly with a fine copy of Jansenius's *Augustinus* (1640). To have so excellent a library at one's home institution, run by a knowledgeable and attentive staff, makes all work lighter. But I have also received much-appreciated aid from the Houghton Library, Harvard (rare editions of Pascal); the Robbins Philosophy Library, Harvard (rare English translations of Malebranche); the rare book collections of Yale and Princeton Universities; the Library Company of Philadelphia; and the Library of the University of Iowa (which supplied a photocopy of the English translation of Malebranche's *Treatise of Morality*).

I am also deeply indebted to the Graduate School of the University of Wisconsin, Madison, for giving me a Romnes

Fellowship that made European research possible in 1980, and for giving me a summer grant in 1982. And the Department of Political Science in Madison has for thirteen years provided me with a home, learned and congenial colleagues, and a fine work-atmosphere. For all of these I am well and truly grateful.

As this book goes to press, I have learned of the death of Ferdinand Alquié—the greatest French Malebranche-scholar of his generation (together with Henri Gouhier). The impress of Alquié's *Le cartésianisme de Malebranche* (1974) is visible on almost every page of my book, and the death of so brilliant an historian of philosophy is a blow not just to Malebranche studies but to the understanding of Descartes and Kant as well.

I will add only, finally, that without my wife's patience and forbearance this work would never have appeared. It was she who put up with my absences, and who is a presence who makes my whole scholarly life possible. She was also a fine judge of *The General Will before Rousseau*, and could well have produced the work herself. No one has ever been helped more than I, and in a sense I am only the person who has actually written down what should be viewed as a collaborative effort.

Cambridge, Massachusetts
August 1985

THE GENERAL WILL BEFORE ROUSSEAU

O N E

THE GENERAL WILL ESTABLISHED: FROM PAUL AND AUGUSTINE TO PASCAL AND MALEBRANCHE

"The phrase 'general will,' " says the eminent Rousseau scholar Judith Shklar, "is ineluctably the property of one man, Jean-Jacques Rousseau. He did not invent it, but he made its history."[1] And he made that history by giving the notion of *volonté générale* a central place in his political and moral philosophy. Rousseau himself insists that "the general will is always right,"[2] that it is "the will that one has as a citizen"—when one thinks of the common good and not of one's own "particular will" (*volonté particulière*) as a "private person."[3] Even virtue, he says, is nothing but a conforming of one's personal *volonté particulière* to the public *volonté générale*—a conforming that "leads us out of ourselves," out of egoism and self-love, and toward "the public happiness."[4] If this is well known, it is perhaps only slightly less well known that, at roughly the same time as Rousseau, Diderot used the notions of *volonté générale* and

[1] Judith N. Shklar, "General Will," in *Dictionary of the History of Ideas*, ed. Philip P. Wiener (New York: Charles Scribner's Sons, 1973), vol. 2, p. 275. This fine article should be read as a supplement to Shklar's magisterial *Men and Citizens: A Study of Rousseau's Social Theory*.

[2] Jean-Jacques Rousseau, *Du contrat social*, in *Political Writings*, ed. C. E. Vaughan (Oxford: Basil Blackwell, 1962), vol. 2, pp. 50. (All translations from the French are the author's, unless otherwise indicated.)

[3] Ibid., pp. 35-36.

[4] Rousseau, *Economie politique*, in *Political Writings*, vol. 1, pp. 255ff.; Rousseau, "Le Bonheur Public," in *Political Writings*, vol. 1, pp. 327-329.

volonté particulière in his *Encyclopédie* article, "Droit naturel" (1755), saying that the general will is the rule of conduct that arises from a "pure act of the understanding," an understanding that "reasons in the silence of the passions about what a man can demand of his fellow-man and what his fellow-man has a right to demand of him." It is "to the general will that the individual man must address himself," Diderot adds, "in order to know how far he must be a man, a citizen, a subject, a father, a child"; and that *volonté générale*, which "never errs," is "the tie of all societies."[5]

But if, as Shklar correctly insists, Rousseau "made the history" of the "general will" without inventing it, who, then, should be credited with the invention? Not Diderot; for, as Shklar shows, Montesquieu had already used the terms *volonté générale* and *volonté particulière* in the most famous book (11) of *De l'esprit des lois* (1748).[6] But, where, then, did Montesquieu find those ideas? And how could he count on their being immediately understood, since he used them without explaining them?

The mystery is solved when one realizes that the term *volonté générale* was well established in the seventeenth century, though not primarily as a political idea. In fact, the notion of "general will" was originally a theological one, referring to the *kind* of will that God (supposedly) had in deciding who would be granted grace sufficient for salvation and who would be consigned to hell. The question at issue was: if "God wills that all men be saved"—as St. Paul asserts in a letter to his disciple Timothy[7]—does he have a *general will* that produces universal salvation? And if he does not, why does he will *particularly* that some men not be

---

[5] Denis Diderot, "Droit naturel," in Rousseau, *Political Writings*, vol. 1, pp. 432-433. Cf. Diderot's "Avertissement" to vol. 8 of the *Encyclopédie*, in which he argues for "the superiority of *morale universelle* to all *morales particulières*, which inspire hatred and trouble, and which break or weaken the *lien général et commun*" (cited in P. Hermand, *Les Idées morales de Diderot* [Paris: Presses Universitaires de France, 1923], p. 128).

[6] Shklar, "General Will," pp. 275-276.

[7] 1 Tim. 2:4.

saved? There was a further question as well, namely, whether God can justly save some and condemn others, particularly if (as St. Augustine asserted) those whom God saves are rescued not through their own merit but through unmerited grace conferred by the will of God.[8] From the beginning, then, the notions of divine *volonté générale* and *volonté particulière* were parts of a larger question about the justice of God; they were always "political" notions, in the largest possible sense of the word "political"—in the sense that even theology is part of what Leibniz called "universal jurisprudence."[9] The whole controversy over God's "general will" to save all men—and how this is to be reconciled with the (equally scriptural) notion that "many are called but few are chosen"[10]—was very precisely summed up in a few words from the last work (*Entretiens de Maxime et de Thémiste*, 1706) of Leibniz's contemporary and correspondent, Pierre Bayle: "The God of the Christians wills that all men be saved; he has the power necessary to save them all; he lacks neither power nor good will, and nonetheless almost all men are damned."[11] The effort to explain this state of affairs led directly to the original theory of *volonté générale*.

The controversy about the nature of divine justice is nearly as old as Christian philosophy itself; it was fully aired in the struggles between St. Augustine and the Pelagians, and resurfaced in seventeenth-century disputes about grace between the Jansenists and the Jesuits.[12] The actual terms "general will" and "particular will," however, are not to be found in Augustine or Pelagius, nor, for that

---

[8] At least, this is how many seventeenth-century Augustinians such as Pascal read St. Augustine.

[9] G. W. Leibniz, *Opinion on the Principles of Pufendorf*, in *The Political Writings of Leibniz*, ed. and trans. Patrick Riley (Cambridge: Cambridge University Press, 1972), p. 3.

[10] Matt. 22:14.

[11] Pierre Bayle, *Entretiens de Maxime et de Thémiste*, cited in Elisabeth Labrousse, *Pierre Bayle* (The Hague: Martinus Nijhoff, 1964), vol. 2, p. 377.

[12] Nigel Abercrombie, *The Origins of Jansenism* (Oxford: Clarendon Press, 1936), pp. 3-47, 93ff. A reliable work, though Abercrombie inclines toward Molinism and doubts the orthodoxy of Jansenism.

matter, in Jansenius's *Augustinus* or in the Jesuit Molina—though Jansenius uses the phrase *volonté particulière* once, in passing, in his last extant letter to St.-Cyran.[13] Those terms, in fact, are the modern successors to the Scholastic distinction between the "antecedent" and the "consequent" will of God: according to this doctrine, God willed "antecedently" (or generally) that all men be saved, but after the Fall of Adam he willed "consequently" (or particularly) that only some be saved.[14] The distinction between antecedent and consequent divine will is to be found in Scholastic philosophy as late as Suarez,[15] and even Leibniz used the terms "general" and "particular" interchangeably with the older words,[16] as did Antoine Arnauld, the great Port-Royal logician.[17]

So far as diligent inquiry will reveal, the first work of consequence to use the actual term "general will" was Antoine Arnauld's *Première Apologie pour M. Jansénius* (1644). This work was written to refute a series of anti-Jansenist sermons that had been preached by the theologian Isaac Habert in the Cathedral of Notre-Dame (1642-1643) at the express order of Cardinal Richelieu.[18] (Quite early on, then,

---

[13] Cornelis Jansenius, "172ᵉ Lettre à St.-Cyran" (23 March 1635) in *Les Origines du Jansénisme* I: *Correspondance de Jansénius*, ed. Jean Orcibal (Paris: Vrin, 1947), p. 585. Complaining of the distractions that are keeping him from producing *Augustinus*, Jansenius nonetheless says, "Je crois que ces divertissemens mesmes me sont donnez par une volonté particulière de Dieu."

[14] The Scholastic distinction between "antecedent" and "consequent" will was perfected by Leibniz in sections 22-25 of his *Thiodicée*.

[15] Francesco Suarez, *De divina substantia*, in *Opera omnia* (Paris, 1856), vol. 1, pp. 221ff. Suarez treats antecedent and consequent will precisely with reference to St. Paul's letter to Timothy.

[16] Leibniz, *Theodicy*, ed. A. Farrer (New Haven: Yale University Press, 1952), p. 137: "God wills antecedently the good [e.g., the general salvation of all men] and consequently the best [e.g., the particular salvation of some men]."

[17] Antoine Arnauld, *Réflexions philosophiques et théologiques sur le nouveau système de la nature et de la grâce* (Cologne, 1685), p. 198.

[18] J. Paquier, *Le Jansénisme* (Paris: Librairie Bloud, 1909), pp. 159ff.; Alexander Sedgwick, *Jansenism in Seventeenth-Century France* (Charlottesville: University Press of Virginia, 1977), pp. 50ff.

volonté générale figured in high politics: it didn't have to wait for Robespierre's transmogrified Rousseaueanism, for the claim that the Committee of Public Safety constituted the general will.)[19] Richelieu may well have ordered Habert's anti-Jansenist sermons for the wrong reasons—he was convinced that Jansenius had written a famous anti-French libel called *Mars gallicus*, accusing Richelieu of aiding German Protestants during the Thirty Years' War. Although this proposition is by no means certain,[20] Habert preached publicly against Jansenius at Richelieu's command, and Arnauld, in refuting Habert, developed the notion of *volonté générale*. Even a mistake can give rise to consequential doctrines: Richelieu may have aimed to strike *Mars gallicus* obliquely by hitting *Augustinus* directly, but what he essentially produced was an occasion for the idea of general will to be thrust forward in a publicly conspicuous way.

Before Arnauld's *Première Apologie*, certainly, one does not find the term *volonté générale* in the place or at the time that one might reasonably expect to find it. It does not appear, for example, in the protracted exchange of letters between Descartes' associate Father Mersenne and the Calvinist theologian André Rivet, though the most interesting of these letters date from 1640 (the year of *Augustinus*'s publication) and deal precisely with the universality or nonuniversality of salvation. In these letters Père Mersenne asserts that, in order to avoid horror and desperation, one must believe that "God does not will the damnation of anyone, but [wills] that each be saved, if he wills to cooperate

---

[19] M. Robespierre, *Textes choisis*, ed. J. Poperen (Paris: Editions Sociales, 1958), passim. In his address entitled "Sur les principes de morale politique qui doivent guider la convention nationale dans l'administration intérieure de la république" (February 1794), Robespierre begs that no one permit "qu'aucun intérêt particulier et caché puisse usurper ici l'ascendant de la volonté générale de l'assemblée et la puissance indestructible de la raison." The Revolution's use of terror, he adds, is "moins un principe particulier qu'une conséquence du principe général de la démocratie appliqué aux plus pressants besoins de la patrie" (pp. 131, 118).
[20] Sedgwick, *Jansenism*, pp. 50ff.

in his salvation";[21] Rivet replies that, since many are damned, Mersenne's alleged universal salvation imputes to God "des désirs vains, et des volontés frustratoires" and tries to reestablish "the paradise of Origen," in which even the devils are included.[22] But if the Mersenne-Rivet letter exchange provided a perfect occasion to assert or deny a divine *volonté générale* to save all, the term did not actually appear; and this is probably an indication that before 1644 the expression was not current, even in the writings of a man such as Mersenne, who corresponded with every great figure of the age.[23]

How Jansenism should be defined is beyond the scope of this work; whether it was an orthodox (though severe) Augustinianism or a kind of heterodox semi-Calvinism need not be settled here.[24] What does matter, for present purposes, is that it was the conflict between Jansenism and its critics, Jesuit and otherwise, that served as the occasional cause of a revived dispute over the meaning of the scriptural assertion that "God wills that all men be saved." Justly or not, Jansenius's *Augustinus* was accused—first by Habert's Richelieu-inspired sermons, then by Nicolas Cornet, syndic of the Sorbonne,[25] then by a letter to the Pope drafted by Habert using Cornet's charges, and finally by several papal bulls, including *Cum occasione* and, much later, *Unigenitus*—of having maintained "five propositions" judged "heretical" and "scandalous." The last of the

---

[21] Marin Mersenne, *Correspondance du P[ère] Marin Mersenne*, ed. Cornelis de Waard (Paris: Editions du Centre National de la Recherche Scientifique, 1967), vol. 10, p. 219.

[22] Ibid., p. 287.

[23] Including Descartes (above all) and Hobbes.

[24] See Abercrombie, *Origins of Jansenism*, passim. For a vigorous, and even brilliant restatement of the thesis, originally enunciated by Arnauld and Nicole, that Jansenism was in no sense a "deviant sect," that it was simply what it claimed to be—a restoration of rightly understood Augustinianism—see Jean LaPorte, "Le Jansénisme," in *Etudes d'histoire de la philosophie française au XVIIe siècle* (Paris: Vrin, 1951), pp. 88ff., esp. p. 105: "Il n'y a plus de jansénisme, parce qu'au fond il n'y en a jamais eu."

[25] Sedgwick, *Jansenism*, pp. 50ff.

five propositions imputed to Jansenius asserted that "it is a semi-Pelagian error to say that Jesus Christ died or spilled his blood for all men without exception."[26] Whether the five propositions were, in fact or in effect, contained in the *Augustinus*, as the Jesuits maintained, or were malicious fabrications of Cornet and Habert designed to ruin the reputation of St. Augustine as *the* "doctor of grace," as the Jansenists insisted,[27] what is indisputable is that, when Jansenists such as Arnauld and Pascal tried to defend Jansenius, they had to show that the bishop of Ypres had correctly (that is, in the manner of St. Augustine) understood the notion that *Deus vult omnes homines salvos fieri*: that a truly general will to save all was fully reconcilable with the Jansenist notion that only the "elect" actually enter the Kingdom of Heaven. In short, had Jansenius and his principal apologists not tried to restrict radically the meaning of St. Paul's letter to Timothy, the question of just and justifiable "general will" might never have become one of the great disputes of the seventeenth century. The whole tradition of *volonté générale* thus began life as a mere gloss on a passing phrase in a letter of St. Paul.[28]

Antoine Arnauld, then, invented, or at least first made visible, the notion of general will; but he did this, ironically enough, as part of a Jansenist effort to minimize (without annihilating) the notion that all are saved, that salvation is "general." In Antoine Arnauld, the "general will" is as little general as possible. In the *Première Apologie pour M. Jansénius*, Arnauld acknowledges the nominal existence of a "general will of God to save all men" but immediately narrows this generality by insisting, with Jansenius, that it is "semi-Pelagian" to construe St. Paul's letter to Timothy *au*

---

[26] Ibid. For an excellent new study of the fifth proposition, see Lucien Ceyssens, "La Cinquième des Propositions condamnées de Jansénius: Sa portée théologique," in *Jansénius et le jansénisme dans les Pays-Bas*, ed. J. van Bavel (Louvain: Peeters, 1982).

[27] Paquier, *Le Jansénisme*, pp. 163ff.

[28] Ibid., pp. 150ff.

pied de la lettre, to understand divine *volonté générale* as requiring salvation "generally for all men in particular, without excepting any of them." God's saving will is "general," Arnauld argues, only in the sense that it applies "to all sorts of conditions, of ages, of sexes, of countries," but it does not rescue every last single man *en particulier*.[29] Indeed, he insists—and here Jansenist rigorism is at its clearest—that

> it is certain that the source of all the errors of the semi-Pelagians is [their] not being able to endure the absolute and immutable decree of God, who . . . chose, from all eternity, without any regard for merit, a certain number of men, whom he destined for glory; leaving the others in the common mass of perdition, from which he is not obliged to pull them.[30]

Since God is not obliged to pull all men from perdition, his "general will" to save them all is attenuated, to put it mildly. In slightly later works, such as his *Apologie pour les Saints Pères* (1651), Arnauld carries this attenuation further still. God's antecedent will for the salvation of all men, he insists, "is only a simple *velléité* and a simple wish, which involves no preparation of means" to effect; his *volonté générale* "is based only on a consideration of human nature in itself, which was created for salvation," but which, since the Fall, has richly deserved perdition. Actually, Arnauld goes on, one could even say that God had a *volonté générale* to save "the devils," who were once angels; but fallen angels, like fallen men, are now damned. All this is clearer, in Arnauld's view, if one sees that God's judgments, which are "very just" though "very secret," are like the decisions of an earthly judge who condemns a thief or a murderer to death, but who "at the same time wills and wishes, by an

---

[29] Arnauld, *Oeuvres de Messire Antoine Arnauld* (Brussels: Culture et Civilisation, 1967), vol. 15-16, pp. 184-185.
[30] Ibid., p. 246.

antecedent will," that the life of this criminal, considered simply "as a man and as a citizen," be saved.[31]

Obviously, Antoine Arnauld tries to weaken the force of "God wills that all men be saved" in two main ways: sometimes by diminishing the compass of "all," sometimes by shrinking the meaning of "will." As Jean la Porte has shown in his brilliant pro-Jansenist *La Doctrine de Port-Royal*, it is characteristic of St. Augustine and the Augustinians (including, usually, the Jansenists) to attempt to pare down the term "all," while it is typical of St. Thomas and the Thomists to deflate divine "will."[32] St. Augustine, in *De correptione et gratia* and in the *Enchiridion*, glosses "all" to mean all *kinds* of persons (of all professions, ages, sexes, countries); this equation of "all" with "some" (provided they are distributed over "all" categories) is most often favored by Arnauld. For the Augustinians, then, God wills to save not all men but all *sorts* of men; in the magnificent Latin of the *Enchiridion*,

> omnes homines omne genus hominum intelligamus per quascumque differentias distributum, reges, privatos, nobiles, ignobiles, sublimes, humiles, doctos, indoctos, integri corporis, debiles, ingeniosos, tardicordes, fatuos, divites, pauperes, mediocres, mares, feminas, infantes, pueros, adolescentes, juvenes, seniores, senes; in linguis omnibus, in moribus omnibus, in artibus omnibus, in professionibus omnibus.[33]

On this point, at least, the claim that Jansenius was a perfectly orthodox Augustinian seems warranted, for in the section of *Augustinus* entitled "De gratia Christi Salvatoris," Jansenius urges that, if one wants to avoid Pelagian and semi-Pelagian heresy in interpreting "God wills that all

---

[31] Arnauld, *Oeuvres*, vol. 18, p. 112.

[32] Jean LaPorte, *La Doctrine de Port-Royal: Les Vérités sur la grâce* (Paris: Vrin, 1923), pp. 250-251.

[33] St. Augustine, *Enchiridion*, in *Oeuvres de S. Augustin* (Paris: Desclée de Brouwer et Cie, 1947), vol. 9, p. 290.

men be saved," one must understand "all" to refer, not to a divine salvific will "for each and every single man" (*pro omnibus omnino singularibus hominibus*), but rather to a will for the salvation of every kind of man (*pro omni genere hominorum*)—Jews and Gentiles, servants and free men, public and private persons, wise and unwise. One should add, however, that in his effort to reduce "all" men to the "elect," Jansenius also relies on other Patristic writings. In particular, he invokes St. Prosper's argument that Christ died for all men only in the sense that his sacrifice was sufficient to redeem all, but that the actual effect of his death was to redeem only a few—or, as Jansenius paraphrases St. Prosper, "Christum omnes redimisse sufficienter, non efficienter."[34] Nonetheless, Jansenius relies mainly on St. Augustine and on the notion that "all" really means "some."

Aquinas's method, occasionally followed by Arnauld, as in the *Apologie pour les Saints Pères*, is very different. He preserves what one is tempted to call the natural meaning of "all"—La Porte calls it the "unforced" meaning[35]—and makes "will" the variable term, saying in *De veritate* that "God wills by an antecedent [or general] will that all men be saved, by reason of human nature, which he has made for salvation; but he wills by a consequent will that some be damned, because of the sins that are in them."[36]

In view of Arnauld's diminishing of "general will," whether by Augustinian or Thomistic means—a general will that he calls "inefficacious" and a mere wish, and that he compares to earthly death sentences for murder—it should come as no surprise that Arnauld particularly admired St. Augustine's *De correptione et gratia*, the anti-Pelagian work that is hardest on the general salvation of all men. So much did Arnauld relish this work, indeed, that he published a French translation of it in 1644, to which he added a somber and powerful introduction. In this intro-

---

[34] Jansenius, *Augustinus* (Louvain, 1640), book 3, chapter 20, p. 376.
[35] Cited in LaPorte, *Doctrine de Port-Royal*, p. 251.
[36] Ibid., pp. 251-252.

duction he warns Christians against falling into the "criminal pride" of the "Pelagians" and of the philosophers, who through "unhappy presumption" treat man as independent;[37] he once again minimizes the generality of salvation, this time nearly to the vanishing point:

> There are no mysteries which God hides so well from proud sages, as the mysteries of grace; for there are no others so opposed to the wise folly of the world, and to that spirit of pride which cannot suffer this sovereign Empire which God exercises over his creatures through his different judgments of pity and of justice— which can be secret, but which can only be very equitable, giving grace to some, because he is good, and not giving it to others, because he is just; and not doing wrong to anyone, because, all being guilty, he owes nothing to anyone, as St. Augustine says so many times.[38]

Here, of course, any general will to save all has all but disappeared. But even here, what remains of *volonté générale* has political and moral implications; after all, it is "just" and "equitable" that God not act on his original general wish that all be saved, because all are guilty and hence cannot rightly complain of not receiving the grace that would save them. In Arnauld, God's "equitable" operation, his "sovereign Empire," begins with a general will, even if it rightfully ends with something radically different—though Arnauld would have felt no need to defend God's cause had he not feared that giving grace to only some *might* be viewed as an inequitable and arbitrary "acceptation of persons."[39] It is one of the great ironies of the history of ideas that *volonté générale* should be thrust into prominence by a

---

[37] St. Augustine, *De la correction et de la grâce*, trans. Antoine Arnauld (Paris, 1644), p. 4.

[38] Ibid., p. 7.

[39] This, of course, was to be Rousseau's argument against unequally conferred grace in *La Nouvelle Héloïse*.

thinker who thought that will very little "general" indeed; it is a still greater irony that the greatest partisan of general will, Rousseau, should in his theological writings have denied flatly the "efficacious" grace and the predestination that, for Arnauld, are the very things that reduce *volonté générale* to a mere "inefficacious wish."[40]

If it was Antoine Arnauld who apparently invented the terms *volonté générale* and *volonté particulière*, it was a far greater Jansenist, Blaise Pascal, who was the first to use the notions of *généralité* and *particularité* in works (the *Pensées* and the *Ecrits sur la grâce*) that are still read. (The works of Arnauld, in forty-three enormous volumes, are today almost unknown.)[41] Even in Pascal's *Ecrits sur la grâce* (c. 1656), the notion of *volonté générale* has political overtones; he uses it in considering whether God can justly dispense sufficient grace for salvation only to those who merit it, or whether by *volonté absolue* he can simply damn some and save others. The notion of an arbitrary *volonté absolue* he connects with Calvinism (a doctrine "injurious to God and insupportable to men"), while the notion of *volonté générale* he traces to the disciples of St. Augustine. According to Pascal, Augustine's disciples believed that, before the Fall of Adam, "God had a *volonté générale et conditionnelle* to save all men," whereas after the Fall he willed, by a *volonté absolue* arising from pity, that some men still be saved, though none merited it. Pascal plainly favors this version of Augustinianism. The Calvinists, in denying that God ever, even before the Fall, had a *volonté générale* to save all men, fall into an "abominable opinion" that injures common sense; the Pelagians, in holding that God had a *volonté générale, égale et conditionelle* to save all men and that this *volonté générale* remained constant even after the Fall, so that God sent Christ

---

[40] Ibid.
[41] Except for the *Port-Royal Logic*, which has been repopularized through the efforts of Noam Chomsky.

into the world to help all men *merit* salvation, fall into an opposite excess by depriving God wholly of any *volonté absolue*, even after the sin of Adam.

Only Augustinianism, in combining a pre-Fall *volonté générale* with a post-Fall *volonté absolue*, Pascal says, strikes a proper balance between the polar errors of granting too much to God (Calvinism) or too much to men (Pelagianism).[42]

So anxious is Pascal to demonstrate the rightfulness of God's (Augustinian) operation—pre-lapsarian *volonté générale* followed by post-lapsarian *volonté absolue*—that he uses the word "justice" or its cognates no fewer than six times in the central paragraphs of the *Premier Ecrit sur la grâce*:

> In the condition of innocence, God could not with justice damn a single man. God could not even refuse to men the graces sufficient for their salvation.
>
> In the condition of corruption, God could with justice damn the entire mass; and those who are being born today without being rescued by baptism are damned and eternally deprived of the beatific vision, which is the greatest of evils.
>
> Considering these two conditions [which are] so different, they [the Augustinians] have formed two different opinions concerning the will of God for the salvation of men.
>
> They claim that, in connection with the state of innocence, God had a general and conditional will [*une volonté générale et conditionelle*] to save all men, provided that they willed it through free will, aided by sufficient graces which He gave them for their salvation, but which do not determine them infallibly to persevere in the good.
>
> But that Adam, having through his free will misused this grace, and having revolted against God through a

---

[42] Blaise Pascal, *Ecrits sur la grâce*, in *Oeuvres de Blaise Pascal*, ed. L. Brunschvicg (Paris: Librairie Hachette, 1914), vol. 11, pp. 133-152.

movement of his will and without the slightest impulsion from God (which would be destestable to imagine), has corrupted and infected the entire mass of men, such that humankind has become the just object of the anger and indignation of God. They understand that God has divided this mass, all equally guilty and wholly worthy of damnation; that He has willed to save a part [of the mass of men] through an absolute will based on His pure and gratuitous pity, and that, leaving the other part in its damnation and in which He could with justice leave the entire mass, He previewed either the particular sins that each [person] would commit, or at least the original sin of which they are all guilty, and that, following this prevision, He willed to condemn them.

"To this end," Pascal goes on, God "sent Jesus Christ to save absolutely and by very efficacious means those whom He has chosen and predestined from this mass," so that it was only for the chosen that Christ "willed absolutely to merit salvation through his death"; he "never had this same will for the salvation of the others who have not been delivered from this universal and just perdition." The Augustinians further believe

that, nonetheless, some of those who are not predestined have been called for the good of the Elect, and thus to participate in the redemption by Jesus Christ. That it is the fault of these persons [who are "called" but not predestined] that they do not persevere; that they could do so, if they willed, but that, since they are not of the number of the elect, God does not give them the efficacious graces without which they will never will it [salvation]. And thus there are three kinds of men: some who never come to the faith; others who come to it but who, not persevering, die in mortal sin; the last who come to the faith and who persevere in it with charity until death. Jesus Christ never had an absolute will that the first [group] receive the slightest grace through His death, since indeed they have received none.

He willed to redeem the second [group]; He gave them graces that would have led them to salvation, if they had used them well; but He did not will to give them that singular grace of perseverance, without which one cannot use [other graces] well.

But as for the final [group], Jesus Christ willed their salvation absolutely, and led them to it by certain and infallible means.[43]

That "final group," evidently, is no longer all men *en gé-néral*. Pascal, indeed, in accordance with his professed Augustinianism, follows the method of St. Augustine's *Enchiridion* in reducing the salvation of all men to a smaller "elected" number: "the elect of God form a universality which is sometimes called *a world* because they are scattered throughout the world, sometimes *all*, because they make up a totality, sometimes *several*, because they are several between themselves, sometimes *few*, because they are few in proportion to the totality of the abandoned."[44]

Pascal uses the notion of *volonté générale* only a handful of times in the *Ecrits sur la grâce*, and the corresponding notion of *volonté particulière* does not appear at all in these writings. But in the *Pensées*, Pascal uses the idea of *volonté particulière* in a striking way that reminds one of Rousseau. Beginning with the observation that *volonté* "will never be satisfied,

---

[43] Ibid., pp. 135-137.

[44] Ibid., pp. 148-149. The finest of all commentaries on the *Ecrits sur la grâce* is that of Jan Miel in his invaluable *Pascal and Theology* (Baltimore: Johns Hopkins Press, 1969), pp. 65ff., esp. p. 191: "In looking at Pascal's own attempts to write real theology—the so-called *Ecrits sur la Grâce*—we discover that although the doctrine is Jansenist, the style is not. Here Pascal shows not just a clarity and conciseness that contrast strongly with the style of an Arnauld, but as always an originality of approach." For an exhaustive study of Pascal's Augustinianism, based on a minute reading of the writings of both figures, see Philippe Sellier, *Pascal et Saint Augustin* (Paris: A. Colin, 1970), passim.

even if it should be capable of everything it wills," Pascal goes on to ask the reader to "imagine a body full of thinking members."

Imagine a body full of thinking members. . . . If the feet and the hands had a *volonté particulière*, they would never be in order except by submitting this *volonté particulière* to the *volonté première* which governs the whole body. Outside of it, they are in disorder and unhappiness; but in willing the good of the body, they will their own good. . . . If the foot was always ignorant of the fact that it belonged to the body and that there was a body on which it depended, if it had had only knowledge and love of itself, and if it came to know that it belonged to a body on which it depended, what regret, what confusion about its past life, to have been useless to the body which influenced its life.[45]

[45] Pascal, *Pensées*, in *Oeuvres*, vol. 2, pp. 381-384. The best recent treatment of this passage is to be found in the chapter on Pascal in Nannerl O. Keohane's *Philosophy and the State in France* (Princeton: Princeton University Press, 1980), p. 280: "There are a number of striking similarities between Pascal's ideal community and the secular version of such blessedness held out by Rousseau in the *Contrat social*. . . . In both communities, individuals lose the narrow self to discover the true self in the whole. . . . In both communities there is the same stress on the intimate connection between the body and its members, the harmonious subordination of the *volonté particulière* to the *volonté générale*." Keohane adds that, for will to be generalized, both Pascal and Rousseau require "the intervention of a suprahuman liberator": God for Pascal, the Legislator for Rousseau. Her interpretation is of the greatest value. In his "Pascal on Justice," in *The Review of Politics* 46 (April 1984), pp. 212ff., A. J. Beitzinger confines Pascal's notion of *volonté générale* to the religious sphere, denying it any political significance: "Accepting fully the common will of the Mystical Body, the 'hateful self' is annihilated and replaced by the 'redeemed self' which identifies with Christ. . . . The separated member becomes a 'thinking member' who works to better the world not in the love of power but in the power of love" (p. 238). For Beitzinger, this kind of membership both transcends and precludes "an identification with such ephemeral, provisional entities as . . . a Rousseauean 'general will' " (p. 239). Cf. the comparable argument of Jean Mesnard, *Pascal* (Paris: de Brouwer, 1965), p. 132, that the "body full of thinking members" is concerned only with "la subordination du chrétien au Christ." Granting the enormous differences that

To make it clear that he is thinking of bodies in general (including "bodies politic") and not just natural bodies, Pascal goes on to say that "one must incline to what is general: and leaning toward oneself is the beginning of all disorder, in war, in policy, in economy, in the particular body of man. Thus the will is depraved."[46] But that depravity can be overcome if we remember that "the members of [both] natural and civil communities incline toward the good of the body," that the members can rise above the "injustice" of self-absorption.[47] To be sure, an inclination toward a ruling *volonté première* is achieved in Pascal through unmerited grace, and in Rousseau through education; nonetheless, the parallel is striking. Thus, almost a century before Rousseau, the reader of Pascal could have learned that *volonté particulière* involves disorder and self-love and that not to incline toward *le général* is "unjust" and "depraved."[48]

One should be quite clear about what Pascal is doing, for it turns out to be absolutely decisive for the next century of French political and moral thought: for Malebranche, for Diderot, for Rousseau. In Pascal's *Ecrits sur la grâce, généralité* begins with God's pre-lapsarian "will" (recounted in 1 Timothy 2) that all men be saved. Then, this "general will," viewed as something divine, is transferred to another strand of Pauline doctrine—namely, the notion of a body and its members in 1 Corinthians 12. In Pascal's reworking (or rather, fusing) of Paul's letters, the members of the body should avoid *particularité* and *amour-propre* and should incline toward *le général* (the good of the body).[49] Just what Pascal has done becomes clear only if one looks at St. Paul's letter to the Corinthians, then compares Pascal's reading of it with a more orthodox and cautious one, such as John

---

separate Pascal and Rousseau, it still seems that Keohane has grasped something missed by Beitzinger and Mesnard.

[46] Pascal, *Pensées*, in *Oeuvres*, p. 385.

[47] Ibid. "Thus we are born unjust, for each inclines toward himself."

[48] Ibid. The *Ecrits sur la grâce*, however, were not fully published until 1908-1912.

[49] Ibid., pp. 381-385.

Locke's in his *Paraphrase and Notes* on 1 Corinthians, and, finally, looks at a representative reflection or echo of Pascal's operation in the century that comes after him.

St. Paul's letter, in the standard seventeenth-century English version, argued that

> the body is not one member, but many. If the foot shall say, 'Because I am not the hand, I am not of the body': is it therefore not of the body? . . . Now are they many members, yet but one body.
>
> And the eye cannot say unto the hand, 'I have no need of thee': nor again, the head to the feet, 'I have no need of you.'
>
> . . . There should be no schism in the body; but . . . the members should have the same care one for another.
>
> And whether one member suffer, all the members suffer with it: or one member be honoured, all the members rejoice with it.
>
> Now, ye are the body of Christ, and members in particular.[50]

Locke, with characteristic sobriety and caution, takes care to read St. Paul's letter as applying only to the church, and never extends the Pauline distinction between a body and its members to "bodies politic" in the manner of Pascal. "God," Locke carefully argues, "hath fitted several persons, as it were so many distinct members, to several offices and functions in the Church . . . if any one have not that function, or dignity, in the Church, which he desires . . . he does not thereby cease to be a member of the Church."[51] The almost obsessive repetition of "Church," together with the phrase "as it were"—which makes being a "member" *metaphorical*—clearly restricts St. Paul. Pascal, by contrast,

---

[50] St. Paul, 1 Cor. 12, cited by John Locke in *A Paraphrase and Notes on St. Paul's First Epistle to the Corinthians*, in *The Works of John Locke*, 11th ed. (London: Otridge & Son et al., 1812), vol. 8, pp. 168-169.

[51] Locke, *A Paraphrase and Notes*, vol. 8, p. 168.

brilliantly expands and politicizes St. Paul's letter with the superb imagination ("imagine a body full of thinking members") that Locke soberly and designedly avoids. (Given the doctrine of the *Second Treatise*, one would not expect Locke to view a body politic in the way that Pascal does; in that *Treatise*, members stand in a contractual, not an "organic," relationship.)[52]

For all those French *moralistes* who come after Pascal and who are struck by his reading of 1 Corinthians 12 (in the light, one might say, of 1 Timothy 2) men would do well to will as God first willed—generally. Here there is a large irony: men after the Fall must try to will generally, though their inability to will generally (*à la Dieu*) is what led to their Fall. They failed to imitate God when they were pure, and must now strive to do so while corrupt. No wonder Pascal hopes for unmerited grace![53]

That 1 Corinthians 12 (read in a more or less Pascalian way) continued to weigh heavily in the works of Pascal's successors is evident. Rousseau, for example, insists on the importance of the passage in his *Letter to Archbishop Beaumont*.[54] Sometimes, however, even in Pascal himself, Rousseau's secularization of *généralité* and body-membership is anticipated; in the *pensée* numbered 480 in the Brunschvicg edition, Pascal had reworked 1 Corinthians 12 into the claim that "to make the members happy, they must have one will, and submit it to the body."[55] And in his fragment called "Le Bonheur public," Rousseau further transmutes and secularizes language originally traceable to St. Paul and

---

[52] Cf. the author's *Will and Political Legitimacy: A Critical Exposition of Social Contract Theory in Hobbes, Locke, Rousseau, Kant and Hegel* (Cambridge, Mass.: Harvard University Press, 1982), chapter 3.

[53] Pascal, *Ecrits sur la grâce*, p. 150: "Les hommes sont sauvés ou damnés, suivant qu'il a pleu à Dieu de les choisir pour leur donner cette grâce dans la masse corrompue des hommes, dans laquelle il pouvoit avec justice les abandonner tous."

[54] Rousseau, *Lettre à Christophe de Beaumont*, in *Oeuvres complètes de Jean-Jacques Rousseau*, ed. B. Gagnebin and M. Raymond (Paris: Pléiade, 1969), p. 961.

[55] Pascal, *Pensées*, in *Oeuvres*, p. 386.

21

then socialized by Pascal: "Make man one, and you will make him as happy as he can be. . . . For being nothing except by [the body politic], they will be nothing except for her. To the force of constraint you have added that of will."[56]

To be sure, in *pensée* no. 480 Pascal is thinking of *any* "body full of thinking members," while in "Le Bonheur public" Rousseau is thinking (more particularly) of the city. Nonetheless, the lineal descent of Rousseau from St. Paul, read *à la* Pascal, is plain enough. This strand of Pascal's thought was certainly available to Rousseau. Though the so-called "Port-Royal" edition of the *Pensées* offered a truncated and rewritten version of Pascal's manuscripts, the 1678 enlarged edition contained Pascal's insistence that "tous les hommes sont membres de ce corps [de membres pensants]" and that "pour être heureux il faut qu'ils conforment leur volonté particulière à la volonté universelle qui gouverne le corps entier."[57]

Of course, these intimations of Rousseau are not the whole of Pascal's notion of justice; indeed, if one would believe some modern commentators, Pascal was a Montaigne-inspired *mondain* who argued for the absolute relativity of justice ("three degrees of latitude overturn the whole of jurisprudence")[58] and who was either a legal pos-

---

[56] Rousseau, "Le Bonheur Public," p. 326.

[57] Pascal, *Pensées*, 2d Port-Royal ed. (Paris: Chez Guillaume Desprez, 1678), pp. 268-269. See also the "Edition nouvelle" of 1699 (Amsterdam: Chez Henri Wetstein), copy in the Bibliothèque du Musée Calvet, Avignon (examined there in October 1982 by kind permission). In order to be sure which *pensées* were included in, or omitted from, the Port-Royal editions of 1670 and 1678, one should consult Mara Vamos's valuable "Pascal's *Pensées* and the Enlightenment," in *Studies on Voltaire and the 18th Century* (Banbury: Voltaire Foundation, 1972), vol. 97, pp. 5ff., esp. pp. 63-64: "Most French schoolboys would consider it child's play to pass an examination requiring that they identify the author of 'Le silence éternel de ces espaces infinis m'effraie.' . . . Yet Bayle, Vauvenargues, Rousseau, Voltaire, Diderot would have failed a quiz containing such identification questions. These lines, as well as numerous other memorable and thought-provoking ones, had been omitted from the Port-Royal *Pensées*."

[58] See Ira O. Wade, *The Intellectual Origins of the French Enlightenment* (Princeton: Princeton University Press, 1971), pp. 320-322.

itivist worse than Hobbes or a resurrection of Thrasy-machus.[59] This brittle, Pyrrhonist Pascal does indeed make some appearances in the *Pensées*. Who would want to ignore or explain away a passage as brilliant as the following?

> On what shall man found the order of the world which he would govern? Shall it be on the caprice of each individual? What confusion! Shall it be on justice? Man is ignorant of it.
>
> Certainly had he known it, he would not have established this maxim, the most general of all that obtain among men, that each should follow the custom of his own country. . . . We see neither justice nor injustice which does not change its nature with change of climate. . . . Fundamental laws change after a few years of possession; right has its epochs; the entry of Saturn into the Lion marks to us the origin of such and such a crime. A strange justice that is bounded by a river! Truth on this side of the Pyrenees, error on the other side.[60]

The argument that justice and injustice vary with "change of climate" is a striking anticipation of Montesquieu's relativism.[61] Perhaps, after all, such political skepticism and relativism would be natural to one who could say, as Pascal does in the *Pensées*, that if man considers "what he is in comparison with all existence" and regards himself as "lost in this remote corner of nature"—a "mean between nothing and everything," as much "miserable" as "great"—he will learn "to estimate at their true value the earth, kingdoms, cities and himself."[62] In Pascal there seems to be a gulf between *mondain* justice ("being unable

[59] S. M. Mason, *Montesquieu's Idea of Justice* (The Hague: Martinus Nijhoff, 1975), p. xii.

[60] Pascal, *Pensées*, trans. W. F. Trotter, intro. T. S. Eliot (New York: Dutton, 1958), p. 83.

[61] See chapter 4 of the present work.

[62] Pascal, *Pensées*, trans. Trotter, p. 17.

to make what is just strong, we have made what is strong just"),[63] which is comparatively inconsequential becaue it is not "infinite," and that justice which, in its *generality*, resembles the will of God before the Fall.[64]

Despite the importance of Pascal's linking up of *généralité* with the good of *le corps entier*—a collective good to which members must subordinate their *volonté particulière*—it remains true that the fullest and best-known seventeenth-century exposition of the notions of general will and particular will was certainly Malebranche's *Traité de la nature et de*

[63] Ibid., p. 85.

[64] There is also a third distinct notion of justice in Pascal—one that arises in connection with his account of the (fully justified) eternal damnation of unbaptized children. In the *Pensées* (no. 434) Pascal grants that "there is nothing which more shocks our reason" than to say that Adam's sin has "rendered guilty" later generations who, "being so removed from this source, seem incapable of participation in it." But this "transmission" seems to be more than merely shocking and unreasonable. "It seems also very unjust. For what is more contrary to the rules of our miserable justice than to damn eternally an infant incapable of will, for a sin wherein he seems to have had so little a share . . . ? Certainly nothing offends us more rudely than this doctrine." Pascal concludes that, despite the "shocking," "unreasonable," and apparently "unjust" character of this doctrine, we cannot dispense with it: "Man is more inconceivable without this mystery than this mystery is inconceivable to man." It is only human reason—"our miserable justice"—that is offended by the injustice of damnation: it is thus necessary that we abandon "the proud exertions of our reason" in favor of "the simple submissions of reason." The mere fact that a mystery is hidden from our reason does not mean that God cannot justify it. His justice will not resemble "our miserable justice," for our justice is "offended" by holding infants incapable of will accountable for acts committed six thousand years ago. As A.W.S. Baird has argued in his *Studies in Pascal's Ethics* (The Hague: Martinus Nijhoff, 1975), pp. 50-51, this "submission" of reason seems inconsistent with another part of the *Pensées* where Pascal urges that "if we submit everything to reason, our religion will have no mysterious and supernatural element" but quickly adds that "if we offend the principles of reason, our religion will be absurd and ridiculous." Pascal's fideism, while real enough, coexists a little uneasily with a vestigial rationalism. In the end, Pascal places three separate ideas of justice before his readers: the general, the merely legal ("justice is what is established"), and the mysterious or hidden (the justice of a *Deus absconditus*). If the last perhaps matters most to Pascal himself, that does not make his "generalism" unimportant, or his "body full of thinking members" less striking. The intimations of Rousseau are still present.

la grâce (1680). This work, which Leibniz called "admirable,"[65] was one of the most celebrated and controversial writings of its day. It was popularized and defended by Bayle in his journal, *Nouvelles de la république des lettres;*[66] it was attacked by the long-lived and boundlessly productive Arnauld in his *Réflexions philosophiques et théologiques sur le nouveau système de la nature et de la grâce* (1685—forty years after the *Première Apologie pour M. Jansénius);*[67] it was criticized by Fontenelle in his *Doutes sur le système physique des causes occasionnelles* (1686),[68] and, above all, by Bossuet in his *Oraison funèbre de Marie-Thérèse d'Autriche* (1683).[69] If Fénelon's highly critical *Réfutation du système du Père Malebranche sur la nature et la grâce* (c. 1687-1688) remained unpublished until 1829, his opinion of Malebranchian *volonté générale* was tolerably clear in the fourth (1709) of his *Lettres sur la grâce et la prédestination,* written for François Lami.[70] Malebranche defended his own work in an endless running polemic with Arnauld, terminated only by the latter's death in 1694.[71] As late as 1710, Leibniz devoted several large sec-

---

[65] Leibniz, *Theodicy*, p. 254.

[66] Bayle, *Nouvelles de la république des lettres* (May 1684) cited in N. Malebranche, *Oeuvres complètes de Malebranche*, ed. André Robinet (Paris: Vrin, 1966), vol. 8-9, pp. 1152ff.

[67] Arnauld, *Réflexions philosophiques et théologiques* (Cologne, 1685), passim. For a helpful commentary on the thought of Arnauld, see Jean Laporte, *La Doctrine de Port-Royal: La Morale (d'après Arnauld)* (Paris: Vrin, 1951), passim.

[68] B. Fontenelle, *Doutes sur le système physique des causes occasionnelles*, in *Oeuvres complètes* (Paris, 1818), vol. 1, pp. 627ff.

[69] J. B. Bossuet, *Oraison funèbre de Marie-Thérèse d'Autriche*, in *Oeuvres de Bossuet*, ed. B. Velat and Y. Champailler (Paris: Pléiade, 1961), p. 110. See Theodore Delmont, *Bossuet et les Saints Pères* (Geneva: Slatkine, 1970), p. 590ff.

[70] Fénelon, *Réfutation du système du Père Malebranche sur la nature et la grâce*, in *Oeuvres de Fénelon* (Paris: Chez Lefèvre, 1835), vol. 2, pp. 232ff. The fourth of the *Lettres sur la grâce* was published as early as 1718 in Fénelon, *Oeuvres spirituelles* (Antwerp, 1718). A fine commentary on the *Réfutation* is to be found in Henri Gouhier, *Fénelon philosophe* (Paris: Vrin, 1977), pp. 33ff. This book is also the best general introduction to French religious and moral thought in the seventeenth century; see the author's review in *The Philosophical Review* 90 (1981), pp. 285-289.

[71] For a good brief account of this polemic, see Ginette Dreyfus's Intro-

tions of his *Théodicée* to a spirited defense of Malebranche's "general will."[72]

If, then, the notions of *volonté générale* and *volonté particulière* were elaborately treated over a seventy-year period (c. 1644-1715) in published writings of figures as eminent as Pascal, Malebranche, Arnauld, Bayle, Fénelon, Bossuet, Fontenelle, and Leibniz, they can scarcely be said to arise— at least as *terms*—only with Diderot and Rousseau; the only question is whether the original (mainly Malebranchian) formulation of the notions has any political content, or at least political implications.

Even in his first work, *De la recherche de la vérité* (1674-1675), Malebranche had already politicized the (originally theological) general-particular distinction. In a passage that looks back to Pascal (and 1 Corinthians 12) as much as forward to Rousseau, Malebranche argues that even those who work for "their particular interests [*leurs intérêts particuliers*]" can unintentionally advance *le bien public*, provided their secret desire for greatness is moderated by some respect for civility.

> But if all individuals [*tous les particuliers*] seem to be what they really are, if they say frankly to others that they want to be the principal parts of the body they compose, and never the least, this would not be the means for men to join together. All the members of a body cannot be its head or its heart; there must be feet and hands, small as well as great, people who obey as

---

duction to Malebranche's *Traité de la nature et de la grâce*, in Malebranche, *Oeuvres complètes*, vol. 5, pp. xxxviiiff. For a fuller account, see Dreyfus's edition of *Nature et grâce*, 1680 ed. (Paris: Vrin, 1958), pp. 47ff.

[72] Leibniz, *Theodicy*, pp. 254ff. For a fuller view of the Malebranche-Leibniz *rapport*, see André Robinet, *Malebranche et Leibniz: Relations personnelles* (Paris: Vrin, 1955), esp. pp. 403ff. See also Gaston Grua, *Jurisprudence universelle et théodicée selon Leibniz* (Paris: Presses Universitaires de France, 1953), pp. 192ff.

well as those who command. And if each should say openly that he wants to command and never obey, as indeed each naturally wishes, it is clear that all political bodies [*tous les corps politiques*] would destroy themselves, and that disorder and injustice would reign over all.[73]

Here, as in all of Malebranche, unlimited pursuit of *intérêt particulier* is linked to "disorder," "injustice," and "the dissolution of society," while love for a general *bien public* yields "civility" (if not quite "charity").

But it was Malebranche's *Traité de la nature et de la grâce* that constituted his most important contribution to the notion of general will. The occasional cause of *Nature et grâce* was the request of the theologian Michel Le Vassor, who had been converted from Jansenism by Malebranche, for a short treatise on grace usable in connection with his lectures on theology at a Paris seminary. (Le Vassor, whose defection from Jansenism had distressed Arnauld and the Port-Royalists, finally abandoned Malebranchism as well, emigrated to Holland, became a Calvinist associated with Bayle [another former Malebranchian], and is remembered—when at all—for his witticism that Jansenius had read St. Augustine "avec les lunettes de Calvin.") Le Vassor's Malebranche-inspired lectures on grace were popular enough to prompt an alarmed Arnauld to request a meeting with Malebranche; this meeting was attended not only by Le Vassor, Malebranche, and Arnauld, but also by Arnauld's disciple, the Oratorian Father Pasquier Quesnel, whose *Réflexions morales* later occasioned an enormous conflict within the French church, culminating in the condemnation of 101 Quesnelian-Jansenist propositions in Pope Clement XI's *Unigenitus*.[74]

---

[73] Malebranche, *De la recherche de la vérité*, in *Oeuvres complètes*, vol. 2, pp. 118-119.

[74] For a good account of the composition and publication of *Nature et grâce*, see Dreyfus's Introduction, pp. xxiiff.

At this famous meeting, Arnauld's volubility denied Malebranche much opportunity to clarify his views; the *Traité de la nature et de la grâce* is a full working-up—for Arnauld's benefit—of the shorter treatise prepared for Le Vassor. To be sure, that shorter treatise was itself a working-up of a few paragraphs on grace from the sixteenth "Eclaircissement" of *De la recherche de la vérité*, which Malebranche had appended to the third edition in 1678. In this "Eclaircissement," which was scrapped in the final editions of the *Recherche*, Malebranche argues that, "while God wills to save us all," the fact that he operates through "the simplest means"—through uniform *volontés générales*, not through a multiplicity of *volontés particulières*—means that some will *not* be saved. (Here "general will" is no longer a mere synonym for "antecedent will"; *volonté générale* is now associated with Cartesian constancy, uniformity and economy.) This was to be elaborated in *Nature et grâce*, but the sixteenth "Eclaircissement" of the *Recherche* contains a defect that was not carried over into the *Traité* and that doubtless led to the final abandoning of this "Eclaircissement." Urging again that God acts "always by the simplest means . . . in virtue of general wills," Malebranche observes that the Ten Commandments were written by the ancient Jews over their doorways and argues that this "spared God a particular will, if one can speak in this way, to inspire these [righteous] thoughts in them."[75] Obviously, a perfect being does not need to be "spared" anything, even a *volonté particulière*, since the notion of need is meaningless for such a being. This is best pointed out, nearly a hundred years later, in the theological *Briefwechsel* between Julie de Wolmar and St. Preux that Rousseau inserts in book 6 of *La Nouvelle Héloïse*, in which Julie mockingly points out to the Malebranchian St. Preux that only human beings need economy, that God does not need man to "abridge his

---

[75] Malebranche, *Recherche de la vérité*, pp. 506, 508. On the question of how far Malebranche is an orthodox Cartesian, see Ferdinand Alquié, *Le Cartésianisme de Malebranche* (Paris: Vrin, 1974), pp. 243ff.

work" for him by following ready-made general rules. (St. Preux responds that "it is worthy of his wisdom to prefer the simplest means.")[76] A similar thought must have crossed Malebranche's mind—even in the sixteenth "Eclaircissement" he says, "if one can speak in this way"— and in *Nature et grâce* the simplicity and generality of God's action is grounded, not in any need for economy or sparing divine labor, but in the notion that simplicity and generality best *express* divine perfection.[77]

In the "Premier Eclaircissement" of the *Traité de la nature et de la grâce*, one sees at once that Malebranche is not going to treat divine *volonté générale* as something confined to theology, to questions of grace and merit; one sees that he intends to treat general will as something that is manifested in *all* of God's operations—as much in the realm of nature as in that of grace. Malebranche argues that "God acts by *volontés générales* when he acts as a consequence of general laws which he has established." Nature, he adds, "is nothing but the general laws which God has established in order to construct or to preserve his work by the simplest means, by an action [that is] always uniform, constant, perfectly worthy of an infinite wisdom and of a universal cause."[78] God, on this view, does not act by *volontés particulières*, by lawless ad hoc volitions, as do "limited intelligences" whose thought is not "infinite."[79] Thus, for Malebranche, "to establish general laws, and to choose the simplest ones which are at the same time the most fruitful, is a way of acting worthy of him whose wisdom has no limits." On the other hand, "to act by *volontés particulières* shows a limited intelligence which cannot judge the consequences or the effects of less fruitful causes."[80]

---

[76] Cited in Emile Bréhier, "Les Lectures malebranchistes de J.-J. Rousseau," *Revue internationale de philosophie* 1 (1938-1939), pp. 113-114.

[77] Malebranche, *Nature et grâce*, in *Oeuvres complètes*, vol. 5, p. 47: God is obliged "to act always in a way worthy of him, in simple, general, constant and uniform ways."

[78] Ibid., pp. 147, 148.

[79] Ibid., p. 63.

[80] Ibid., p. 166.

Even at this point, Malebranche's argument, though mainly a theological one, contains some points that could be read "politically": the general will manifests itself in general laws that are "fruitful" and "worthy" of infinite wisdom, whereas particular will is "limited," comparatively unintelligent, and lawless—but these terms are not very different from Rousseau's characterizations of *volonté générale* and *particulière* in *Du contrat social*, especially when Rousseau argues that *volonté générale*, in the form of general laws, never deals with particular cases.[81] One need not jump to any premature conclusions, however, since Malebranche himself occasionally politicizes his argument, particularly in his effort to justify God's acting (exclusively) through *volontés générales*. If "rain falls on certain lands, and if the sun roasts others . . . if a child comes into the world with a malformed and useless head . . . this is not at all because God wanted to produce those effects by *volontés particulières*; it is because he has established [general] laws for the communication of motion, whose effects are necessary consequences." Thus, according to Malebranche, "one cannot say that God acts through caprice or ignorance" in permitting malformed children to be born or unripe fruit to fall. "He has not established the laws of the communication of motion for the purpose of producing monsters, or of making fruits fall before their maturity"; he has willed these laws "because of their fruitfulness, and not because of their sterility."[82] Those who claim that God *ought*, through special, ad hoc *volontés particulières*, to suspend natural laws if their operation will harm the virtuous or the innocent, or that he ought to confer grace only on those who will ac-

---

[81] Rousseau, *Du contrat social*, p. 49: "When I say that the object of the laws is always general, I mean that the law considers subjects as a body and actions in the abstract; never a man as an individual, or a particular action." There is never, he adds, "a general will concerning a particular object."

[82] Malebranche, *Nature et grâce, in Oeuvres complètes de Malebranche*, vol. 5, p. 32.

tually be saved by it, fail to understand that it is not worthy of an infinitely wise being to abandon general rules in order to find a suppositious perfect fit between the particular case of each finite being and a *volonté particulière* suited to that case alone.[83]

By this point, evidently, the theological notion of *volonté générale* is becoming politicized. *Volonté générale* originally manifested itself in general laws that were wise and fruitful; now that will, expressed in those laws, is *just* as well, and it is quite wrong to say that God ought to contrive a *volonté particulière* suited to each case, even though the generality of his will and of his laws will mean that grace will occasionally fall on a hardened heart incapable of receiving it.[84] God, Malebranche urges, loves his wisdom more than he loves mankind ("c'est que Dieu aime davantage sa sagesse que son ouvrage"),[85] and his wisdom is expressed in general laws, the operation of which may have consequences (monstrous children, unripened fruit) that are not *themselves* willed and that cannot therefore give rise to charges of divine caprice or ignorance.

If Malebranche, in pleading the "cause" of God (to use Leibniz's phrase),[86] views divine *volonté générale* as issuing in wise and just laws, the *Traité de la nature et de la grâce* is further (and quite explicitly) politicized by an analogy that Malebranche himself draws between a well-governed earthly kingdom and a well-governed Creation. He begins with an argument about enlightened and unenlightened will: "The more enlightened an agent is, the more extensive are his *volontés*. A very limited mind undertakes new schemes at every moment; and when he wants to execute one of them, he uses several means, of which some are al-

---

[83] Ibid., pp. 63-64, 166 (*inter alia*).
[84] Ibid., pp. 50-51.
[85] Ibid., p. 47.
[86] Leibniz, *Theodicy*, p. 62. For a fuller treatment of Leibniz's notion of divine justice, see the author's "An Unpublished MS of Leibniz on the Allegiance Due to Sovereign Powers," in *Journal of the History of Philosophy* 11 (July 1973), pp. 324ff.

ways useless." But a "broad and penetrating mind," he goes on, "compares and weighs all things: he never forms plans except with the knowledge that he has the means to execute them."[87] Malebranche then moves to his political analogy: "A great number of laws in a state"—presumably a mere concatenation of many *volontés particulières*—"often shows little penetration and breadth of mind in those who have established them: it is often the mere experience of need, rather than wise foresight, which has ordained them." God qua legislator has none of these defects, Malebranche claims: "He need not multiply his *volontés*, which are the executive laws of his plans, any further than necessity obliges." He must act through *volontés générales* "and thus establish a constant and regulated order" by "the simplest means." Those who want God to act, not through "les loix ou les volontés générales," but through *volontés particulières*, simply "imagine that God at every moment is performing miracles in their favor." This partisanship for the particular, Malebranche says—in an astonishingly Rousseauean vein—"flatters the self-love which relates everything to itself," and "accommodates itself quite well" to ignorance.[88]

Malebranche certainly believed that those who imagine a God thick with *volontés particulières* will use that alleged divine particularism to rationalize their own failure to embrace general principles. Indeed, he appeals to the notion of *particularisme* in attempting to explain the lamentable diversity of the world's moral opinions and practices. In the *Traité de morale* (1684) Malebranche argues that although "universal reason is always the same" and "order is immutable," "morality changes according to countries and according to the times." Germans think it virtuous to drink to excess; European nobles think it "generous" to fight duels in defense of their honor. Such people "even imagine that

[87] Malebranche, *Nature et grâce*, in *Oeuvres complètes de Malebranche*, vol. 5, p. 46.
[88] Ibid., p. 63.

God approves their conduct," that, in the case of an aristo-
cratic duel, he "presides at the judgment and . . . awards
the palm to him who is right." Of course, one can only
imagine this if one thinks that God acts by *volontés particulières*. And if even he is thought to operate particularly, why
should not men as well? The man who imputes particular
wills to God by "letting himself be led by imagination, his
enemy," will also have his own *"morale particulière*, his own
devotion, his favorite virtue." What is essential is that one
abandon *particularisme*, whether as something ascribed to
God or as something merely derived from human "inclina-
tions" and "humors." It is "immutable order" that must
serve as our "inviolable and natural law," and "imagination" that must be suppressed. For order is general, while
imagination is all too particular.[89]

Malebranche's notion that those who believe that they
are the beneficiaries of a miraculous *Providence particulière*
are suffering from acute egomania is strongly reinforced in
the 1683 *Méditations chrétiennes*. In the eighth *méditation*
Malebranche insists that "the New Testament [*la nouvelle alliance*] is in perfect conformity with the simplicity of natural
laws," even though those general laws "cause so many
evils in the world." The New Testament promises *des biens
éternels* to the just as compensation for their patience in en-
during monstrous children and unripened fruit; therefore,
it is "not at all necessary that God perform miracles often"
in order to deliver the just from their "present evils." To be
sure, Malebranche concedes, under the Old Testament,
miracles—or, at least, what are called miracles—were more
necessary; the ancient Jews, who lacked Christ's salvific
grace and who were "un peu grossiers et charnels,"
needed, or at least asked for, exceptions in their favor from
general and simple laws. This, according to Malebranche,
led God, "at least in appearance," to "trouble the simplicity

[89] Malebranche, *Traité de morale*, ed. M. Adam, in *Oeuvres complètes*, vol.
11, pp. 31-33.

of the laws" in biblical times.[90] But Christians, Malebranche insists, should know better, and must live with the simplicity of (occasionally ruinous) laws; Malebranche condemns those who, "failing to respect the order of nature," imagine that on all occasions God should "protect them in a particular way [*d'une manière particulière*]." Is some people's reliance on God, Malebranche asks rhetorically, a sign of "the greatness of their faith," or rather a mark of "a stupid and rash confidence" that makes them have contempt for human ways? Malebranche does not doubt that the piety of those who claim to be under "une protection de Dieu toute particulière" can often be sincere. That sincerity, however, is commonly "neither wise nor enlightened" but rather, "filled with *amour-propre* and with secret pride." Some people, Malebranche adds, fancy that God is only good insofar as he applies himself to making exceptions to the rules of wisdom; but it should be remembered that "God constantly follows the general laws which he has very wisely established."[91] Here, then, *particularisme* is identified with self-love, rashness, stupidity, and making exceptions to general laws—more or less in the manner of Rousseau.

So wise, constant, and just are God's *volontés générales*, in Malebranche's view, that it is a moral wrong on man's part not to accept and respect these general wills and to make them the measure of human conduct. In one of his numerous defenses of *Nature et grâce*, Malebranche argues that "if God did not act in consequence of general laws which he has established, no one would ever make any effort. Instead of descending a staircase step by step, one would rather throw himself out of the windows, trusting himself to God." Why would it be sin as well as folly to hurl oneself from a window? "It would be sin," Malebranche answers, "because it would be tempting God: it would be claiming to obligate him to act in a manner unworthy of him, or

---

[90] Malebranche, *Méditations chrétiennes et métaphysiques*, in *Oeuvres complètes*, vol. 10, p. 84.
[91] Ibid., pp. 87-88.

through *volontés particulières*"; it would amount to telling God "that his work is going to perish, if he himself does not trouble the simplicity of his ways." In addition to sin, of course, hurling oneself would be folly, for one must be mad to imagine that "God must regulate his action by our particular needs, and groundlessly change, out of love for us, the uniformity of his conduct."[92]

For Malebranche's orthodox and conservative critics—most notably Bossuet, whose anti-Malebranchism will be treated shortly—perhaps the most distressing aspect of Malebranche's theory of divine *volonté générale* was the much-diminished weight and value given to literally read Scripture. In *Nature et grâce* Malebranche urges that "those who claim that God has particular plans and wills for all the particular effects which are produced in consequence of general laws" ordinarily rely not on philosophy but on the authority of Scripture to "shore up" their feeling. (The verb and noun are sufficiently revealing.) But, Malebranche argues, "since Scripture was made for everybody, for the simple as well as for the learned, it is full of *anthropologies*" (emphasis in original). Scripture, continues Malebranche, endows God with "a body, a throne, a chariot, a retinue, the passions of joy, of sadness, of anger, of remorse, and the other movements of the soul"; it even goes beyond this and attributes to him "ordinary human ways of acting, in order to speak to the simple in a more sensible way." St. Paul, in order to accommodate himself to everyone, speaks of sanctification and predestination "as if God acted ceaselessly" through *volontés particulières* to produce those particular effects; even Christ himself "speaks of his Father as if he applied himself, through comparable *volontés*, to clothe the lilies of the field and to preserve the least hair on his disciples' heads."

[92] Malebranche, *Réponse au livre de Mr Arnau[l]d, Des vrayes et des fausses idées*, in *Oeuvres complètes*, vol. 6-7, p. 43.

Despite all these "anthropologies" and "as ifs," introduced solely to make God lovable to "even the coarsest minds," Malebranche concludes, one must use the idea of God (qua perfect being), coupled with those non-anthropological scriptural passages that are in conformity to this idea, in order to correct the sense of some other passages that attribute "parts" to God, or "passions like our own."[93] (To make his own non-reliance on Scripture quite plain, Malebranche omitted any reference at all to the Bible in the original [1680] edition of *Nature et grâce*. Later, when, out of prudence, he interpolated a number of scriptural passages in the *Traité*, he took care to set them off from the 1680 text by labelling the new parts "additions" and having them set in a different typeface. Even in the Scripture-laden version of 1684, then, the authority of Scripture is separated—physically separated—from the idea of an *être infiniment parfait*.)[94]

The notion that Scripture represents God as a man who has "passions of the soul" and *volontés particulières* merely to accommodate the weakness of "even the coarsest minds" leads to a difficulty that an Augustinian, and certainly a Jansenist, would find distressing. Pascal had argued that in "Augustinianism" God's pre-lapsarian *volonté générale* to save all men is replaced after the Fall by the election of a few for salvation through *miséricorde*, or "pity" (though none merited it);[95] Arnauld, in the preface to his translation of *De correptione et gratia*, had also stressed an undeserved divine *miséricorde*, which God might with perfect justice have withheld.[96] "Pity," of course, on a Malebranchian view, is a "passion of the soul," but it is only through weakness and anthropomorphism that we imagine these passions to animate God. If an *être parfait* does not

---

[93] Malebranche, *Nature et grâce*, in *Oeuvres complètes de Malebranche*, vol. 5, pp. 61-62.

[94] If one examines the 1684 edition of *Nature et grâce* (Rotterdam: Chez Reinier Leers, 1684), one finds that all the additions to the 1680 text are set in italic type.

[95] Pascal, *Ecrits sur la grâce*, pp. 135-140.

[96] St. Augustine, *Correction et grâce*, p. 7.

really have these passions, it cannot be the case that—as in Pascal—a *volonté générale* to save all is replaced by a pitiful *volonté absolue* to save a few.

Indeed, whereas in Pascal *volonté générale* comes first and gets replaced by *miséricorde*, in Malebranche general will governs the realms of nature and grace from the outset, once the world has been created by a *volonté particulière*. (Even Malebranche treats the Creation as the product of *volonté particulière*, arguing in part 2 of *Nature et grâce* that, until there are created things that can serve as the "occasional" or "second" causes of general laws, those general laws cannot operate.)[97]

Far from abandoning his position when he was accused of "ruining" Providence (in a work such as Jurieu's *Esprit de M. Arnauld*),[98] Malebranche maintained it stoutly in the "Dernier Eclaircissement" of *Nature et grâce*, provocatively entitled "The Frequent Miracles of the Old Testament Do Not Show at All that God Acts Often by Particular Wills," which he added to the fourth edition in 1684. The "proofs" that he has drawn from the idea of an infinitely perfect being, Malebranche insists, make it clear that "God executes his designs by general laws." On the other hand, it is not easy to demonstrate that God operates ordinarily through *volontés particulières*, "though Holy Scripture, which accommodates itself to our weakness, sometimes represents God as a man, and often has him act as men act."[99] Here, as in the main text of *Nature et grâce*, the key notion is weakness, and any notion of divine *volonté particulière* simply accommodates that *faiblesse*. This is why Malebranche can maintain—this time in the "Troisième Eclaircissement" of 1683—that "there are ways of acting [that are] simple, fruitful, general, uniform and constant,"

---

[97] Malebranche, *Nature et grâce*, in *Oeuvres complètes*, vol. 5, pp. 67-68.

[98] Pierre Jurieu, *L'Esprit de M. Arnau[l]d* (Deventer: Jean Colombius, 1684), pp. 80ff., esp. p. 80: "Je ne scay si le P. Malebranche a eu un ami assez fidele, pour lui apprendre qu'il n'y a jamais eu de Livre plus généralement désapprouvé que [*Nature et grâce*]."

[99] Malebranche, *Nature et grâce*, in *Oeuvres complètes*, vol. 5, p. 204.

and that manifest "wisdom, goodness, steadiness [and] immutability in those who use them." On the other hand, there are also ways that are "complex, sterile, particular, lawless and inconstant," and that reveal "lack of intelligence, malignity, unsteadiness [and] levity in those who use them."[100] Thus, a very effective heap of execrations is mounded around any *volonté particulière*, which turns out to be complex, sterile, lawless, inconstant, unintelligent, malignant, and frivolous.

Indeed, for Malebranche it is precisely *volonté particulière*, and not *volonté générale*, that "ruins" Providence. In his *Réponse à une dissertation de M. Arnauld contre un éclaircissement de la nature et de la grâce* (1685), he argues that, if Arnauld's insistence on miracles and constant divine *volontés particulières* does not "overturn" Providence, it at least "degrades it, humanizes it, and makes it either blind, or perverse."

> Is there wisdom in creating monsters by *volontés particulières*? In making crops grow by rainfall, in order to ravage them by hail? In giving to men a thousand impulses of grace which misfortunes render useless? In making rain fall equally on sand and on cultivated ground? But all this is nothing. Is there wisdom and goodness in making impious princes reign, in suffering so great a number of heresies, in letting so many nations perish? Let M. Arnauld raise his head and discover all the evils which happen in the world, and let him justify Providence, on the supposition that God acts and must act through *volontés particulières*.[101]

It is Malebranche's view, in fact, that the classical "theodicy problems" of reconciling a morally and physically imperfect world with God's "power," "goodness," and "wisdom" can *only* be solved by insisting that God wills

[100] Ibid., p. 180.
[101] Malebranche, *Réponse à une dissertation de M. Arnauld contre un eclaircissement de la nature et de la grâce*, in *Oeuvres complètes*, vol. 6-7, pp. 591-592.

generally. Malebranche states these problems starkly in *Nature et grâce*:

> Holy Scripture teaches us on [the] one hand that God wills that all men be saved, and that they come to a knowledge of the truth; and on the other, that he does everything that he wills: and nonetheless faith is not given to everyone; and the number of those that perish is much greater than that of the predestined. How can one reconcile this with his power?

> God foresaw from all eternity [both] original sin, and the infinite number of persons that this sin would sweep into Hell. Nonetheless he created the first man in a condition from which he knew he would fall; he even established between this man and his posterity relations which would communicate his sin to them, and render them all worthy of his aversion and his wrath. How can one reconcile this with his goodness?

> God frequently diffuses graces, without having the effect for which his goodness obliges us to believe that he gives them. He increases piety in persons almost to the end of their life; and sin dominates them at death, and throws them into Hell. He makes the rain of grace fall on hardened hearts, as well as on prepared grounds: men resist it, and make it useless for their salvation. In a word, God undoes and re-does without cease: it seems that he wills, and no longer wills. How can one reconcile this with his wisdom?[102]

According to Malebranche, these "great difficulties" are cleared up by the generality and simplicity of divine will. Its possession of these characteristics also explains how a being who loves order can permit disorder. "God loves men, he wills to save them all," Malebranche asserts, "for order is his law." Nonetheless, God "does not will to *do*

---

[102] Malebranche, *Nature et grâce*, in *Oeuvres complètes*, vol. 5, pp. 47-48.

what is necessary in order that all [men] know him and love him infallibly," and this is simply because "order does not permit that he have practical *volontés* proper to the execution of this design. . . . He must not disturb the simplicity of his ways."[103] Or, as Malebranche puts it in his *Réponse* to Arnauld's *Réflexions* on *Nature et grâce*,

> The greater number of men are damned, and [yet] God wills to save them all. . . . Whence comes it, then, that sinners die in their sin? Is it better to maintain that God does *not* will to save them all, simply because it pleases him to act in that way, than to seek the general reason for it in what he owes to himself, to his wisdom, and to his other attributes? Is it not clear, or at least is it not a feeling in conformity with piety, that one must throw these unhappy effects back onto simplicity—in one word onto the divinity of his ways?[104]

In his final work, published in the year of his death (1715), Malebranche reformulated this argument in an even stronger way—a way that Leibniz, among others, found excessive.

> Infinity in all sorts of perfections is an attribute of the divinity, indeed his essential attribute, that which encloses all the others. Now between the finite and the infinite, the distance is infinite; the relation is nothing. The most excellent of creatures, compared to the divinity, is nothing; and God counts it as nothing in relation to himself. . . . It seems to me evident, that God conducts himself according to what he is, in remaining immobile, [even while] seeing the demon tempt, and man succumb to the temptation. . . . His immobility

---

[103] Cited in Ginette Dreyfus, *La Volonté selon Malebranche* (Paris: Vrin, 1958), p. 114.

[104] Malebranche, *Réponse au livre 1 des réflexions philosophiques*, in *Oeuvres complètes*, vol. 8-9, p. 721. Cf. p. 722: "S'il [Dieu] avoit une volonté absolue de sauver tous les hommes, sans avoir egard à la simplicité des moyens, il est certain qu'il les sauveroit tous."

bears the character of his infinity. . . . If God, in order to stop the Fall of Adam, had interrupted the ordinary course of his *providence générale*, that conduct would have expressed the false judgment that God had counted the worship that Adam rendered him as something, with respect to his infinite majesty. Now God must never trouble the simplicity of his ways, nor interrupt the wise, constant and majestic course of his ordinary providence, by a particular and miraculous providence. . . . God is infinitely wise, infinitely just, infinitely good, and he does men all the good he can— not absolutely, but acting according to what he is. . . . [105]

After this, Malebranche's insistence that, nonetheless, "God sincerely wills to save all men" rings a little hollow. It is no wonder that Leibniz, for all his general agreement with Malebranche, should complain that "I do not know whether one should have recourse to the expedient [of saying] that God, by remaining immobile during the Fall of man . . . marks [in that way] that the most excellent creatures are nothing in relation to him." For Leibniz, that way of putting the matter can be abused, and can even lead to "the despotism of the supralapsarians."[106] Perhaps the "immobility" passage was the one that the Jesuit Rodolphe Du Tertre had in mind when he published a three-volume attack on Malebranche even as the Oratorian lay on his deathbed; in the final volume of his *Réfutation d'un nouveau système de métaphysique proposé par le Père Malebranche*, Du Tertre argues that

> according to our author [Malebranche], God wills to save all men in this sense, that the ways . . . that he was indispensably obliged to follow in the execution of

[105] Malebranche, *Réflexions sur la prémotion physique*, in *Oeuvres complètes*, vol. 16, p. 118.
[106] Leibniz, letter to Malebranche (December 1711), cited in Malebranche, *Oeuvres complètes*, vol. 19, p. 815.

his work, will cause to enter into the future Church the most men that simplicity and generality will permit. [God] wills that all men be saved in this sense, that if there could be some other order of grace, equally worthy of him and more useful to men . . . he would have chosen it, or rather he would have been necessitated by his wisdom to choose it, in order not to contradict his attributes. There once again one sees what Father M[alebranche] calls God's true will that all men be saved—though at the same time he assures us that God cannot save more than he does save, without performing miracles that immutable order, which is his necessary law, does not permit him to perform. . . .

This means that the new theologian judges it suitable, for good reasons, to give the name "true and sincere will" to a chimerical *velléité* which it pleases him to imagine in God with respect to the salvation of men; such that, according to [Malebranche's] dictionary, to say that God truly wills that all men be saved is really to say that God would will this, if it could be, though it cannot be: that he would will it, supposing an impossible hypothesis, which would be that there is another way of acting [that is] more advantageous to men, and at the same time equally worthy of his attributes.[107]

Evidently, Malebranche was able to please neither the Jesuits, at one extreme, nor the Jansenists, at the other: for the Jesuits, Malebranche's God saves too few men, while for the Jansenists, he saves too many—and would apparently save all, if his generality and simplicity did not forbid

---

[107] Rodolphe Du Tertre, *Réfutation d'un nouveau système de métaphysique proposé par le Père Malebranche* (Paris: Chez Raymond Mazières, 1715), pp. 275-277. (The only available copy of Du Tertre's work is in the Bibliothèque Nationale, Paris—through whose courtesy the author was able to examine the *Réfutation* in November 1982.) Du Tertre had been an ardent Malebranchian, but was ordered by his Jesuit superiors to relinquish his views; unlike his fellow Jesuit and one-time friend Y. M. André, he followed orders.

it. (As Ginette Dreyfus has correctly said in her helpful *La Volonté selon Malebranche*, "God wills to save all men, but wisdom forbids him to act in such a way that they would actually be saved."[108] Generality, then, "saves" God, though it fails to save all men.)

According to Malebranche, the theodicy problems that generality and simplicity are meant to solve *must* have a resolution, because the radical imperfection and evil in the universe are all too real, not merely apparent. If they were merely apparent, one could perhaps appeal to the notion of a mysterious *Dieu caché* whose inscrutable ways discover real good in seeming evil. However, this is not Malebranche's view. "A monster," he declares, "is an imperfect work, whatever may have been God's purpose in creating it."

> Some philosophers, perverted by an extravagant metaphysics, come and tell me that God wills evil as positively and directly as the good; that he truly only wills the beauty of the universe . . . [and] . . . that the world is a harmony in which monsters are a necessary dissonance; that God wants sinners as well as the just; and that, just as shadows in a painting make its subjects stand out, and give them relief, so too the impious are absolutely necessary in the work of God, to make virtue shine in men of good will.[109]

Those who reason along these lines, in Malebranche's view, are trying to resolve moral dilemmas by appealing to aesthetic similes; but the method will not serve. "Shadows are necessary in a painting and dissonances in music. Thus it is necessary that women abort and produce an infinity of monsters. What a conclusion!" He ends by insisting, "I do not agree that there is evil only in appearance." Hence, *volonté générale* alone, which wills (positively) the good and

---

[108] Dreyfus, *Volonté selon Malebranche*, p. 114.

[109] Cited in André Robinet, *Système et existence dans l'oeuvre de Malebranche* (Paris: Vrin, 1965), pp. 104–105.

only *permits* evil as the unavoidable consequence of general and simple laws, is the sole avenue of escape from theodicy problems if one calls evil "real." For Malebranche, as for Rousseau in the following century, only *généralité* is positively good and truly justifiable.[110]

Another of the aspects of *volonté générale* that Malebranche's critics found distressing was the possibility that it had been derived or extracted from a Cartesian notion of general laws of uniform motion (in physics) and simply grafted onto the realm of grace.[111] This suspicion was borne out by a careful reading of some passages from *Nature et grâce*. In the *Premier Discours* of the *Traité*, Malebranche finds a parallel between generality in nature and in grace, but he *begins* with nature, and finds in grace no more than a kind of analogue to nature. "Just as one has no right to be annoyed by the fact that rain falls in the sea, where it is useless," Malebranche argues, so also one has no right "to complain of the apparent irregularity according to which grace is given to men." Useless rain and useless grace both derive from "the regularity with which God acts," from "the simplicity of the laws which he follows." Malebranche reinforces the nature-grace parallel, in which nature seems to be the model for grace, by calling grace a "heavenly rain which sometimes falls on hardened hearts, as well as on prepared souls."[112] This horticultural language, of course—which Malebranche himself claimed to have used primarily to persuade Cartesians, not Scholastic theologians[113]—did nothing to dispel the suspicion of traditionalists like Bossuet that Cartesian generality and uniformity might be used in radical ways, to the detriment of traditional teachings

---

[110] See particularly Alberto Postigliola, "De Malebranche à Rousseau: Les Apories de la volonté générale et la revanche du 'raisonneur violent,' " in *Annales de la Société Jean-Jacques Rousseau* (Geneva: Chez A. Jullien, 1980), vol. 39, pp. 134ff. (For a full treatment of this excellent piece, see chapter 5 of the present work.)

[111] This was the fear of both Arnauld and Bossuet; see note 114.

[112] Malebranche, *Nature et grâce*, in *Oeuvres complètes*, vol. 5, p. 50.

[113] Ibid., p. 7.

about grace based on Scripture and patristic writings. This kind of suspicion—best expressed by Bossuet himself when he says, in a letter dealing with Malebranchism, that he sees "a great struggle against the Church being prepared in the name of Cartesian philosophy"[114]—was certainly not relieved by Malebranche's insistence that "what Moses tells us in *Genesis* is so obscure" that the beginning of the world can be explained *à la Descartes* better than any other way.[115] "Obscurity" is no more welcome than "anthropology" or "as if."

The fear of orthodox Christian moralists that Malebranche had permitted a Cartesian physics to invade and infect the sphere of metaphysics, including ethics, was not wholly groundless. In the *Recherche de la vérité*, Malebranche "Cartesianizes" everything, not least human volition and action:

> Just as the author of nature is the universal cause of all the movements which are in matter, it is also him who is the general cause [*cause générale*] of all the natural inclinations which are in minds. And just as all movements proceed in a straight line [*en ligne droite*], if there are no foreign and particular causes which determine them, and which change them into curved lines through their opposing forces; so too the inclinations which we receive from God are right [*droites*], and they could not have any other end than the possession of the good and of truth if there were not any foreign cause, which determined the impression of nature towards bad ends.[116]

Like Kant a century later, here Malebranche is playing with the different senses of "droit" (meaning both "straight" and "right") and of "curved" (which can mean

---

[114] Bossuet, letter to Marquis d'Allemans (May 1687), in Malebranche, *Oeuvres complètes*, vol. 18, p. 445.

[115] Malebranche, *Réponse au livre* I, p. 780.

[116] Malebranche, *Recherche de la vérité*, p. 45.

"crooked" in a moral sense).[117] This same kind of playing can be found in Rousseau's most famous single assertion about general will: "La volonté générale est toujours droite, mais le jugement qui la guide n'est pas toujours éclairé."[118] However, the key point in connection with Malebranche is that the language of Cartesian physics has been imposed on morality and psychology; however briefly, Malebranche resembles Hobbes in accounting for everything in terms of general *motion*.[119] Moreover, that *généralité*, in Malebranche as in Rousseau, always has supreme weight: if the God of Pascal and Arnauld permanently abandons a primitive *volonté générale* to save all in favor of a very particular pity for the elect, Malebranche's God moves as quickly as possible away from an embarrassingly particularistic Creation and toward the generality and simplicity that later shape *Du contrat social*.

Some of the contemporary opponents of Malebranche—particularly the orthodox Cartesian Pierre Régis—thought that the notion of a just and justifiable divine *volonté générale* was "political" in a wholly bad sense, that Malebranche had confused divine governance with ordinary human governance and hence had politicized theology. "I shall not say," Régis observes, "that God acts by *volontés générales*, or by *volontés particulières*, because these two kinds of will cannot be suitable to a perfect being." If God acted only through *volontés générales*, this would mean "that he willed things only in a general way, without descending to anything particular, as a king governs a kingdom through general laws, not having the power to guide each subject." A mere king falls back on general laws and *volontés générales*

---

[117] Immanuel Kant, "Einleitung in der Rechtslehre," sec. E, *Die Metaphysik der Sitten*, in *Immanuel Kants Werke*, ed. Ernst Cassirer (Berlin: Bruno Cassirer Verlag, 1922), vol. 7, p. 34.

[118] Rousseau, *Du contrat social*, p. 50.

[119] See Labrousse, *Pierre Bayle*, vol. 2, pp. 592ff.

only because of political impotence, but "God cannot have *volontés générales* . . . because these *volontés* suppose an impotence in God which I cannot attribute to him." Since the notion that God operates through *volontés particulières* is no better, in Régis's view ("it would follow that the nature of God would be composed of as many different wills as there are particular things which God wills, which is repugnant to his simplicity"), it must be the case that "God acts by a simple, eternal and immutable will which embraces indivisibly and in a single act everything that is and will be."[120]

Malebranche, as it happens, had an answer to this kind of charge. In the seventh of his *Méditations chrétiennes et métaphysiques* (1683), he warns that when one says that God "permits certain natural disorders, such as the generation of monsters, the violent death of a good man, or something similar," one must not imagine that there is an autonomous "nature" to which God has given some of his power and that acts independently of God, "in the same way that a prince lets ministers act, and permits disorders which he cannot stop." God *could* stop all "disorders" (though a prince cannot) by acting through a multiplicity of *volontés particulières*, which would remedy all particular evils. Acting in this fashion, however, would derogate from the simplicity of his ways; God, Malebranche argues, "does good because he wants his work to be perfect," and he *permits* (rather than *does*) evil not because he "positively and directly" wills it but because "he wants his manner of acting to be simple, regular, uniform and constant, because he wants his conduct to be worthy of him and to wear visibly the character of his attributes."[121] Thus, for Malebranche, to act by *volontés générales* and general laws does not mani-

---

[120] Pierre-Sylvain Régis, *Cours entier de philosophie ou système général selon les principes de M. Descartes* (Amsterdam: Huguetan, 1691), vol. 1, pp. 92, 93. For a commentary on Régis's thought, see Genevieve Lewis, *Le Problème de l'inconscient et le cartésianisme* (Paris: Presses Universitaires de France, 1950).

[121] Malebranche, *Méditations chrétiennes*, pp. 76, 77.

fest a quasi-political impotence at all: God can will anything, but acting through *volontés particulières* would not be
worthy of him. What he can do is simply a question of
power; what he actually wills is a question of wisdom and
justice.

If there were critics of Malebranche who claimed that he
had illegitimately thought of God as a mere earthly king,
there were others who thought that political analogies
were, in themselves, perfectly acceptable, and that Malebranche had simply pitched upon false ones. In his *Réflexions sur le système de la nature et de la grâce* (1685), Arnauld argues that "there is no contradiction whatever [in the fact]
that God wills by a *volonté absolue et particulière* the contrary
of what he wills *en général* by an antecedent will, just as a
good king wills by an antecedent will that all his subjects
live contentedly, though by a consequent will he executes
those who disturb public tranquility by murders and vio-
lence."[122] In Arnauld's view, Malebranche's theory of general justice suffers from the defect of virtually equating *volonté générale*, general law, wisdom, justice, and "the
simplest means"; these terms, according to Arnauld, are
not equivalent, and what "wisdom" requires (e.g., the rem-
edying of particular evils) may not be attainable by "the
simplest means"—either for God or for a human ruler.[123]

For Arnauld, Malebranche's fatal confusion is the confla-
tion of general will and general law; in fact, the operation of

---

[122] Arnauld, *Réflexions philosophiques et théologiques*, in *Oeuvres*, vol. 39, p.
198. For a fine account of Arnauld's criticisms of Malebranche, see Ginette
Dreyfus's Introduction to her edition of Malebranche's *Nature et grâce*, pp.
47ff.

[123] Arnauld, *Réflexions philosophiques et théologiques*, in *Oeuvres*, pp. 174ff.
"It has never been said that it is not to act by a *volonté particulière*, when one
wills each particular effect positively and directly, though in conformity to
a general law. Otherwise Jesus Christ, having had a general law which he
always had in view—which was to follow in all things the orders of his
father—would have to be said never to have willed, by *volontés particulières*, everything which he did in particular for the redemption of the human race." One must conclude, therefore, *contra* Malebranche, that "God
acts by *volontés particulières* in consequence of general laws" (p. 175).

a general law may contain a divine *volonté particulière*. In "proving" this, Arnauld has recourse to Scripture, which Malebranche had minimized. "If one considers a particular effect," Arnauld begins in the *Réflexions philosophiques et théologiques*, "and if one finds nothing but conformity to general laws of nature, one has reason to say, with respect to this effect, that God has acted according to general laws." However, since this particular effect has many "remote causes," one would have to be assured that there has never been a particular divine intervention in this causal sequence before one could say absolutely that any particular effect was "*only* a consequence of the general laws of nature." One would have, in short, to be omniscient. Now, who, Arnauld asks triumphantly, can "assure us of this, without a prodigious temerity, and without ruining the faith we have in Providence?"[124]

But Arnauld does not content himself with the impossibility of proving that Providence has *not* intervened somewhere in the causal chain; he relies mainly on Scripture. It is precisely the Old Testament that "recounts to us that a stone, falling high from a tower, smashed the head of Abimelech, son of Gideon, who had had all his brothers, save one, killed." One cannot reasonably doubt, argues Arnauld, that this stone "observed the general laws of the movement of heavy things," and that it crushed Abimelech's head "according to the laws of the communication of movement"; nevertheless, this generality of law does not *exclude* a divine particular will at all:

> One can thus say that God acted, in injuring this wicked man, according to the general laws of nature, which he himself established. But does it follow from this that he acted only according to these laws, and that he had not the slightest *volonté particulière* in this matter? To judge of this, let us look farther back. This rock fell from this tower. Was it by itself? No. It was a

[124] Ibid., p. 177.

woman who threw it. Now who can doubt that God led the will and the hand of this woman, if one considers that Scripture teaches us that this happened through a just vengeance of God, which had been predicted by the youngest of the children of Gideon, who had escaped the cruelty of his brother?[125]

If one could look back, one would often find a particular divine contribution to effects that *seem* to be "only consequences of the general laws of nature." It is Scripture that teaches us where to find these hidden particular interventions. To deny these interventions is to deny that God can realize justice in this world—by punishing Abimelech, for example. Malebranchian generality thus undercuts justice and wisdom; it forbids God to do in particular what justice requires and makes him the slave of his own simplicity. If one wants to see how these *volontés cachées* of God operate in human history, Arnauld adds in a later chapter, one should repair to Bossuet's *Histoire universelle*—so full of "light" and "insight"—which reveals particular Providence always operating behind "the human causes of the establishment and decline of great Empires."[126] In short, for Arnauld it is a Malebranchian confusion to identify general law with general will, for *loi générale* can "carry out" a divine *volonté particulière*. Between Arnauld and Malebranche there is no middle ground that can be jointly occupied. For Arnauld, Scripture limits what philosophy can reveal about God; for Malebranche, it is philosophy that limits Scripture (and its "anthropologies").

Actually, Arnauld's thesis that generality does not invariably produce justice is very much like an argument that Aristotle puts forward in the *Ethics*—though Arnauld's aversion to Aristotelianism, at least in its Scholastic forms, prevented him from seeing the similarity. In the *Ethics* Aristotle says that, while laws must of necessity be general or

[125] Ibid.
[126] Ibid., pp. 177, 313.

universal, this is not a pure advantage; every law is "a universal rule," but "there are some things about which a universal proposition cannot be made correctly." As a result, the excessive generality of legal justice must be corrected through the notion of "equity," which relates to *particular* cases and is "better" than legal justice. This, he says, can be summarized by defining "equity" as "a correction of law where law is defective owing to its universality." He adds that whoever insists on general legal justice to the utter exclusion of equity is "a martinet for justice in a bad sense."[127] Though the Aristotelian notion that general law is only generally (not invariably) good could have served Arnauld to advantage, he does not rely on Aristotle's authority—which would not have impressed Malebranche, either. However, Arnauld's criticisms finally brought Malebranche to argue only that God "ordinarily" acts by *volontés générales* and "not often" by *volontés particulières*.[128] This grudging admission opened the door, however narrowly, to Fénelon's point that "not often" is an indeterminate notion, that the frequency of *volontés particulières* must be relative to what "wisdom" requires.[129] And this may be why Malebranche uses the notion of *volonté générale* somewhat sparingly in his later works.[130]

Without attempting to claim, with Régis, that Male-

---

[127] Aristotle, *Ethics*, book 5, 1137bff., cited in Aristotle, *Politics*, trans. Ernest Barker (Oxford: Clarendon Press, 1946), Appendix II, pp. 368, 369.

[128] Malebranche, *Réponse à une dissertation de M. Arnauld*, pp. 493ff.: "I believe that God does not often act by *volontés particulières*, and that ordinarily he follows the general laws which he has prescribed for himself."

[129] Fénelon, *Réfutation du système du Père Malebranche*, pp. 258-259: "But in what consists that which the author [Malebranche] calls 'rarely'? Is there a fatal number of exceptions which God is obliged to use up, beyond which he can will nothing except in accordance with general laws? Would one dare to say this?" See also Gouhier's commentary, described in note 70.

[130] Nevertheless, when Malebranche wrote a seventeenth "Eclaircissement" of *Recherche de la vérité* for the last edition published under his supervision (1712), he still insisted that "God acts by laws or by *volontés générales.*" For this "Eclaircissement," see *Oeuvres complètes*, vol. 3, p. 346.

branche's *Traité de la nature et de la grâce* is mainly political, is it not at least possible that his theological argument about the divine mode of operation is full of half-political notions that were readily politicizable in the hands of Diderot and Rousseau? Consider: Malebranche's *volonté générale* takes the form of general law, as in Diderot and Rousseau. That will and that law are just, wise, and constant. *Volonté particulière*, by contrast, is lawless: it hopes for miracles in favor of itself; it manifests self-love and limited intelligence. To be sure, to secularize and politicize this argument completely is not merely to modify Malebranche; to "bracket" God wholly out of the argument is to bracket out more than one leaves behind, at least from Malebranche's perspective. And yet, if one performs this modification, this bracketing, one is left with the residual notions of wise, just, constant general law (*volonté générale*) on the one hand and with lawless, comparatively unintelligent *amour-propre* (*volonté particulière*) on the other. But how far is this from Rousseau?

Of course, Malebranche's original argument is "political" only in a somewhat attenuated sense—in the sense that all theodicies or justifications of God are quasi-political; thus it is interesting that the ideas of *volonté générale* and *volonté particulière* recur in a less theological, more "practical" form in Malebranche's *Traité de morale* (1684). In this work, which opens with a brief account of general law and of particular will, Malebranche observes that "all the precepts of morality depend absolutely" on the means whereby "our hearts are touched by feelings proper to our end"—those feelings being (positively) "the love of order" and (negatively) the "arresting" of *amour-propre*.[131] These positive and negative

---

[131] Malebranche, *Traité de morale* (Lyon, 1697), vol. 2, pp. 248ff. Malebranche's distinction between the general and the particular pervades this work. At one point (vol. 2, p. 7) he urges that "it is for each to examine his particular duties in relation to general and essential obligations"; at another (vol. 2, p. 37) he argues that, while individual persons are "des êtres particuliers" who have difficulty in finding "un bien général et commun" when something like private property is at issue, nonetheless reason, which all share, is an indivisible "bien commun."

feelings are roughly comparable to the kinds of feelings that Rousseau wants to generate through education in the *Economie politique*—particularly on the negative side, since Rousseau argues that *amour-propre* is a "contemptible activity which absorbs all virtue and constitutes the life and being of little minds," and that virtue consists in conforming one's *volonté particulière* to one's *volonté générale*.[132]

A certain passage in the *Traité de morale* is still more suggestive of Rousseau—this time, the Rousseau of *Inégalité*. In part 2, chapter II of *Morale*, Malebranche argues that "human nature being equal in all men, and made for reason, it is only merit which ought to distinguish between us, and reason [which ought] to lead us." Thanks to sin, however, "men, though naturally all equal, have ceased to form between themselves a society based on equality, under a single law of reason." Force, or "the law of brutes," has "become the mistress among men"; the ambition of some and the need of others has forced everyone to abandon God and "universal reason, their inviolable law" and to choose "visible protectors against enemy force."[133] If one transforms Malebranche's "sin" into Rousseau's first acquisition of property,[134] and Malebranche's "law of reason" into Rousseau's "sentiment of humanity,"[135] then there is a sub-

[132] Rousseau, *Economie politique*, pp. 256, 248: "Do you want the general will to be accomplished? Make all *volontés particulières* relate to it; and since virtue is nothing else but the conformity of *volonté particulière* to *la générale* . . . make virtue reign."

[133] Malebranche, *Traité de morale*, in *Oeuvres complètes*, pp. 188-189.

[134] Rousseau, *Discours sur l'inégalité*, in *Political Writings*, vol. 1, p. 169: "The first [man] who, having enclosed some land, bethought himself to say, 'This is mine,' and found men simple enough to believe him, was the true founder of civil society. What crimes, what wars, what murders, what miseries and horrors would not have been spared the human race by him who, pulling up the stakes and knocking down the stones, cried to his fellow-men: 'Guard against listening to this impostor; you are lost if you forget that the fruits [of the earth] are for everyone, and that the earth belongs to no one.' " For Rousseau, the first acquisition of property is a kind of "original sin."

[135] Ibid., pp. 160ff., esp. p. 162: "Thus it is certain that pity is a natural

stantial parallel between this passage of the *Traité de morale* and *Inégalité*: natural equality is destroyed by the sinful ambition of some, and the need of others necessitates "visible protectors." Thus, the entire Malebranchian practical philosophy can be made to look remarkably Rousseauean.

It is only fair to say "can be made to look," since it takes a great deal of transforming and "bracketing" to get from Malebranche to Rousseau. The distance from Malebranche to Diderot's version of *volonté générale* may be a little shorter. After all, Diderot's general will is a quite general moral "rule of conduct" applicable between men, between a man and his society, or even between societies, whereas Rousseau's *volonté générale* is slightly more *particulière*: it is *for* and *within* a highly particular society and not for the whole "human race" (Diderot). Diderot's rather abstract "rule of conduct," then, is close to Malebranche's "law," just as Malebranche's "reason" is close to Diderot's "pure act of the understanding." And is it pure chance that, just as Malebranche urges that *volonté générale* takes the form of laws valid for all creatures, none of whom ought to insist on miracles in their favor, Diderot defines law produced by *volonté générale* as "made for all, and not for one"?[136]

In his last work, the *Réflexions sur la prémotion physique*, published in the year of his death (1715), Malebranche found an opportunity to show that his notions of *volonté générale* and general law have a general political significance that can be used in refuting theories of justice that rely primarily on sovereign power, such as Hobbes's. This anti-Hobbesian view, like the idea of "general will," later turned up in Montesquieu and in Rousseau. The *Réflexions* were a commentary on Laurent Boursier's quasi-Jansenist *De l'action de Dieu sur les créatures* (1713)—a large section of which at-

---

sentiment which, moderating in each individual the activity of self-love, aids in the mutual conservation of the whole species."

[136] Diderot, "Droit naturel," pp. 432, 433.

tempted to refute Malebranche's theory of the divine *modus operandi*. In *De l'action de Dieu* Boursier treats God as a "sovereign" whose will is unrestricted by any necessity to act only through general laws ("God has willed [the world] thus, because he willed it")[137] and argues that Malebranche's notion of divine wisdom renders God "impotent."[138] "The sovereign who governs," Boursier claims, whether God or a prince, "causes inferiors to act as he wills." He does this through "command": "He interposes his power in order to determine them." And "inferiors," for their part, act only "because they are excited and determined by the prince . . . they act in consequence of his determination."[139]

Since God is a powerful sovereign who has willed the world to be what it is simply "because he has willed it," one cannot say that he prefers a Malebranchian generality or "the simplest means," or, indeed, that he prefers anything at all; the "greatness and majesty of the Supreme Being" must make us realize that "everything that he can will with respect to what is outside himself" is "equal" to him. Malebranche, Boursier complains, does not see that God can equally will whatever is in his power: "What an idea of God! He wishes, and he does not accomplish; he does not like monsters, but he makes them; he does not attain the perfection which he desires in his works: he cannot fashion a work without defects . . . his wisdom limits his power. A strange idea of God! An impotent being, an unskilful workman, a wisdom based on constraint, a sovereign who does not do what he wills, an unhappy God."[140]

In his response to Boursier's theory of sovereignty based on will, command, and power, Malebranche actually aban-

---

[137] Laurent Boursier, *De l'action de Dieu sur les créatures* (Paris: Babuty, 1713), p. 70. (Substantial extracts from Boursier's work are printed as an appendix to Malebranche, *Oeuvres complètes*, vol. 16, pp. 199ff.)

[138] Ibid., p. 76: "C'est que sa sagesse le rend impuissant."

[139] Ibid., p. 36.

[140] Ibid., pp. 47, 79.

dons the terms *volonté générale* and *volonté particulière* (conceivably because of the constant criticisms of Régis, Arnauld et al.), but he does not abandon the concepts for which the terms stood; thus, *volonté générale* and general law become "eternal law," while *volonté particulière* becomes *volonté absolue et bizarre* (which is more striking still). "My present design," Malebranche says, "is to prove that God is essentially wise, just and good . . . that his *volontés* are not at all purely arbitrary—that is to say that they are not wise and just simply because he is all-powerful . . . but because they are regulated by the eternal law . . . a law which can consist only in the necessary immutable relations which are among the attributes and perfections which God encloses in his essence." The ideas that we have of wisdom, justice, and goodness "are quite different from those that we have of omnipotence." To say that the *volontés* of God are "purely arbitrary," that "no reason can be given for his *volontés*, except his *volontés* themselves," and that everything that he wills and does is just, wise, and good because he is omnipotent and has a "sovereign domain" over his creatures—is "to leave the objections of libertines in all their force."[141]

The notion that God wills in virtue of eternal law, not simply through the bare possession of sovereign domain, leads Malebranche to a criticism of Hobbes (and Locke) that is an interesting expansion of his notion of *volonté générale;* this criticism recurs in Montesquieu and then in Rousseau. "If," Malebranche says, "God were only omnipotent, and if he were like princes who glory more in their power than in their nature," then "his sovereign domain, or his independence, would give him a right to everything, or he would not act as [an] all-powerful [being]." If this were true of God, then "Hobbes, Locke and several others would have discovered the true foundations of morality: authority and power giving, without reason, the right to do whatever

---

[141] Malebranche, *Prémotion physique*, pp. 93, 101, 104.

one wills, when one has nothing to fear." This legal-positiv-ist view of either human or divine justice Malebranche char-acterizes as "mad," and those who attribute this mode of operation to God "apparently prefer force, the law of brutes (that which has granted to the lion an empire over the ani-mals), to reason."[142]

However unfair this may be to Hobbes, and still more to Locke—though at least Hobbes does actually say, in chap-ter 31 of *Leviathan*, that "irresistible power" carries with it a right to "dominion"[143]—Malebranche's last work shows that he thought that rule through *volontés* that are *particu-lières* or *absolues* or (even) *bizarres* was wrong in either hu-man or divine governance, and that rule through eternal laws that are of general validity is right. Of course, Male-branche was not alone in this; since Descartes' time a con-troversy had raged over the question of whether there *are* any eternal laws that God "finds" in his understanding and "follows" in his volitions.[144] Leibniz (following Plato's *Eu-*

---

[142] Ibid., pp. 93, 98.

[143] Hobbes, *Leviathan*, ed. M. Oakeshott (Oxford: Basil Blackwell, 1957), chapter 31, p. 234: "To those therefore whose power is irresistible, the do-minion of all men adhereth naturally by their excellence or power." As for Locke, Malebranche may be thinking of the passage in *The Reasonableness of Christianity* in which Locke argues that "those just measures of right and wrong which . . . [ancient] . . . philosophy recommended, stood on their true foundations. . . . But where was it that their obligation was thor-oughly known and allowed, and they received as precepts of a law . . . ? That could not be, without a clear knowledge and acknowledgement of the law-maker, and the great rewards and punishments, for those that would, or would not obey him" (in *Works of John Locke*, vol. 7, p. 144). Malebranche would not have approved the notion that the "just measures of right and wrong" derive their whole force from reward, punishment, and obedi-ence. For a fuller treatment of these passages from Hobbes and Locke, see the author's *Will and Political Legitimacy*, chapters 2 and 3.

[144] For a fuller treatment of this point, see the author's Introduction to *Political Writings of Leibniz*, pp. 6ff. See also Jean-Luc Marion, "De la créa-tion des vérités éternelles au principe de la raison: remarques sur l'anti-cartésianisme de Spinoza, Malebranche, Leibniz," in *Dix-septième Siècle*, vol. 37, No. 2, April/June 1985, pp. 143-164; and Geneviève Rodis-Lewis, "La création des vérités éternelles: polémiques sur la création des possi-bles et sur l'impossible dans l'école cartésienne," in *Studia Cartesiana* (Am-sterdam: Quadratures, 1981), vol. 2, pp. 105-123.

thyphro)[145] put forward a theory of general, non-arbitrary divine justice in his *Théodicée* (1710) that was very close to Malebranche's and criticized Hobbes along (roughly) Malebranchian lines in his *Opinion on the Principles of Pufendorf*.[146] Thus, arguments against Hobbism based on the notion that there are eternal laws of justice were certainly not scarce at the turn of the eighteenth century, and Malebranche was in perfect accord with Leibniz in disputing Hobbes (and Descartes) on this point.

In connection with his doctrine that God never operates through a *volonté* that is *absolue* or *bizarre*, but only through love of the eternal law, which is "co-eternal" with him, Malebranche designs one of the strikingly imaginative stage settings that even Voltaire found impressive:

> If God were only all-powerful, or if he gloried only in his omnipotence, without the slightest regard for his other attributes—in a word, without consulting his consubstantial law, his lovable and inviolable law—how strange his plans would be! How could we be certain that, through his omnipotence, he would not, on the first day, place all of the demons in heaven, and all the saints in hell, and a moment after annihilate all that he had done! Cannot God, *qua* omnipotent, create each day a million planets, make new worlds, each more perfect than the last, and reduce them each year to a grain of sand?[147]

Fortunately, according to Malebranche, though God is in

---

[145] Plato, *Euthyphro* 9E–10E in *Plato: The Collected Dialogues*, ed. E. Hamilton and H. Cairns (New York: Bollingen, 1961), pp. 178-179.

[146] Leibniz, *Principles of Pufendorf*, pp. 64ff.: "Neither the norm of conduct itself, nor the essence of the just, depends on his [God's] free decision, but rather on eternal truths, objects of the divine intellect, which constitute, so to speak, the essence of divinity itself. . . . Justice, indeed, would not be an essential attribute of God, if he himself established justice and law by his free will." For an appreciation of the limits of Leibniz's Platonism, see the author's "An Unpublished MS of Leibniz on the Existence of God," in *Studia Leibnitiana* (Hannover), 1984.

[147] Malebranche, *Prémotion physique*, p. 100.

58

fact all-powerful and "does whatever he wills to do," nonetheless he does not will to do anything except "according to the immutable order of justice." This is why Malebranche insists, in four or five separate passages of the *Réflexions sur la prémotion physique*, that St. Paul always said "O altitudo divitiarum Sapientiae et Scientiae Dei" and never "O altitudo voluntatis Dei." Will can be willful, if its only attribute is power, and that attribute is the one that Boursier (and Hobbes) wrongly endow with excessive weight.[148]

It is not only in the *Prémotion physique* that hostility to Hobbes (or at least the popular idea of Hobbism) appears; as early as 1688, in the *Entretiens sur la métaphysique*, Malebranche argues that "the just and the unjust, as well as the true and the false, are not at all mere inventions of the human mind, as some corrupted spirits have claimed." It is the view of these *esprits corrompus*—above all, Hobbes—Malebranche suggests, that men have made laws for themselves solely for their mutual preservation; that it is on self-love that these laws are based; that Hobbesian social contractors "have agreed between themselves, and by that [alone] they are obligated to each other." For a Hobbist, Malebranche complains, it is not because the laws are "just in themselves" but only out of egoism that one "must observe the laws of the country in which one lives"; for the same Hobbist, "everything is naturally permitted to all men," and "each individual [*particulier*] has a right to everything."[149] This doctrine, which Leibniz attacked along similar lines in his *Meditation on the Common Concept of Justice* and *Caesarinus Fürstenerius*, Malebranche stigmatizes in a memorable (if not entirely fair) paragraph. In Hobbes, he says,

> law is a foreign power; and if I were the most powerful I would regain all my rights. Can one say anything

---

[148] Ibid., pp. 72, 93, 122, etc.

[149] Cited in Henri Gouhier, *Malebranche* (Paris: Lecoffre, 1929), pp. 168-69. An excellent selection of Malebranche texts with good commentaries.

more brutal and more insane? Force has ceded to the lion an Empire over the other brutes; and I grant that it is often through force that men usurp [power] over each other. But to believe that this is permitted, and that the strongest has a right to everything, such that he can never commit the slightest injustice—this is assuredly to range oneself among the animals, and to make of human society a collection of brute beasts.[150]

Strictly speaking, Malebranche and Leibniz share enemies (especially Hobbes) rather than agree perfectly; they are only in general accord on "general will." Even in the *Théodicée*, which maximizes the area of agreement, Leibniz takes care to distance himself slightly from *Nature et grâce*. It is quite true, he urges, that "the events which are born of the execution of general laws are not at all the object of a *volonté particulière* of God" and that "one can even imagine that this way of acting through *volontés générales* seemed preferable to him (though some superfluous events . . . had to result from it) to another way [that was] more complex." However, Leibniz will not say, with Malebranche, that God "derogates" from *loix générales* when and if he performs a miracle; even miracles are only the applications of a divine law, though that law may remain unknown to finite intelligences ("the character of miracles . . . is that one cannot explain them through the natures of created things").[151]

The notion that human finitude may keep men from seeing the real generality of the divine laws that give rise to miracles is plainer and clearer in some of Leibniz's private notes on Malebranche. In his 1685 observations on Malebranche's *Réponse au livre des vraies et des fausses idées*, Leibniz first summarizes Malebranche's doctrine, then notes in the margin that "everything done by wisdom is done by *des loix générales*, or rules or principles; and God always acts wisely. Thus even miracles are in the general order, that is

[150] Ibid.
[151] Cited in Robinet, *Malebranche et Leibniz*, p. 408.

to say in general laws. But that which makes them miracles, is that they do not follow the notions of [human] subjects and cannot be predicted by the greatest finite mind that one can simulate."[152]

The following year, in notes on some of Antoine Arnauld's letters to Malebranche, Leibniz relates to mathematics his belief that the merely apparent "particularity" of miracles arises from the inability of finite minds to conceive divinely general laws: "In my opinion none of the actions of God are exceptions, but conform to general rules. And just as there is no line, freely made by hand, however irregular it appears to be, which cannot be reduced to a rule or a definition, in the same way the consequences of God's actions comprise a certain quite regular disposition, without any exception."[153] Here Leibniz's view was no doubt that, if Malebranche had been a better mathematician, he would have operated with a more adequate idea of generality.

Leibniz explicitly politicizes his notion of God's generality (even in miracles) in a manuscript from c. 1700 entitled *Conversation sur la liberté et le destin.* After talking about the "order of justice" in the best of all possible worlds that God has chosen to produce, and after enlarging on the "usefulness" of divinely appointed "pains and compensations" ("right is always based on the general utility"), Leibniz goes on to discuss God's *volontés générales,* which "serve as a rule," and his *volontés particulières,* which are "not at all an exception to the rule" (if one understands true generality). God's two kinds of will are "different without being contrary," and one can even say that the particular is subordinated to the general. As for human conduct, "we can only govern ourselves through the known will of God, which is general, that is to say through the orders which he has given us" (such as the Commandments). (Leibniz admits that *généralité* is not always clung to in practice; in *Mars*

---

[152] Ibid., p. 202.
[153] Ibid., p. 222.

Christianissimus (1683) he complains that "the majority of men [have] the habit of considering their *interest particulier* rather than the public good . . . the *bien général du Christianisme.*")[154]

Despite some disagreements with Malebranche, Leibniz could send a copy of the *Théodicée* to the Oratorian in the confident belief that most of it would prove congenial, and Malebranche's acknowledgement of Leibniz's present ("you prove quite well . . . that God . . . must choose the best") showed Leibniz to be right.[155] A shared Augustinian Platonism and love of eternal mathematical order formed the *rapport* between Malebranche and Leibniz; and, if Malebranche was a more nearly orthodox Cartesian than his Hannoverian correspondent, even the Oratorian shared Leibniz's distaste for the Cartesian notion that God creates mathematical, logical, and moral truth *ex nihilo.*[156]

It seems clear, moreover, that this Malebranchian-Leibnizian (ultimately Platonic) notion of justice as general laws not merely willed by someone with sovereign domain found its way into Montesquieu and, in a somewhat different form, into Rousseau. Treating Hobbes in "a few thoughts" originally intended for his *Traité des devoirs* (1725), Montesquieu complains, using Malebranchian imagery, that "Hobbes wants to do to men what lions themselves do not do"—that is, be in a natural state of war. But, says Montesquieu (anticipating Rousseau), it is not a state of nature that is violent: "It is only by the establishment of societies that some [men] abuse others and become the strongest; before that, they are all equal."[157] (That, in a line, summarizes Rousseau's argument against Hobbes in *L'Etat de guerre.*)[158] Rousseau, of course, always argues along

---

[154] Cited in Gaston Grua, *Leibniz: Textes inédits* (Paris: Presses Universitaires de France, 1948), vol. 2, p. 483. For *Mars Christianissimus*, see *Oeuvres de Leibniz*, ed. Foucher de Careil (Paris: Didot Frères, 1861), vol. 3, pp. 1-2.
[155] Cited in Robinet, *Malebranche et Leibniz*, p. 417.
[156] See Alquié, *Cartésianisme de Malebranche*, pp. 226ff.
[157] Montesquieu, *Oeuvres complètes* (Paris: Pléiade, 1949), vol. 1, p. 1140.
[158] Rousseau, *L'Etat de guerre*, in *Political Writings*, vol. 1, pp. 293ff.

Malebranchian-Leibnizian-Montesquieuean lines that power and justice are wholly distinct: "Force is a form of physical power; I am at a loss to see how it can produce any moral consequences."[159] According to Rousseau, only a society's general will transforms the mere fact of power into right.[160] But this is how Malebranche, too, viewed the *volonté générale* of God: if it rests on the mere fact of omnipotence, then it cannot be called just.

[159] Rousseau, *Du contrat social*, p. 26.
[160] Ibid. "The strongest is never strong enough to be the master always, if he does not transform his power into right, and obedience into duty. . . . To yield to force is an act of necessity, not of will . . . in what sense can it be a duty?"

THE GENERAL WILL
UNDER ATTACK:
THE CRITICISMS OF BOSSUET,
FÉNELON, AND BAYLE

In selecting representative contemporary criticisms of Malebranche's theory of general will one cannot do better than to choose the works of Bossuet and of Bayle. Both offer striking criticisms of Malebranchism, but from radically different perspectives; Bossuet was a pillar of the Catholic church and a close ally of the French monarchy, while Bayle was a Calvinist emigré to Holland who was tolerated by neither French church nor state. Bossuet represented an inspired and eloquent perfect orthodoxy, while Bayle was an independent intellectual frequently accused of undercutting all orthodoxy.[1] Despite these enormous differences, both developed influential critiques of Malebranchism during roughly the same period—from the early 1680s to their nearly coinciding deaths (Bossuet in 1704, Bayle in 1706). Bayle began as a strong Malebranchist, then moved slowly but steadily away, while Bossuet began with violent antipathy and ended with slight and partial sympathy. Nonetheless, Bossuet and Bayle almost certainly count (together with Antoine Arnauld) as the most important antagonists

[1] See Elisabeth Labrousse, *Pierre Bayle* (The Hague: Martinus Nijhoff, 1964), passim, and Henri Gouhier, *Fénelon philosophe* (Paris: Vrin, 1977), pp. 33ff.

of Malebranchian *volonté générale* at the end of the seventeenth century.

If Arnauld was influential enough so that some of his partisans succeeded in having the *Traité de la nature et de la grâce* placed on the Index at Rome in 1690,[2] the still more formidable opponent was Bossuet—Bishop of Meaux, preacher to the Court at Versailles, tutor to the Dauphin. Bossuet showed an unabating hostility to Malebranchian *volonté générale*, first in his *Oraison funèbre de Marie-Thérèse d'Autriche* (1683), then in his correspondence with Malebranche's disciple, the Marquis d'Allemans, and finally in his commissioning of Fénelon's *Réfutation du système du Père Malebranche sur la nature et la grâce* (which Bossuet corrected and annotated in his own hand, but finally did not publish).[3] Of course, Bossuet's great *Discours sur l'histoire universelle* (1681) is built on the notion of a *Providence particulière*, which Malebranche had tried so hard to overturn, just as his *Politique tirée des propres paroles de l'Ecriture Sainte* relied on the very "anthropologies" that Malebranche had scorned. It was only in 1697, when Malebranche published his *Traité de l'amour de Dieu*, which argued against Fénelonian "quietism" and disinterested love, that Bossuet—now locked in combat with Fénelon—finally began to countenance a part of Malebranchism, and even to make some slight use of the term *volonté générale* in his magistral *Défense de la tradition et des Pères*, which was left unfinished (with a massive fragment on grace in St. Augustine) at his death in 1704.[4]

---

[2] For details of the condemnation of Malebranche's work, see Malebranche, *Oeuvres complètes de Malebranche*, ed. André Robinet (Paris: Vrin, 1966), vol. 19, pp. 550-558.

[3] See Gouhier, *Fénelon philosophe*, pp. 33ff.

[4] J. B. Bossuet, *Oeuvres complètes de Bossuet* (Bar-le-Duc, France: Louis Guérin, 1870), vol. 5, pp. iiiff. (a brief historical account of the composition of the *Défense*). For a good, short account of Bossuet's political views and writings, see the Introduction to Bossuet, *Politique tirée des propres paroles de l'Ecriture Sainte*, ed. and intro. Jacques Le Brun (Geneva: Librairie Droz, 1967), pp. vii-xxxi.

If Bossuet ended his career with a partial countenancing of general will—though within very narrow, nonpolitical limits—he also began that career with a view of the general and the particular that is not wholly unrelated to Malebranchism. In a sermon on Providence, preached at the Louvre in 1662, Bossuet argues that the "remarkable difference" between *les causes particulières* and *la cause universelle* (God) is that particular causes—such as heat and cold, human desires and counter-desires—oppose and cancel each other, while the universal cause "encloses both the whole and the parts within the same order." And he pursues the distinction between the *particulière* and the *universelle* in a moral tone rather like that of Malebranche's *Nature et grâce*.

> Whoever attaches himself to particular causes—or, let us say it more plainly, whoever wants to obtain a benefit from a Prince; whoever wants to make his fortune in a circuitous way, finds other claimants who counter him, finds unforeseen collisions which cross him: a scheme fails to work in time, and the machine breaks down; intrigue fails to have its effect; hopes go up in smoke. But whoever attaches himself immutably to the whole and not to the parts; not to proximate causes— to the powerful, to favor, to intrigue—but to the *cause première et fondamentelle*, to God, to his will, to his providence, finds nothing which opposes him, nothing which troubles his plans.[5]

While this is not exactly Malebranchism, the merely particular is cast in an unflattering light by being linked with "circuitousness," "collision," "breaking down," "intrigue," and "smoke," while the universal is "providential." And one cannot help noticing that the wish to be benefited by a prince is lumped with smoke and intrigue.

Just one year later, in 1663, Bossuet preached the *oraison*

---

[5] Bossuet, "Sermon sur la Providence," in *Oeuvres de Bossuet*, ed. B. Velat and Y. Champailler (Paris: Pléiade, 1961), p. 1070.

funèbre of his benefactor, Nicolas Cornet, the syndic of the Sorbonne who had first identified (Jansenists would say "constructed") the "five propositions."[6] Without specifically affirming, against the Jansenists, that God has a still-efficacious general will to save all men, Bossuet nonetheless praises Cornet for the "exquisite knowledge" of Scripture and of the writings of Saints Augustine and Thomas that permitted him, in conjunction with "the best minds of the Sorbonne," to identify "these five propositions," which go beyond "the just limits by which truth is separated from error" and manifest the "singularity" and "peculiarity" of new opinions. To be sure, Bossuet concedes, the leading Jansenists were "great men, eloquent, bold, strong and luminous minds"; but they were also "more capable of pushing things to the extreme" than of being moderate—though they were quite right to oppose the Jesuitical laxity that Bossuet equally castigates. In the face of the "zealous and powerful" Jansenist party within the Sorbonne, Nicolas Cornet "worked usefully among these tumults, convincing some through his doctrine, restraining others by his authority, animating and sustaining everyone through his constancy." The praise of the characters (if not the thoughts) of the Jansenists, coupled with an assault on Jesuitical latitudinarianism reminiscent of Pascal's *Lettres provinciales*, allows Bossuet to steer a middle course between "terrible excesses" of rigor and worldliness.[7] Nevertheless, it could really please no orthodox Jansenist to hear the five propositions stigmatized as "singular," "peculiar," and "error," for that must mean—if the fifth proposition is as erroneous as the rest—that it is *not* a "semi-Pelagian" heresy to read "God wills that all men be saved" *au pied de la lettre*. A Jan-

---

[6] For the view that the five propositions were constructed or fabricated, not "found" in Jansenius's *Augustinus*, see Jean LaPorte, "Le Jansénisme," in *Etudes d'histoire de la philosophie française au XVIIe siècle* (Paris: Vrin, 1951), pp. 88ff.

[7] Bossuet, *Oraison funèbre de Nicolas Cornet*, in *Oeuvres*, ed. Velat and Champailler, pp. 51, 50, 44.

senist, indeed, would wish that St. Paul had ceased his letter writing with Romans 9, with the doctrine that God
"hath mercy on whom he will have mercy, and whom he
will he hardeneth . . . hath not the potter power over the
clay, of the same lump to make one vessel unto honor, and
another unto dishonor?"[8] The clay of Romans can certainly
be modeled into "the elect"; it is Paul's letter to Timothy
that is harder to shape to Jansenist ends. By condemning
the fifth proposition, Bossuet tacitly reaffirms God's general will to save all men.

By 1680, however, when Bossuet first read Malebranche's *Nature et grâce*, his thought had begun to change.
He is said to have written *pulchra, nova, falsa* on his published copy, and by June 1683 he was expressing his doubts
about divine general will (in general) and his "horror" of
Malebranchian *volonté générale* (in particular) in a letter to a
fellow bishop.[9] But the decisive, and very public, turn came
in September 1683 with the rhetorically superb *Oraison funèbre de Marie-Thérèse d'Autriche*, pronounced by Bossuet
during the funeral of the Queen of France at St. Denis, in
the presence of the Dauphin and of the Court.[10] The central
passage of this remarkable funeral oration (which was
quickly published) is aimed clearly and obviously at Malebranche's "general will":

> What contempt I have for those philosophers who,
> measuring the counsels of God by their own thoughts,
> make him the author of nothing more than a certain
> general order, out of which the rest develops as it may!
> As if he had, after our fashion, only general and con-

---

[8] Rom. 9:18, 21. One might reasonably say that the whole question of
volonté générale is a theological byproduct of later efforts to reconcile St.
Paul with himself—to make this passage from Romans coexist with 1 Tim.
2:4.

[9] Bossuet, letter to Neercassel (June 1683), in N. Malebranche, *Oeuvres
complètes de Malebranche*, ed. André Robinet (Paris: Vrin, 1966), vol. 18, pp.
248-249.

[10] See Bossuet, *Oeuvres*, ed. Velat and Champailler, pp. 1235-1236, for
notes concerning this *Oraison funèbre*.

fused views, and as if the sovereign intelligence could not include in his plans particular things, which alone truly exist.[11]

Bossuet—who has begun by equating the "general" with the "confused" and by adroitly re-aiming the charge of anthropomorphism at Malebranche himself—loses no time in drawing a purely political moral from this particularism: God has "ordained," in all nations, *les familles particulières* who ought to govern those nations, and, still more *en particulier*, he has ordained the precise persons within those families who will help a ruling house "to rise, to sustain itself, or to fall." Since "it is God who gives [the world] great births, great marriages, children and posterity," it is certainly God who particularly gave Queen Marie-Thérèse to France. (Bossuet supports this claim with numerous Old Testament citations, particularly Genesis 17:6, where God tells Abraham, "Kings will issue from you.")[12]

Bossuet does not hesitate to use the language of grace to reinforce this political particularism. God, he argues, has "predestined" from all eternity the world's political "alliances and divisions"; by giving France a Hapsburg queen through *une grâce particulière*, he has drawn together Austrian counsel and French courage (which are the *caractères particuliers* of those nations), much as he earlier gave the virtue of clemency to the kings of Israel. Theological notions are piled up to particularly striking effect in a passage that begins by lamenting the "rarity" of purity in men, but more especially in "the great."

And nonetheless it is true, Messieurs, that God, through a miracle of his grace, has been pleased to choose, among kings, some pure souls. Such was St. Louis [IX], always pure and holy since childhood; and Marie-Thérèse, his daughter, [who] received this fine

[11] Bossuet, *Oraison funèbre de Marie-Thérèse d'Autriche*, in *Oeuvres*, ed. Velat and Champailler, p. 110.
[12] Ibid., pp. 110, 1238nn.

inheritance from him. Let us enter, Messieurs, into the plans of Providence, and let us admire the goodness of God . . . in the predestination of this Princess.[13]

Here, of course, grace is "a miracle" and therefore precisely *not* something general; the queen is particularly "predestined" to rule by God's choice. To be sure, such rule was not the queen's chief attribute; what really mattered was her piety. "She tells you," Bossuet insists, "through my mouth . . . that greatness is a dream, that joy is an error, that youth is a flower that withers, and that health is a deceiving name." Nonetheless, he ends by admonishing the Dauphin to ask God—"as Solomon did"—for the wisdom that will make him worthy of the throne of his ancestors.[14] And "asking," of course, supposes a *Providence particulière* that can intervene in human affairs to *give* what is asked for.

Incidentally, Bossuet's notion that Malebranchian "generality" cannot account for anything as particular as "great births" reappears, but transmogrified, in the work of the French Spinozist Pierre-Valentine Faydit, who in his *Remarques sur Virgile et Homère et sur le style poetique de l'Ecriture Sainte* (1705) offers a grotesque dramatization of Malebranche's alleged contempt for everything particular. Imagining Malebranche attending a *Te Deum* for the birth of Louis XIV's great-grandson, the Duc de Brétagne, Faydit asks Malebranche, "What are you doing here, Father? You laugh in your soul and up your sleeve at our devotion, and you say to yourself that we are quite simple and great idiots to believe that it is God who, by a *volonté particulière*, has accorded health to the King, and has given a son to his grandson." Bossuet himself, of course, with his marmoreal splendor of style, would never have stooped to anything so *outré*; but the *outré* was Faydit's specialty, whether in a nasty ad

---

[13] Ibid., pp. 109-111.
[14] Ibid., p. 133.

hominem attack on Fénelon (*Télémacomanie*)[15] or in the famous anti-Malebranchian couplet:

> Lui qui voit tout en Dieu
> N'y voit pas qu'il est fou.[16]

The present point is simply that Bossuet's *Oraison funèbre*—published in October 1683—was widely known, and sometimes recast in base material.

Bossuet actually sent a copy of this published version to Malebranche, who felt constrained to thank the bishop for his thoughtful gift.[17] Bossuet's criticism of *volonté générale* was not always quite so public, however; indeed, the lengthiest of his refutations of general will is to be found in a 1687 letter to the Malebranchian Marquis d'Allemans, who had tried to represent (or re-present) Malebranche's *Nature et grâce* in a way that Bossuet could accept. Bossuet begins this very long letter by complaining that d'Allemans has not in the slightest succeeded in making *Nature et grâce* more palatable; he refers to Malebranche, with withering sarcasm, as "your infallible doctor" and "your master." "I notice in you," Bossuet tells the marquis, "nothing but an attachment, which grows every day more blind, to your patriarch," though his "ridiculous" theory of nature and grace is "a perfect *galimatias*."[18]

To be more exact, in Bossuet's view Malebranche does not really offer nature *and* grace at all: he offers just nature, and grace vanishes. (The "naturalization" of grace that was later to delight Voltaire only horrified Bossuet.)[19] It is bad

---

[15] Cited in Paul Vernière, *Spinoza et la pensée française* (Paris: Presses Universitaires de France, 1954), vol. 1, p. 181.

[16] On Faydit's treatment of Malebranche's philosophy, see Malebranche, *Oeuvres complètes*, vol. 20, pp. 364ff.

[17] Ginette Dreyfus, Introduction to Malebranche, *Traité de la nature et de la grâce*, 1680 ed. (Paris: Vrin, 1958), pp. 127ff. ("l'opposition commune de Bossuet et de Fénelon").

[18] Bossuet, letter to the Marquis d'Allemans (May 1687), in Malebranche, *Oeuvres complètes*, vol. 18, p. 444.

[19] Voltaire, *Dictionnaire philosophique*, s.v. "grâce," cited in Ferdinand

71

enough, Bossuet complains, that Malebranche prides himself on having "explained Noah's Flood through the operation of natural causes," but if d'Allemans continues to follow Malebranche, "he will lead you to find, in those same causes," the Israelites' passage through the Red Sea as well as all other scriptural "marvels of this kind." If one means by natural causality the "effects which happen through the force of the first laws of movement," then Malebranchian generality will finally "render everything natural, even to the resurrection of the dead and the healing of those born blind."[20] (Bossuet turned out to be as prescient as he was conservative; Rousseau was to argue only eighty years later in the Malebranche-colored *Lettres écrites de la montagne* that the raising of Lazarus was no "supernatural operation," but a misreported "live interment," and that one should doubt particular changes in the order of nature.)[21]

Much of this "heresy" (as Bossuet does not hesitate to call it) arises from misunderstood Cartesianism:

For on the pretext that one should admit only what one clearly understands—which, within certain limits, is quite true—each person gives himself freedom to say: I understand this, I do not understand that; and on this sole foundation, one approves or rejects whatever one likes. . . . Thus is introduced, under this pretext, a liberty of judging which involves advancing with temerity whatever one thinks, without regard for tradition.[22]

Alquié, *Le Cartésianisme de Malebranche* (Paris: Vrin, 1974), pp. 443-444: "Toute la nature, tout ce qui existe, est une grâce de Dieu. . . . La grâce de faire croître un arbre de soixante et dix pieds est accordée au sapin, et refusée au roseau. Il [Dieu] donne à l'homme la grâce de penser, de parler et de le connaître." Alquié himself adds (p. 444): "Ici, l'assimilation de la nature et de la grâce est complète. Malebranche, assurement, n'opère pas cette identification. Mais, en naturalisant la grâce, il prépare de telles pensées."
[20] Bossuet, letter to the Marquis d'Allemans, p. 444.
[21] Jean-Jacques Rousseau, *Lettres écrites de la montagne*, in *Rousseau: Oeuvres complètes* (Paris: Editions du Seuil, 1971), vol. 3, p. 424n.
[22] Bossuet, letter to the Marquis d'Allemans, p. 445.

This clearly refers to Malebranche's notion that one must conceive God through the idea of an *être parfait*, and not through (allegedly historical) "anthropologies." But this preference for ideas, this contempt for tradition, leaves Bossuet "terrified" and fearful of "great scandal"; heretics, he says, always "begin with novelty," move on to "stubbornness," and end with "open revolt."[23]

Bossuet concludes his letter—spoken, he says, "as one does to a friend"—with a final, chilling remark about thinking that one can "do" theology because one "knows physics and algebra"; he reminds Malebranche's disciple that one cannot favor both Malebranchian *volonté générale* and Bossuet's own *Histoire universelle* (which d'Allemans had praised).

> It is easy for me to show you that the principles on which I reason are directly opposed to those of your system. . . . There is a great difference in saying, as I do, that God leads each thing to the end which he proposes for it by the means which he [actually] follows, and in saying that he contents himself with giving some general laws, from which result many things which enter only indirectly into his plans. . . . I turn away from your ideas of general laws.[24]

Bossuet was perfectly right, of course, in characterizing his own *Histoire universelle* as a work built on *Providence particulière*, not on general laws. "Remember, Monseigneur," Bossuet admonishes the Dauphin at the end of the *Histoire*, "that this long chain of particular causes, which make and unmake empires, depends on the secret decrees of Divine Providence." It is God who "holds the reins of every kingdom and holds every heart in his hands." Moreover, his action in shaping universal history is completely particular: "Should he wish to see a conqueror, he will spread terror

---

[23] Ibid., p. 446.
[24] Ibid., p. 447.

before him . . . should he wish to see legislators, he will send them his spirit of wisdom and foresight."[25] Bossuet—after virtually anticipating Hegel's "cunning of history" by urging that, thanks to secret Providence, rulers "achieve either more or less than they plan," and that "their intentions have always led to unforeseen consequences"—concludes with an apotheosis of *Providence particulière* that Montesquieu must have had in mind (if only to oppose it) when he wrote *Considerations on the Greatness and Decline of the Romans* fifty years later.

> Thus God reigns over every nation. Let us no longer speak of coincidence or fortune; or let us use those words only to cover our ignorance. What is coincidence to our uncertain foresight is concerted design to a higher foresight, that is, to the eternal foresight which encompasses all causes and all effects in a single plan. Thus all things concur to the same end; and it is only because we fail to understand the whole design that we see coincidence or strangeness in particular events.[26]

It is precisely the *Histoire universelle* that is cited at a crucial juncture in the work that Bossuet commissioned from the Abbé Fénelon in 1686-1687; this *Réfutation du système du Père Malebranche sur la nature et la grâce*, corrected and (in some parts) rewritten or amplified by Bossuet himself, is

---

[25] Bossuet, *Discours sur l'histoire universelle*, in *Oeuvres de Bossuet* (Versailles: J. A. Lebel, 1818), vol. 35, p. 556.

[26] Ibid., p. 557. Montesquieu was surely thinking of this passage—if only to refute it through Malebranchian *généralité*—when he wrote the key paragraph of chapter 18 of his *Considerations on the Greatness and Decline of the Romans*: "It is not chance that rules the world. . . . There are general causes, moral and physical, which act in every monarchy, elevating it, maintaining it, or hurling it to the ground. All accidents are controlled by these causes. And if the chance of one battle—that is, a particular cause—has brought a state to ruin, some general cause made it necessary for that state to perish from a single battle. In a word, the main trend draws with it all particular accidents" (trans. D. Lowenthal [Ithaca: Cornell University Press, 1968], p. 169).

perhaps the most important philosophical contribution that Bossuet made to anti-Malebranchism—even if Bossuet was only the occasional cause, and Fénelon the true cause, of the *Réfutation*.[27] In this work, apparently commissioned after Bossuet became dissatisfied with his own attempted refutation of *volonté générale*, Fénelon begins with a reasonably fair résumé of *Nature et grâce*. Nevertheless, he thinks that he has found a fatal flaw in Malebranche's admission that God acts only usually, but not invariably, through general wills and general laws, that he sometimes (though "rarely") acts through *volontés particulières*.

> But in what consists that which the author [Malebranche] calls 'rarely'? These words signify nothing, unless they mean that there is a certain small number of *volontés particulières* which order permits to God outside the general laws, after which he can will nothing particularly. If order permits to God this small number of *volontés particulières*—order never permitting anything but the most perfect—it follows not only that these *volontés particulières* do not diminish in the slightest the simplicity of God's ways, but even that it is more perfect of God to mix some *volontés particulières* in his general plan, than to limit himself absolutely to his *volontés générales*.[28]

(In his corrections, Bossuet complains at this point that Fénelon should not confuse God's simplicity with his perfection. "Multiplicity [of divine wills] may well not be contrary to perfection," Bossuet urges, "but it is always [contrary] to simplicity." This is logically unimpeachable; the "simple" is *necessarily* nonmultiple, and the "perfect" may or may not involve multiplicity.)[29]

Fénelon, still stressing simplicity rather than perfection,

[27] See Gouhier, *Fénelon philosophe*, pp. 33ff.
[28] François Fénelon, *Oeuvres de Fénelon* (Paris: Chez Lefevre, 1835), vol. 2, p. 258.
[29] Ibid., p. 258n.

goes on to imagine a hypothetical case in which order has permitted God to have a hundred *volontés particulières*. He then asks himself a rhetorical question: "What, then, is this 'simplicity' which is able to accommodate a hundred [particular] wills, which even requires them, but which invincibly rejects the hundred and first?" In a passage that is extremely effective, though perhaps not entirely fair, he adds that "if God did not have these hundred *volontés particulières*, he would cease to be God; for he would violate the order which requires them, and would not act with the greatest perfection. If he had the hundred and first *volonté*, he would also cease to be God; for he would destroy the simplicity of his ways."[30]

It is certainly not the case, Fénelon goes on, that the hundred and first *volonté particulière* is "of another nature" than the first hundred; all are equally "exceptions to the general rule." He ends with the striking question, "Is there a fatal number of exceptions which God is obliged to use up, after which he can will nothing except according to general laws? Would one dare to say this?"[31] Even if, as Bossuet's annotations argue, a multiplicity of *volontés particulières* would contradict only "simplicity," but not necessarily "perfection," this is an effective passage.

The political moral of all this is drawn by Fénelon several chapters later, in a section entitled, "That Which the Author [Malebranche] Says about *Volontés Particulières* Destroys, through Its Consequences, All Divine Providence." Sometimes, Fénelon argues, Providence "acts against general rules, through miracles" (as in the parting of the Red Sea); this particularism is obviously morally and politically important, since the Jews *deserved* to escape from the Egyptians. Sometimes, however—and this seems to matter more—Providence creates a *parallel* between general laws and "particular plans"; she "uses the wills of men, in which

[30] Ibid., pp. 258-259.
[31] Ibid., p. 259.

she inspires whatever pleases her, to cause even in matter itself movements which seem fortuitous, but which are related to events which God wills to draw from them." It was exactly in this way, Fénelon insists, that Alexander the Great "conceived the ambitious plan of conquering Asia: in that way he was able to fulfil the prophecy of Daniel." If one examines all the revolutions of great empires, which are "the greatest spectacle which can sustain our faith," one sees that "Providence has raised or leveled them to prepare the way for the Messiah, and to establish his endless reign." And in a footnote, he indicates that on this point it is Bossuet's *Histoire universelle* that ought to be consulted.[32] (In this chapter, significantly, Bossuet found nothing at all to fault.)[33]

By the 1690s, Bossuet had lost his one-time disciple Fénelon to Mme. Guyon, "quietism," and the "disinterested love of God," and there was something of a rapprochement with Malebranche.[34] Hence, in his *Défense de la tradition et des Pères*, which he began in 1693 as a refutation of Richard Simon's *Histoire critique des principaux commentateurs du Nouveau Testament*,[35] he allowed himself to use the concept of general will—though mainly in the thirteenth book, which he added to the manuscript in 1702. Even here, he refuses to use *volonté générale* in Malebranche's expanded sense, as something coextensive with wisdom, constancy, even justice, but is careful to restrict the term to a narrowly circumscribed realm of grace. Indeed, he talks simply about St. Augustine's interpretation of the Pauline assertion that "God wills that all men be saved"—the very claim that started the whole controversy over general will.

St. Augustine's difficulty, Bossuet argues, was that of

---

[32] Ibid., p. 270, 270n.

[33] See Bossuet's notes to Fénelon's *Réfutation*, in Fénelon, *Oeuvres*, pp. 270n-273n.

[34] See Gouhier, *Fénelon philosophe*, pp. 77ff.

[35] Theodore Delmont, *Bossuet et les Saints Pères* (Geneva: Slatkine, 1970), pp. 590ff.

knowing why the will to believe was not given equally to all men, if God truly wills that all men be saved. St. Augustine had two related problems as well: first, how one can say that God wills something that "does not happen" (since some are damned, not saved), and second, how one can reconcile God's general will with human free will. In Bossuet's view, St. Augustine overcomes all of these difficulties quite admirably by "saying that God truly wills to save all men, but that, since he wants to do this without depriving them of their natural liberty, it is also through the latter that they perish." St. Augustine supposes that, if all men are not saved, the obstacle comes not at all from "the *volonté* of God, which is *générale*," but from the will of man, which opposes God. (In the end, this "opposition" gets punished, precisely through some men's being damned.)[36]

Bossuet grants that St. Augustine does not invariably maintain that God has a general will to save all men. Indeed, in *De correptione et gratia*, Bossuet concedes, Augustine seems to say that "all" men in St. Paul's assertion refers simply to "the predestined." Bossuet insists, however, that one must recall that in this and other late writings St. Augustine was combatting the Pelagians, who "amused the world by calling nature 'grace' " and maintained that grace was given to all equally and indifferently. It was the aim of St. Augustine, Bossuet continues, "to preach the grace by which we are Christians"; he finally concludes that while God as creator willed generally that all men be saved, God as redeemer reduced this "all" to Christians.[37] This, of course, is fairly close to what Pascal says about a *volonté générale* to save "all" being replaced, after the Fall, by a will to save a smaller number—though Bossuet, no Jansenist, is careful not to speak of the "elect."

Even when he is willing to employ *volonté générale*, then, Bossuet is careful to restrict it radically. He does not extend

---

[36] Bossuet, *Défense de la tradition et des Pères*, in *Oeuvres complètes*, 1870 ed., vol. 5, p. 324.
[37] Ibid., pp. 357-359.

the term to cover "bodies politic," as Pascal does, nor does it become coextensive with legality, as in Malebranche. Hence, one can conclude that, with the exception of the purely theological *Défense de la tradition et des Pères*, Bossuet adhered in the main to his providentialist particularism—which, *inter alia*, saved Louis XIV from being a mere consequence of a general law. Of all those who use the term "general will" in the late seventeenth century, Bossuet uses it in the *least* general way.[38]

If Bossuet said a great deal (most of it negative) about *volonté générale*, he did little to prepare it for Montesquieu's extensive secularization and politicization of the term in *De l'esprit des lois*. Indeed, at first sight it looks as if there is a missing link in the "translation" of general will from a primarily theological notion into a primarily political one—though one should recall that Pascal had used the notions of *généralité* and *particularité* with respect to bodies politic. That missing link is supplied by an important writer who was completely familiar with the theological use of the notions *volonté générale* and *volonté particulière* and who frequently used those notions in a purely political sense: Pierre Bayle, *philosophe de Rotterdam*.[39] It was Bayle, especially, who undertook this secular conversion, paving the way first for Montesquieu's further transformations and then for Rousseau's "making the history" of the general will. (To be sure, one can find other links between the seventeenth and eighteenth centuries. If Bayle is most important, one can still admit that Cardinal Polignac's *Anti-Lucrèce*, written in the 1720s, stresses the notion that, "if rain falls in the sea or in a wilderness," it is because these natural facts are "particular effects of *loix générales* estab-

[38] Except, of course, for the late works of Antoine Arnauld *contra* Malebranchian *généralité*.

[39] For an appreciation of Bayle's knowledge of (particularly Malebranchian) theology, see Labrousse, *Pierre Bayle*, vol. 2, pp. 187ff.

lished for the governance of the universe."[40] That purely Malebranchian thought is *slightly* politicized by being linked to the notion of "governance"; interestingly, Polignac read the *Anti-Lucrèce* to Montesquieu when the latter visited Rome in 1729.[41] Nevertheless, Bayle's secularization of *volonté générale* is far more radical and thoroughgoing.)

Though a Calvinist, Bayle was briefly (c. 1680-1685) a Malebranchist as well;[42] indeed, nothing did more to spread the European fame of Malebranche's *Nature et grâce* than Bayle's glowing review (May 1684) in his universally diffused journal, *Nouvelles de la république des lettres*. The hypothesis that "God acts through a general will which prescribes only a small number of simple and uniform laws," Bayle argues, is quite suitable for justifying "several things which cause pain to minds of the second rank." (Is this slightly left-handed compliment an intimation of hostility to come?) When these minds ask why "nature produces so many monstrous things," or why "in the order of grace there are so many things which shock our reason," a Malebranchian can reply that they are consequences of the general laws that God has chosen, and that God loves his own wisdom "infinitely more than all his works." Though one may not agree with everything in Malebranche's *Nature et grâce*, one is still "forced to admit that no one has ever, perhaps, formed so well-linked a system in so little time"—a system that manifests the vast and penetrating genius of its author.[43]

Bayle's decisive work in this vein is the thoroughly Malebranchian *Pensées diverses sur la comète* (1682), the general aim of which is to overturn superstition by demonstrating that the comet that alarmed Europe in December 1680 was

[40] Melchior de Polignac, *L'Anti-Lucrèce, Poème sur la réligion naturelle*, trans. de Bougainville (Paris: Desaint et Saillant, 1749), vol. 2, p. 304.

[41] Robert Shackleton, "Bayle and Montesquieu," in *Pierre Bayle, le philosophe de Rotterdam*, ed. P. Dibon (Amsterdam: Elsevier, 1959), p. 147.

[42] See Alquié, *Cartésianisme de Malebranche*, pp. 16-17.

[43] Pierre Bayle, *Compte rendu du Traité de la nature et de la grâce*, from the *Nouvelles de la république des lettres* (May 1684), in Malebranche, *Oeuvres complètes*, vol. 8-9, pp. 1153-1156.

produced by Malebranchian general laws, that it was not a sign of *Providence particulière* or a portent of doom. If God wants to instruct the world through something miraculous, Bayle argues, he sends persons (Christ, for example) who shine "with the brilliance of excellent virtues" that only the "voluntarily blind" can ignore; he does not merely send a flying rock signifying "at most the anger of heaven." If all the martyrs and prophets have not overcome idolatry, Bayle observes tartly, why should one expect much from "a mute flame, which naturally inspires only a feeling of apprehension?"[44]

Those who have read Malebranche's *Nature et grâce*, Bayle goes on, will have understood that "the events which are born of the execution of general laws of nature, are not the object of a *volonté particulière* of God." And this Malebranchian generality, in Bayle's view, is usable in "resolving a thousand difficulties which are raised against divine Providence."

> If we are permitted to judge the actions of God, we can say that he does not will all particular events because of the perfection they contain, but simply because they are linked to general laws which he has chosen to be the rule of his operations. . . . One can even imagine that the simplicity and uniformity of this way of acting, joined with an infinite fecundicity, seemed preferable to him, to another way of acting [which was] more complicated but more regular, even though some superfluous events had to result from this.[45]

So clearly does Bayle adhere to Malebranche at this point in his career that he even copies Malebranche's treatment of morality as a kind of analogue to law-governed nature. Just as it would be "ridiculous" to claim that God ought to depart from laws of nature "when a rock falls on a fragile vase which is the delight of its owner," so also it is ridiculous to

---

[44] Bayle, *Pensées diverses, Ecrites à un docteur de Sorbonne*, 4th ed. (Rotterdam: Chez Reinier Leers, 1704), vol. 2, pp. 452-453.
[45] Ibid., pp. 462-463.

claim that God should abandon generality "to stop an evil man from enriching himself by despoiling an *homme de bien*." Indeed, Bayle outstrips Malebranche in the purity of his Malebranchism by urging that it is as unjust to wish that an evil man become sick through a divine *volonté particulière* as it is unreasonable to hope that a rock that falls on a vase will not break it. In the same chapter of the *Pensées diverses*, Bayle extracts a political moral from his tale of the fragile vase and the evil man by urging that if "a mere governor of a city will be laughed at, if he changes his rules and his orders as many times as it pleases anyone to murmur against him," this is even more true of God, "whose laws concern so universal a good." Can God "derogate from his laws, because today they fail to please someone, tomorrow someone else?" Can one, Bayle asks, "form falser ideas of a *Providence générale*?"[46]

This hyper-Malebranchism Bayle carries over into a still more extended political analogy—located, appropriately enough, in a chapter of the *Pensées diverses* called "That There Is Nothing Worthier of the Greatness of God Than to Maintain General Laws." Some people say, Bayle begins, that God *ought* to intervene particularly in nature to stop the birth of "monsters" that might later be worshipped by "idolators"; but these people do not reflect that "there could be nothing more unworthy of a *cause générale*, which sets all others in motion by a simple and uniform law, than to violate that law at every moment, in order to prevent murmurings and superstitions." In just the same way, Bayle insists, "there is nothing which gives us a higher idea of a monarch, than to see that he, having wisely established a law, maintains it in vigor for all and against all," without suffering the prejudice of an individual [*un particulier*] or the "interested recommendations of a favorite" to restrict the law's generality. He adds, as much *à la Rousseau* as *à la Malebranche*, that, "of all the things which are capable of throwing the state into monstrous confusion," the worst is "to derogate from the laws, to change them, to mutilate them, to stretch them, to abridge them" in proportion as *des particuliers* have "domestic views" that accommodate these alterations. It is true enough, Bayle grants, that human limitation seems to necessitate that *les politiques* correct their laws through declarations and interpretations. It remains true, however, that "the more a law is maintained without alteration, the more also it shows the great sense and the great vision of him who made it."[47] In this assertion, Malebranche is recalled and Rousseau is foreshadowed: it is a "monstrously confused" state in which *des particuliers* deprive law of its generality; and statesmen should strive to imitate the constancy of the divine *volonté générale*. In the *Pensées diverses*, the politically rightful and the general are exactly equivalent.

In the second edition of the *Pensées diverses* Bayle added a section arguing that even the Reformation had been brought about by *particularisme*. Shortly before the Council of Trent, he points out, a group of cardinals and bishops told Pope Paul III that the readiness of his predecessors to "derogate from the canon laws" and to "listen to counsels of flattery" constituted the "Trojan horse" that led to "all the abuses which have inundated the Church." Centuries earlier, Innocent IV had been told that papal particularism had derogated from the laws, leading to a "deluge of inconstancy, a lack of faith, and an obstacle to the tranquility of Christianity."[48] Here, very effectively, particularity is linked with flattery, abuse, and inconstancy, while generality is associated with lawfulness, faith, and tranquility.

To be sure, in the *Nouvelles Lettres critiques sur l'histoire du calvinisme* (1684), written only slightly later than the *Pensées diverses*, Bayle shows as much affinity with a Hobbesian

[47] Ibid., pp. 455-457.
[48] Ibid., pp. 456-457: "Il est d'ailleurs indubitable, que la nécessité ou se trouvent les Politiques de corriger leurs loix . . . suppose en eux une intelligence bornée." This is the very language of Malebranche's *Nature et grâce*.

politics based on passion and fear as with a Rousseauean politics grounded in *généralité*. For Bayle, this arises simply from the fact that there is a regrettable (and very large) gap between what politics might be and what it actually is. He begins the political part of the *Nouvelles Lettres* in the familiar Malebranchian-Rousseauean tone of the *Pensées diverses*: "It is more glorious to be led by universal reason, which relates all things to the general good of the universe, than by *une raison particulière*."[49] Shortly, however, Bayle reflects that *la raison universelle* has little efficacy, given the depressing facts of human psychology; this leads him to a more careful (and quasi-Hobbesian) passage in which a general-particular distinction is still present but has lost some of the color of *Nature et grâce* and has assumed some of the hues of *Leviathan*. In this passage Bayle argues that, while pure reason alone is not the motive of human actions, a purely instrumental reason can help to achieve ends dictated by passion—above all, security and the avoidance of death.

"It is necessary," Bayle begins, "to distinguish the reason which precedes the passions" from the reason "which follows in their train." The former is "a certain faculty of the soul which judges things by general principles, and by universal ideas of honor, of justice, of perfection." However, the purely instrumental reason, which is preceded by feelings and instincts, judges everything only by relation to the particular condition [*l'état particulier*] in which one finds himself. In that (more or less Hobbesian) condition, reason has willed that men "confederate" in order to be delivered from "perpetual disquiet"; but this reason is one that "accommodates itself to fear" and "consults" only what "is useful in our present condition," rather than "the general ideas of the good, the beautiful, the great and the honorable."[50]

[49] Bayle, *Nouvelles Lettres critiques sur l'histoire du calvinisme*, in *Oeuvres diverses de M. Pierre Bayle* (The Hague: Compagnie des Libraires, 1737), vol. 2, p. 282.
[50] Ibid.

It would be better, of course, if men had "formed societies through considerations worthy of a reasonable creature"—if they had been willing to perfect themselves, and
not live like beasts. However, it has proven necessary in
human politics "to use a more efficacious means, namely
fear, the love of repose, and some other similar passions."[51]
Despite these concessions to Hobbism, Bayle's groupings
of terms show plainly what would be better; universal reason is "glorious" and points out "the general good," while
la raison particulière is forced by necessity to accommodate itself to passion—above all, fear. Thus, in Bayle there is a tension between a Malebranchian-Rousseauean ideal of *généralité* and an awareness that Hobbes may have been more
nearly right than either Malebranche or Rousseau would
ever admit.[52]

After the revocation of the Edict of Nantes in 1685, followed by the death of his brother, a Calvinist pastor, in a
French prison,[53] Bayle published an uncharacteristically
violent anti-Catholic polemic entitled *Ce que c'est que la
France toute catholique sous le règne de Louis Le Grand*. As a
commentator has noted, one of the most interesting fea-
tures of *La France toute catholique* is "the bitter use Bayle
makes of Malebranche's theology," particularly his *generalism*.[54] (Perhaps Bayle had begun to feel that some "particular" evils—including his own personal disasters of 1685—
could not be explained away as consequences of uniform
laws.) The revocation of the Edict, followed by fresh persecution of non-Catholics, Bayle argues, was "the best lesson
in Malebranchism that could be given; for if it were worthy
of God to act often through *volontés particulières* and through
miracles, would he have suffered that a Church as cor-

---

[51] Ibid.

[52] Malebranche shows an unabating hostility to Hobbes; see *Réflexions
sur la prémotion physique*, in Malebranche, *Oeuvres complètes*, vol. 16, p. 98.

[53] See Elisabeth Labrousse, Introduction to Bayle, *Ce que c'est que la
France toute catholique* (Paris: Vrin, 1973), pp. 7ff.

[54] C. Brush, *Montaigne and Bayle* (The Hague: Martinus Nijhoff, 1966), p.
239.

rupted as yours should grow to the point that it has—a Church which, through the enormity of its maxims and the baseness of some of its dogmas has merited the horror and contempt of all the world?"[55]

"Let us say, then," Bayle concludes savagely, "with this Oratorian Father, that God, loving his wisdom better than anything else, prefers that his conduct bear the character of a wise agent . . . than that it remedy . . . the evils that happen in the world."[56] Bayle does not yet, despite his ferocious sarcasm, call Malebranchism a "pious fraud" (one of the favorite epithets of his *Dictionnaire historique et critique*); but he is clearly moving toward his later view that general will does not *really* explain the evils of the world.[57]

Even so, that later view is not yet wholly realized in *La France toute catholique*, for in other parts of the work there are remnants of Malebranchian generality to which Bayle gives a plainly political turn. He begins in a sarcastic vein, saying that, if Louis XIV had always intended to revoke the Edict of Nantes ("as he assures us in the preface to the Edict"), then he ought to have revoked it by "the shortest way, which is always that of an able worker," and not by "act after act, some of which destroyed each other." Here the Malebranchian idea of an "able" God, working "simply," has been ironically grafted onto the vacillations of Louis XIV. Just slightly later, however, one cannot be sure that the tone is still ironic. Bayle complains that, just before the revocation, Louis's council first permitted Huguenot ministers to baptize children, then (afterwards) permitted them to celebrate marriages ("it is as if the judges who had condemned a criminal to be hanged in three days ordained that he change prisons every two months"), and finally avows,

I have always had some antipathy to the hypotheses of

---

[55] Bayle, *La France toute catholique*, p. 62.
[56] Ibid.
[57] See note 70, below.

Père Malebranche, but I grant, sir, that your [the Catholics'] way of acting gives me a taste for what he says. I find something unworthy in a wise mind when it makes so many *arrêts particuliers*, when it advances, steps back, goes to the right, goes to the left, when it retracts, re-explains itself—in one word when it lives from day to day, that is to say, making new rules at each session of the council. This, I say, seems to me so far from the idea of perfection . . . that I begin to believe, with this new philosopher, that God acts only through a small number of general laws.[58]

After this—and one cannot be sure just how far Malebranchism is being used and how far abused—Bayle concludes that Louis's inconsistencies are "unworthy of a good and wise politics." Given his view in the *Pensées diverses* that good politics should be as general as possible, one cannot be certain whether Bayle is attacking Louis XIV for his inconsistency or for the sheer wrongness of his Huguenot policy. In any case, Louis's particularism proves that a *really* perfect ruler must operate very differently.

Whatever may have been Bayle's doubts about the adequacy of Malebranchism by the time he wrote *La France toute catholique*, he continued to use Malebranche's distinction between *le particulier* (as something bad) and *le général* (as something good) in an important work from c. 1686, the *Commentaire philosophique sur ces paroles de l'évangile selon S. Luc, chap.* XIV, *vers* 23, '*Et le maître dit au serviteur: "Va par les chemins et par les hayes, et contrains-les d'entrer, afin que ma maison soit remplie." '* The central point of the *Commentaire* was to show that Scripture should be interpreted not through "literal sense" but through "natural light"—that, if a literal reading seemed to make Scripture advocate crimes (such as constraining French Protestants to enter the Catholic church), then the literal interpretation must be rejected in favor of an "equitable" reading.[59]

---

[58] Bayle, *La France toute catholique*, p. 46.
[59] Bayle, *Commentaire philosophique*, in *Oeuvres diverses*, vol. 2, p. 368.

It is precisely in connection with equity and *lumière natu-relle* that Bayle takes up the familiar general-particular distinction. "Without exception," he begins, "one must submit all moral laws to this natural idea of equity," which "enlightens every man coming into the world." But, Bayle goes on, in the language of *Recherche de la vérité*, "since passion and prejudices only too often obscure the ideas of natural equity," he could wish that a man who wants to know those ideas well "consider them *en général*, and leaving his *intérêt particulier* out of account, as well as the customs of his country." It may happen that "a sharp passion" will persuade a man that something "very useful" and "very pleasant" to himself is "in conformity to reason," or that he may be swayed by "the force of custom." To avoid this, Bayle argues, he could wish that a man "who wants to know natural light distinctly" in its relation to morality be able to "raise himself above his personal interest, and the custom of his country, and ask himself *en général*, 'Is such-and-such a thing just? And, if it is a question of introducing it into a country where it is not in use . . . would one see, if one examined it coldly, that it is just enough to merit being adopted?' "[60] This last part, which anticipates Rousseau's *Du contrat social*, book 4, chapter 2 ("when a law is proposed in the assembly of the people, what the voters are being asked is . . . whether or not it is in conformity with the general will"),[61] ends by praising "that universal and original light which emanates from God in order to show all men the general principles of equity"—general principles that are the "touchstone" of all *loix particulières*, "not even excepting those which God has revealed to us in an extraordinary way."[62]

If, then, Bayle insists, a casuist tells us that Scripture has

[60] Ibid., p. 379.

[61] Rousseau, *Du contrat social*, in *Political Writings*, ed. C. E. Vaughan (Oxford: Basil Blackwell, 1962), vol. 2, p. 106.

[62] Bayle, *Commentaire philosophique*, p. 106.

particularly revealed to him that "it is good and holy to curse one's enemies" or to persecute the faithful, we must shun him and turn our eyes toward "natural religion fortified and perfected by the Gospel." Then we shall hear "that interior truth which speaks to our spirit without saying a word, but which speaks quite intelligibly to those who pay attention," while the "pretended" Scripture of the casuist will be unmasked as a "bilious vapor of temperament." Even a particular fact produced by God through "special Providence" is not "the light which leads us," and does not derogate from "the positive law which is universally promulgated for all men in the Gospel," which requires all men to be meek and forgiving. Still less does particular Providence derogate from "the natural and eternal law which supplies all men with the idea of honorability." Bayle ends the opening part of the *Commentaire philosophique* with the wholly Malebranchian thought that "universal reason, which illuminates all minds," will never be denied to those who are attentive and do not permit corporeal objects to "fill up the capacity of their soul," nor passions to "excite" their hearts.[63]

By the 1690s, Bayle's doubts about Malebranchism began to overcome his vestigial respect for the doctrine; and in the *Réponse aux questions d'un provincial* he indicates exactly why his views changed and who did the changing. At the time of his review of *Nature et grâce* and of the *Pensées diverses sur la comète*, Bayle relates, he had been among those who believed that Malebranche had resolved many difficulties through general will and general law. Without now denying that Malebranche's system is "the work of a superior genius, and one of the greatest efforts of the human spirit," Bayle avows that, "after having read the books of M. Arnauld against this system, and after having considered well the vast and immense idea of the sovereignly perfect being," he can no longer embrace Malebranchian general-

[63] Ibid.

ity. The idea of an *être parfait* no longer conveys to Bayle what it seemed to convey to Malebranche; the true idea of God "teaches," Bayle argues, that "there is nothing easier for God than to follow a simple, fecund and regular plan, which is, at the same time, suitable for all creatures." It is only "a limited intelligence" (Malebranche's own phrase, now turned against him) that takes more pride in its own ability than in its "love for the public good." All of this Bayle quickly turns in a purely political direction:

A prince who causes a city to be built may, through a false taste for grandeur, prefer that it have an air of magnificence, and an architecture of bold and singular character, though at the same time very inconvenient for its inhabitants, than that, with less magnificence, it allow them to enjoy all sorts of conveniences. But if this prince has a true greatness of soul, that is, a strong disposition to make his subjects happy, he will prefer convenient but less magnificent architecture, to magnificent but less convenient architecture.[64]

From this architectural fable—which is not sufficiently well-designed to be fatal to Malebranche—Bayle concludes that, however well-intentioned "our legislators" on earth may be, they can still never "invent rules which are convenient for all individuals [*particuliers*]"; the limitation of these legislators' enlightenment forces them to fall back on general laws, which, everything considered, are "more useful than damaging."[65] Here generality is something *settled for* but (as in Aristotle) not invariably equitable.[66] But God does not suffer from this problem, since he is "infinite in power and in intelligence."[67] *Why* he does not suffer, why the theodicy problems that drive Malebranche to the general

[64] Bayle, *Réponse aux questions d'un provincial*, in *Oeuvres diverses*, vol. 3, pp. 812, 825, 826.
[65] Ibid.
[66] Aristotle, *Ethics* 3. 1137bff.
[67] Bayle, *Réponse aux questions*, p. 826.

will vanish if one takes note of divine power and intelligence, is not made clear, at least in this work. The probable answer is that, for Bayle, philosophy cannot solve theodicy problems satisfactorily; in the end, one must rely on faith, not reason, in explaining (or rather believing in) the justice of God's operation. As Bayle himself says in the *Dictionnaire historique et critique*, a man is "happily disposed toward faith when he knows how defective reason is. This is why Pascal and others have said that in order to convert the libertines they should make them realize the weakness of reason and teach them to distrust it."[68] This fideism, Bayle's final (and apparently sincere) position, is radically at variance with Malebranche's insistence in the *Traité de morale* that "faith passes away, but intelligence exists eternally."[69] In the end, a fideism like Bayle's cannot coexist with a rationalism like Malebranche's, nor can it hope to find in divine *volonté générale* a model of justice that can be approximately realized on earth.

Despite the fideism of the *Dictionnaire* and Bayle's increasing doubts about a link between generality and justice, there is an important passage in this work—the article dealing with Sarah, wife of the Prophet Abraham—in which precisely that Malebranchian link is maintained. In "Sarah," Bayle considers the ways in which various Christian theologians have tried either to excuse or to condemn Sarah's conduct (recounted in *Genesis*) in countenancing Abraham's impregnation of her servant Agar after Sarah's sterility had led to the impossibility of her bearing a child for Abraham. Bayle argues that St. Augustine's effort to justify Abraham's adultery and Sarah's connivance in *The City of God* is not "une bonne apologie," and that the attempts of St. Ambrose are no better. All of the efforts of the early church fathers to excuse Abraham and Sarah are implausible and even unworthy: "The liberty which Calvin took in

---

[68] Bayle, *Historical and Critical Dictionary*, ed. R. Popkin (Indianapolis: Library of Liberal Arts, 1965), s.v. "Pyrrho."

[69] Malebranche, *Traité de morale*, in *Oeuvres complètes*, vol. 11, p. 34.

strongly censuring this action of Sarah and of her husband, is incomparably more useful to Christian morality, than the care which the Fathers took to justify Abraham and his wife." Using a Malebranchian general-particular distinction, Bayle then indicates just what is unjustifiable, not only in the conduct of Abraham and Sarah, but, still more, in the efforts of Augustine and Ambrose. Those Fathers, through their apologies, sacrificed *les intérêts généraux de la moralité* to "the reputation of a particular person [*un particulier*]."[70] To show more plainly that morality is a general interest, while an individual reputation is only particular, Bayle remarks that even the Patriarch Abraham, yielding to lust, was as susceptible to "the snares of Satan" as are "manifestly criminal persons," and that Augustine's justificatory efforts involve a morality more lax than that of the Jesuits Bauni and Escobar—those accommodating latitudinarians so ferociously attacked by Pascal in the *Lettres provinciales*.[71] (It was surely no accident that Bayle pitched upon the very figures that Pascal—justly or not—had saddled with permanently horrible reputations.)[72] In Bayle's "Sarah," then, the *intérêt général de la moralité* is pitted against Satanic snares, manifest criminality, and Jesuitical laxity; and these should not be admitted, according to Bayle, just to justify *un particulier*, even one who happened to be a prophet.

King David comes in for a similarly harsh treatment in the *Dictionnaire*, couched once again in the language of *généralité* and *particularité*. Following a vivid description of some of King David's crimes, including several massacres and the killing of Uriah, Bayle observes that "the profound respect that one ought to have for this great king" should not blind one to the "blemishes" that disfigured his life;

---

[70] Bayle, *Dictionnaire historique et critique* (Rotterdam, 1720), vol. 3, s.v. "Sarah."

[71] Blaise Pascal, *Les [Lettres] Provinciales*, ed. Louis Cognet (Paris: Garnier Frères, 1965), pp. 72ff. It is in the *Cinquième Lettre* above all that Pascal ridicules the Jesuit doctrine of probabilism as enunciated by Bauni and Escobar.

[72] Ibid., pp. liff. of Cognet's Introduction.

otherwise, some will fancy that "it suffices, in order for an action to be just, that it have been done by certain people whom we venerate." Nothing could be "more fatal . . . to Christian morality" than this countenancing of crimes carried out by great men: "It is important for true religion that the life of the orthodox be judged by general ideas of rightness and of order [*par les idées générales de la droiture et de l'ordre*]." Bayle concludes with virtually the same words that he applies to Sarah and Abraham: "There is no middle ground: either these actions [of King David] are worthless, or actions similar to them are not evil. Now, since one must choose one or the other of these two possibilities, is it not better to place the interests of morality above the glory of an individual [*la gloire d'un particulier*]?"[73] From "Sarah," of course, one recalls that the "interest of morality" is precisely *general*; one must not try to derive *la morale naturelle* from the (frequently bad) conduct of someone who does "great wrong to the eternal laws."[74]

In Bayle's late work, the article "Sarah" (as well as its nearly identical companion piece, "King David") is exceptional for its vestigial Malebranchism; more characteristic of his doubts about the worth of *généralité* is the piece on which he was working at the time of his death in 1706, the *Entretiens de Maxime et de Thémiste*. The *Entretiens* are nominally a refutation of Isaac Jaquelot's *Examen de la théologie de Mr. Bayle* (1705), but Jaquelot's *Examen* is itself a doctrinaire restatement of Malebranche, gratuitously coupled with some non-Malebranchian ideas. Bayle's final work, then, is an oblique commentary, not on Malebranche *en soi*, but on comparatively unintelligent, secondhand *Malebranchisme*. Even so, Jaquelot's *Examen* serves as the occasional cause of a more general inquiry into the worth of generality.[75]

---

[73] Cited in Elisabeth Labrousse, *Pierre Bayle* (Paris: Editions Seghers, 1965), pp. 136-137.

[74] Ibid., p. 137.

[75] Bayle, *Entretiens de Maxime et de Thémiste*, in *Oeuvres diverses*, vol. 4, pp. 3ff.

If in early works such as the *Pensées diverses* Bayle had linked generality with justice and wisdom, in the *Entretiens* he was concerned to show that always operating generally might (wrongly) keep wise agents from departing from general laws and *volontés générales* even when goodness itself dictated such a departure. Jaquelot imagines, Bayle argues, that "God could not have prevented the Fall of Adam without performing a miracle unworthy of his wisdom," without derogating from general laws. Here, Bayle complains, "the least philosopher" will properly point out that, according to Scripture, "God performed a great number of miracles [that were] incomparably less useful and less necessary" than impeding the Fall of Adam—though it remains true that generality is worth *something* and that, therefore, God will not derogate from general laws "unless it is a question of stopping a dreadful corruption of morals" and unless "an infinity of miseries is going to inundate the human race." If this corruption and inundation will take place, however, *without* a particular divine intervention, Bayle is clear that *généralité* must yield: "The salvation of the people is the supreme law, *salus populi suprema lex esto*. It would be sinning against the laws of government not to be willing to derogate from the old laws, when the people's safety is at stake. Thus one shocks natural enlightenment if one supposes that, when it is a question of the safety of the human race, God would not have willed to derogate from general laws."[76] Obviously, one wills to derogate from general laws by a *volonté particulière*.

In later sections of the *Entretiens*, Bayle goes on to say that an insistence on the constant operation of general laws places (merely) aesthetic standards above moral ones. If a "pagan philosopher" were to examine Jaquelot's notion of *généralité*, he argues, he would be told that God "only created the world in order to show his power and his infinite knowledge of architecture and of mechanics," that his

[76] Ibid., pp. 57-58.

attribute of being "good" and "the friend of virtue" had "no part in the construction of his great work." Bayle then imagines what the "pagan philosopher" might have said: "What a God is M. Jaquelot's God! He prides himself only on knowledge; he prefers to let the whole human race perish than to suffer that some atoms move faster or slower than general laws demand. He would not disorder the slightest thing in the symmetry of his work in order to stop vice from ruling men, and would [instead] expose the whole of human-kind to disorders and to countless and appalling miseries."[77]

Bayle goes on to argue that *lumière naturelle* supplies men with a very different notion of God, with goodness as his chief attribute; thus, if he had to choose "between a physical irregularity and a moral irregularity, he would choose the former." If the "architecture of the universe" has some defect, Bayle says, that harms no creature; but "if moral evil is introduced among men," that is an injury that spreads over "an infinity of subjects." If Jaquelot places the uniform operation of general laws above human safety—if he gives greater weight to the aesthetic than to the moral—then he makes God's rule "resemble extremely the project of an enemy."[78]

To drive home this last point, Bayle compares Jaquelot's God (who *"ne se pique que de science"*) to Alexander the Great and Caesar, while contrasting this God with a better one, who more nearly resembles Titus and Marcus Aurelius:

> Natural enlightenment shows us manifestly that nothing is more suitable to true greatness . . . than to use one's power and knowledge for the happiness of others. We are more stupified by the glory of Alexander and of Caesar, than by that of Titus and of Marcus Aurelius; but this is only a tumult of the imagination. Let the tempest be calmed: consult pure reason,

[77] Ibid., p. 62.
[78] Ibid., p. 63.

and she will tell you that the Alexanders and the Cae-
sars deserve to be detested, because they only used
their valor, their military knowledge, their minds, in
order to ruin people, and for spilling human blood; and
that the beneficent temper of Titus and of Marcus Aurelius is a title of honor infinitely more glorious than
the trophies and the victories of the most famous con-
querors.[79]

To be sure, Jaquelot's God "prides himself" on *science
générale*, not on *science militaire*; but, like Caesar, he would
be the people's enemy if he loved his own knowledge more
than "the public good." This, says Bayle, is just what Jaquelot's God actually does; his refusal to depart from *généralité*, even to save the human race, means "that God's
power must have had the first place; that his infinite knowledge of architecture and of mechanics must have had the
second; and that his goodness must have had the third." To
be more exact, goodness could not even have occupied the
third rank, since God's preference for constancy and uniformity over moral good "bears all the characteristics of
hatred or of indifference to the human race."[80] Bayle's
suggestion that one can learn this by letting the tumult of
imagination subside and by consulting reason is perfectly
Malebranchian,[81] but his attack on generality is perfectly
anti-Malebranchian. And so Bayle finally sets Jaquelot, his
Malebranche surrogate, to one side, and confronts the Oratorian himself one last time. Even Père Malebranche, "the
inventor of the system of general laws," Bayle says, allows
that God *sometimes* departs from generality and acts
through *volontés particulières*; thus, it is absurd for either
Malebranche or Jaquelot to assert that God could not have
saved all men without harming his own attributes. Here

[79] Ibid.
[80] Ibid., p. 66.
[81] Malebranche, *De la recherche de la vérité*, in *Oeuvres complètes*, vol. 1, pp.
488ff., esp. pp. 491-492: "On se peut donc servir de sa raison en toutes
choses, et c'est le privilège qu'elle a sur les sens et sur l'imagination."

Bayle puts a final speech into the mouth of his imagined "pagan philosopher":

What! . . . God did nothing but derogate from general laws during the six days of the Creation, in order to form rocks, plants and animals. Could he not have derogated from them a little later in order to spare the human race the moral evil and the physical evil which reign over men, and which will reign eternally in hell? He derogated from these same laws on a thousand less important occasions; could he not derogate from them when it was a question of the salvation or the ruin of the human race, the most noble creature that he had produced in our world?[82]

Near the end of the portion of the *Entretiens* that bears on Malebranchism and *généralité*, Bayle concludes that a Malebranchian God would, through love of his own wisdom, have "subjected himself to the slavery of letting vice rule"; general laws would have "prevailed over goodness and over the love of moral good." The Malebranchian God has found his own *loix générales* to be "so fine, so admirable, so worthy of him" that even though they generate "all the crimes, all the heresies, in a word all the disorders of the human race," he nonetheless "has undertaken the continual and perpetual execution of these laws." And Bayle adds, with characteristic bravery, that a "superior"—even a divine one—can become "criminal" not just by ordaining evil but also through mere permission, through what he calls "connivance": just as (to use his own analogy) a parent who foresees that his virgin daughters will be seduced at a ball and who nonetheless lets them go is as guilty as the seducer.[83]

What matters in Bayle, despite his vacillation between Malebranchian generality and particularism, is that he did

[82] Bayle, *Entretiens*, p. 64.
[83] Ibid., p. 67.

more to politicize *volonté générale* and general law than any-one between Malebranche and Montesquieu. By always in-sisting on the rightness (or wrongness) of general will, and by talking about *généralité* in connection with, say, the reli-gious policies of Louis XIV—the very policies that drove Bayle himself into permanent Dutch exile—Bayle began to shift the emphasis from theodicy to human justice. This he achieved by always relating generality and particularity to some example of human conduct: the irresponsible negli-gence of parents who fail to take the particular steps that will save their children from seduction; the cowardice of the governor of a city who abandons general laws whenever anyone "murmurs" against them; the wisdom of a mon-arch who refuses to let general laws be abridged by the in-terests of *des particuliers*. The obvious vacillation between generality and particularity matters less than the fact that Bayle *is* consistent in one thing: namely, always operating with political and moral examples. For this reason, he is the most important step between Malebranche and Montes-quieu in the gradual secularization of a general will, the his-tory of which was finally "made" by Rousseau.[84] In a series of tiny incremental changes, Bayle is a leap.

[84] For the influence of Bayle on Montesquieu, see Shackleton, "Bayle and Montesquieu," pp. 142-149. For a classic treatment of Bayle's secular-ization of morality, see Paul Hazard, *La Crise de la conscience européenne* (Paris: Boivin et Cie., 1935), vol. 2, pp. 71ff.: "S'il est un homme qui, plus nettement et plus vigoureusement que tous ses predecesseurs, ait affirmé l'independance de la morale et de la religion, c'est Pierre Bayle."

THREE

THE DEPARTURE FROM
GENERAL WILL:
MALEBRANCHE ON MORAL
RELATIONS, ORDER, AND
OCCASIONALISM

In treating Malebranche, it is common enough to speak as if his whole practical philosophy confined itself to elevating *volonté générale* and execrating *volonté particulière*. (In their critiques of Malebranche, Bossuet and Bayle had certainly singled out *généralité* as the main problem, or defect, in the Oratorian's thought.) Pierre Jurieu, writing at the end of the seventeenth century in his *Traitté [sic] de la nature et de la grâce*, insisted that "one can scarcely say how much this thought [of general will] pleases this philosopher, for he loves it to the point of idolatry, and causes it to appear everywhere . . . it is the sole foundation of his system."[1] Pierre-Valentine Faydit, publishing his characteristically venomous *Presbytéromachie* at the turn of the eighteenth century, argued that Malebranche will not "admit any *volontés particulières* in God, outside the case of miracles, which are, according to him, almost as rare as in Spinoza," and that Malebranche's God is a "universal agent" who acts

---

[1] Pierre Jurieu, *Traitté [sic] de la nature et de la grâce* (Utrecht, the Netherlands: Chez François Halma, 1687), p. 160.

only through *des loix générales*.[2] And Sainte-Beuve, writing *Port-Royal* in the middle of the nineteenth century, urged that "Malebranche loves general laws, the *volontés générales* of God, once established; he does not want God to alter them, whether two times or a thousand. . . . He wants the supreme watchmaker to make the world run by itself, or almost all alone, from the first push."[3]

However, the notion of "general will" is not, for Malebranche, as much of a complete practical doctrine as it is later for Rousseau, who argues that any agreement that the sovereign people makes is equitable, provided it is voluntary and general.[4] Voluntariness and generality go far in Malebranche, but they go further still in Rousseau, and the weight of *volonté générale* is sufficient in Malebranche without trying to make it weightier still. It has to yield some room to moral and political ideas that Malebranche took at least equally seriously: above all, the idea that moral laws are "relations of perfection [*rapports de perfection*]" that together constitute order, and that men are only the occasional causes of their own activity, while God is the sole true, or efficacious, or general cause.[5]

But in moving briefly away from *volonté générale* and *volonté particulière*, and in stressing other Malebranchian notions—"order," "relations of perfection," "occasionalism,"

[2] Pierre-Valentine Faydit, *La Presbytéromachie*, in *Annales de philosophie chretiènne* (Paris, 1863), vol. 7, pp. 50ff.

[3] Sainte-Beuve, *Port-Royal* (Paris, 1908), Book VI, p. 387.

[4] Jean-Jacques Rousseau, *Première Version du contrat social*, in *Political Writings*, ed. C. E. Vaughan (Oxford: Basil Blackwell, 1962), vol. 1, pp. 472-473.

[5] For these "new" aspects of Malebranche and *malebranchisme*, see André Robinet, *Système et éxistence dans l'oeuvre de Malebranche* (Paris: Vrin, 1965), passim; Ferdinand Alquié, *Le Cartésianisme de Malebranche* (Paris: Vrin, 1974), passim; Martial Guéroult, *Malebranche: Le Cinq Abîmes de la Providence* (Paris: Aubier, 1959), vol. 3, pp. 147ff.; Pierre Blanchard, *L'Attention à Dieu selon Malebranche* (Lyon: Desclée de Brouwer, 1956), passim; Yves de Montcheuil, *Malebranche et le quietisme* (Paris: Aubier, 1946), pp. 309ff.; Ginette Dreyfus, "Le Problème de la liberté de l'homme dans la philosophie de Malebranche," in *Malebranche: l'Homme et l'oeuvre, 1638-1715* (Paris: Vrin, 1967), pp. 153ff.

and God as *cause générale*—one moves toward the unfolding of French political and moral thought after Malebranche. For the notion of moral law as a *rapport de perfection* turns up in Montesquieu,[6] and Montesquieu then bears on Rousseau, while the idea of order is at the very heart of the "Profession de foi du vicaire savoyard," which is in turn the very heart of *Emile*.[7] And Malebranche's divine *cause générale* later became, after secularization, Montesquieu's notion of (many) *causes générales* (geography, climate, education, *moeurs*) that generate the particular characters of individuals.[8] Every element of Malebranche's philosophy, then, bears on later French social theory.

This is not to say that a perfectly orthodox Malebranchism shapes the whole of eighteenth-century French practical thought. Indeed, for the Malebranchian synthesis of Christianity and Cartesianism to last, Malebranche's successors would have had to continue to see moral *généralité* and scientific *généralité* as perfectly parallel; they would have had to continue to see grace (or, more generally, *la morale*) as a kind of divine rain that falls constantly and indifferently on the just and the unjust. But what might have been foreseen in fact happened: scientific *généralité* tended to separate itself from theology and morality,[9] so that a writer like Montesquieu stresses one side of Malebranchism—general laws, *la physique* often determining *la morale*—while a writer like Rousseau, whose scientific views were

---

[6] See S. M. Mason, *Montesquieu's Idea of Justice* (The Hague: Martinus Nijhoff, 1975), pp. 8-17, 51, 268, and Mark H. Waddicor, *Montesquieu and the Philosophy of Natural Law* (The Hague: Martinus Nijhoff, 1970), pp. 177ff. Both valuable studies bring out Montesquieu's acceptance of the Malebranchian idea that law is a *rapport*—whether *de convenance* or *de perfection*.

[7] See particularly Henri Gouhier, *Les Méditations métaphysiques de Jean-Jacques Rousseau* (Paris: Vrin, 1970), pp. 120ff.

[8] Robert Shackleton, *Montesquieu* (Oxford: Oxford University Press, 1961), pp. 168-169: "The distinction between the First Cause and occasional causes which was made by the author of *De la Recherche de la Vérité* has been carried into history by Montesquieu."

[9] See Alquié, *Cartésianisme de Malebranche*, pp. 443ff.

sound but not central to him, tends to find *généralité* more in the moral sphere (above all, in general will) than in the scientific one. To be sure, Montesquieu still prizes moral *généralité* (most particularly in republics), while Rousseau still sees a general order in nature; but Malebranche's *perfect* fitting together of Cartesianism and Christianity has weakened. Nevertheless, much of eighteenth-century French moral and political thought is still dominated by a slowly disintegrating *christianisme cartésianisé*.[10]

If, finally, one moves briefly away from *volonté générale* and *volonté particulière*, and toward order, practical laws as relations, and occasionalism, one also draws up by that side of Malebranche that was heavily criticized in several late and posthumously published works of John Locke,[11] but also reflected in some parts of Locke's *Essay*, which contains a chapter on divine and civil law (book 2, chapter 28) called "Of Other Relations."[12] The wholly familiar philosophy of Locke may throw a little light on the darker corners of Malebranchism—just as, earlier, it had illuminated Pascal's radically political reading of 1 Corinthians 12.

The less-than-total importance of *volonté générale* in Malebranche becomes clear if one turns from the *Traité de la nature et de la grâce*, which is wholly dominated by the notion of general will, to a work such as the *Traité de morale*, in which one finds different but equally characteristic Malebranchian practical ideas. Since the *Traité de morale* was produced at the very time (1683-1684) that Malebranche was writing the third and fourth "Eclaircissements" of *Nature et grâce*,[13] there is a very smooth transition from the one work

---

[10] See Henri Gouhier, *Fénelon philosophe* (Paris: Vrin, 1977), pp. 19ff.

[11] See Charles J. McCracken, *Malebranche and British Philosophy* (Oxford: Clarendon Press, 1983), chapter 4 ("Locke's Refutation of Malebranche").

[12] John Locke, *An Essay Concerning Human Understanding*, ed. A. C. Fraser (New York: Dover, 1959), pp. 471ff.

[13] For an account of the composition and publication of the *Traité de morale*, see the Introduction to vol. 11 of N. Malebranche, *Oeuvres complètes de*

to the other. Indeed, in the opening chapter of the "Première Partie" of the *Traité de morale*, Malebranche begins with the now-familiar general-particular dichotomy, only by a series of small steps arriving at the notion that there may be something of moral and political value *beyond* the constancy and uniformity of *volonté générale* and *loi générale*. This something he calls "order," or "relations of perfection."

Malebranche begins the *Traité de morale* by observing that, "if God moved bodies by *volontés particulières*, it would be a crime to avoid by flight the ruins of a collapsing building; for one cannot, without injustice, refuse to return to God the life he has given us, if he demands it." If God positively willed everything in particular, "it would be an insult to God's wisdom, to correct the course of rivers, and turn them to places lacking water: one would have to follow nature and remain at rest." Since, however, God acts not through *volontés particulières* but through *des loix générales*, "one corrects his work, without injuring his wisdom; one resists his action, without resisting his will; because he does not will positively and directly everything that he does."[14] He permits disorder, but he loves order.

In Malebranche's view, the case is quite different if one resists or corrects the action of men. "What is true of God is not so of men, of the general cause as of particular causes." When one resists the action of men, one offends them, "for, since they act only by *volontés particulières*, one cannot resist their acts without resisting their plans." However, in resisting God's general laws (manifested in something like the collapse of a building) one not only offends "not at all" but even "favors" God's plans; this is simply because the general laws that God follows do not always produce results

---

Malebranche, ed. André Robinet (Paris: Vrin, 1966). The only extensive commentary on *Morale* in English is Craig Walton's helpful *De la recherche du bien: A Study of Malebranche's Science of Ethics* (The Hague: Martinus Nijhoff, 1972), passim.

[14] Malebranche, *Traité de morale*, in *Oeuvres complètes*, vol. 11, p. 25.

that conform to order, or to "the best work."[15] After all, as Malebranche remarks in *Nature et grâce*, "if one drops a rock on the head of passers-by, the rock will always fall at an equal speed, without discerning the piety, or the station, or the good or evil dispositions of those who pass by."[16] He gives this same thought a complacent cast in the *Méditations chrétiennes*, in which he urges that, by permitting general laws to operate, God lets "the ruins of a house fall on a just person who is going to the aid of an unfortunate, as well as on a villain who is going to cut the throat of an *homme de bien*."[17] Hence, in Malebranche's opinion, there is no moral obligation to allow *les loix générales* to cause death, or even to let their operation inconvenience or displease us. (Precisely the same argument recurs in Rousseau's *Du contrat social*: "All power comes from God, I admit, but so does all illness; does that mean we are forbidden to call a doctor?")[18] "Our duty," Malebranche concludes, "consists then in submitting ourselves to God's law, and in following order"; and we can know this order only through union with "the eternal Word, with universal reason"—the one thing all men share, whatever their particular dispositions.[19]

But what does Malebranche mean in calling this order—something that transcends mere generality—a "relation of perfection"? Now one first encounters Malebranche's theory of moral *rapports* in the opening book of *Recherche de la vérité*, in which he argues that, while truth "consists only in the relations which two or several things have between themselves," moral goodness, by contrast, "consists in the relation of suitability [*rapport de convenance*] that things have to us [men]."[20] Here the key notion is *rapport de convenance*

---

[15] Ibid., p. 26.

[16] Malebranche, *Traité de la nature et de la grâce*, in *Oeuvres complètes*, vol. 5, p. 63.

[17] Cited in Ferdinand Alquié, *Malebranche* (Paris: Seghers, 1977), p. 124.

[18] Rousseau, *The Social Contract*, in *Rousseau: Political Writings*, ed. and trans. F. Watkins (Edinburgh: Nelson, 1953), p. 6.

[19] Malebranche, *Traité de morale*, pp. 26-27.

[20] Malebranche, *De la recherche de la vérité*, in *Oeuvres complètes*, vol. 1, pp. 52-53.

(the same term that Montesquieu later uses to define justice in *Lettre persane* no. 83);[21] *rapports de perfection* do not yet appear. Indeed, it is only in the *Traité de morale* that the first important exposition of Malebranchian "relations" is to be found.

"In supposing that man is reasonable," argues the *Traité de morale*, and even that he belongs to a *société spirituelle* with God, which "nourishes" all minds, one cannot deny that man "knows something of what God thinks, and of the way in which God acts." "In contemplating the intelligible substance of the Word, which alone makes me reasonable," Malebranche continues, "I can clearly see the relations of size [*rapports de grandeur*] which exist between the intelligible ideas which it [the Word] encloses"; these relations are "the same eternal truths that God sees." For God sees, as does a man, that two times two makes four. A man can also discover, "at least confusedly," the existence of relations of perfection [*rapports de perfection*], which constitute the "immutable order that God consults when he acts—an order which ought also to regulate the esteem and love of all intelligent beings."[22]

This is, perhaps, more eloquent than clear, but in a succeeding passage Malebranche fleshes out the notion of "relations of perfection." The reason it is true that "a beast is more estimable than a stone, and less estimable than a man" is that "there is a greater relation of perfection from the beast to the stone, than from the stone to the beast" and "a greater *rapport de perfection* between the beast compared to the man, than between the man compared to the beast." In simpler language, men enjoy a greater degree of perfection than beasts, and beasts, a greater degree than stones. Plainly, Malebranche envisions a hierarchy of more or less

---

[21] Montesquieu, *Persian Letters*, trans. C. J. Betts (Harmondsworth, England: Penguin, 1973), no. 83, pp. 162-163. Betts translates *rapport de convenance* as "relation of suitability." For an excellent study of the notion of moral relations in seventeenth-century thought—in Bossuet and Clark as well as Malebranche—see Mason, *Idea of Justice*, pp. 9ff.

[22] Malebranche, *Traité de morale*, p. 19.

"perfect" beings—their perfection defined in terms of their capacity for union with the Word or universal reason—and holds that one should regulate his esteem in view of degrees of perfection. Thus, for Malebranche, whoever "esteems his horse more than his coachman" does not really see the *rapport de perfection* "which he perhaps thinks he sees." Linking this up with his familiar general-particular distinction, Malebranche adds that the unreasonable horse lover fails to see *la raison universelle*, that he takes his own *raison particulière* for his rule. But to abandon *la raison universelle* and order for *la raison particulière* is to manifest *amour-propre*, "error," and "lawlessness"; thus, the language of *Nature et grâce* reappears and begins to color "order" and "relations of perfection" themselves.[23]

From all of this, Malebranche concludes—following St. Augustine's following of Plato—that "it is evident that there is a true and a false, a just and an unjust," and that this holds "with respect to all intelligences." Just as what is true for God is true for angels and men, so too "that which is injustice or disorder with respect to man is also such with respect to God himself." Just as all minds discover the same *rapports de grandeur*, so those same minds discover "the same truths of practice, the same laws, the same order" when they see the *rapports de perfection* enclosed in the Word.[24]

The "love of order," then, according to Malebranche, is "our principal duty": it is "mother virtue, universal virtue, fundamental virtue." (This order, these "related" perfections, actually *exist* only in God; hence the love of God, of perfection, and of order are equivalent and together constitute Malebranche's version of "charity"—a charity that is extended to men as citizens of God's *société spirituelle*.) "Speculative truths" or *rapports de grandeur* do not "regu-

---

[23] Ibid., p. 21.
[24] Ibid., p. 19.

late" our duties; "it is principally the knowledge and the love of relations of perfection, or of practical truths, which constitute our perfection." Hence Malebranche's closing peroration: "Let us then apply ourselves to know, to love and to follow order; let us work for our perfection."[25]

Is there a relation between *rapports de grandeur* and *rapports de perfection*? In Malebranche's great contemporary and correspondent Leibniz, the answer is plainly "yes," for Leibniz argues (in a letter of 1696) that "order and harmony are . . . something mathematical and which consist in certain proportions."[26] In *Opinion on the Principles of Pufendorf* (1706), a piece that attracted a European reputation thanks to Barbeyrac's French translation, he adds that "justice follows certain rules of equality and of proportion which are no less founded in the immutable nature of things, and in the ideas of the divine understanding, than the principles of arithmetic and geometry." In Malebranche himself, the initial answer appears to be "no," for he calls *rapports de grandeur* "quite pure, abstract, metaphysical," while *rapports de perfection* are "practical" and serve as laws.[27] But one might object that the notions of *rapports de perfection* and of "order" are also quite abstract; as Jeremy Bentham later observed, "the worst order is as truly order as the best."[28]

[25] Ibid., p. 24. On this point see the useful remarks in McCracken, *Malebranche and British Philosophy*, p. 285.

[26] G. W. Leibniz, letter to the Electress Sophie, in *Textes inédits*, ed. Gaston Grua (Paris: Presses Universitaires de France, 1948), vol. 1, p. 379.

[27] Leibniz, *Opinion on the Principles of Pufendorf*, in *The Political Writings of Leibniz*, ed. and trans. Patrick Riley (Cambridge: Cambridge University Press, 1972), p. 71. Malebranche, *Méditations chrétiennes et métaphysiques*, in *Oeuvres complètes*, vol. 10, p. 39: "Or il y a cette différence entre les rapports de grandeur et les rapports de perfection, que les rapports de grandeur sont des veritez toutes pures, abstraites, métaphysiques, et que les rapports de perfection sont des veritez et en même tems des Loix immuables et nécessaires."

[28] Jeremy Bentham, *Book of Fallacies*, in *Works* (Edinburgh: Tait, 1843), vol. 2, p. 441.

Mercier de La Rivière, quoting a line about order from Malebranche's *Traité de morale* ("Order is the inviolable law of minds, and nothing is lawful which does not conform to it") went on to extract from this "order" a (certainly very orderly) theory of authoritarian monarchism, or "legal despotism," in his *L'Ordre naturel et essentiel des sociétés politiques*. (The "irresistible force" of order, Mercier argues, exists to "link up all our opinions" and to "establish a legal and personal despotism" by means of which "all our interests, all our *volontés*, will come to be united with the interest and the *volonté* of the sovereign." According to Mercier, this will form a "common welfare, a harmony, an ensemble which one can regard as the work of a divinity.")[29] Here a number of Malebranchian terms—"order," "will," "divinity"—are transmogrified into a benevolent authoritarianism that is far removed from Malebranche himself. And this proves Bentham's point that "order" is as abstract a term as one could find.

In fact, Malebranche finally abandons the abstractness of "order," as well as his less-than-concrete characterization of "relations of perfection." In *Entretiens sur la métaphysique* (1688), the work commonly accounted his masterpiece, he moves in the direction of Leibniz's virtual identification of proportion or equality in mathematics and in notions of rightness. Malebranche begins the thirteenth section of the eighth *entretien* by calling *rapports de grandeur* "speculative" and *rapports de perfection* "practical" (as in *Morale*), but he then goes on to the view that "relations of perfection cannot be known clearly unless they are *expressed* in relations of size." That two times two equals four, he continues, "is a relation of equality in size, is a speculative truth which excites no movement in the soul—neither love nor hate, neither esteem nor contempt." However, the notion that man is "of greater value than the beast" is "a relation of inequal-

---

[29] Mercier de La Rivière, *L'Ordre naturel et essentiel des sociétés politiques*, in *Physiocrates*, ed. Eugène Daire (Paris: Librairie de Guillaumin, 1846), vol. 2, pp. 637-638.

ity in perfection, which demands not merely that the soul should accept it, but that love and esteem be regulated by the knowledge of this relation or of this truth."[30] Since we ought to love perfection, we ought to love beings closer to divinity in the scale of being in preference to "lower" beings and things. In this way, the unfamiliar notion of *rapports de perfection* is assimilated to the much more familiar idea of a great chain of being; if this makes Malebranchism more ordinary, it also makes it more concrete and intelligible.[31]

This concreteness had already been intimated in the tenth "Eclaircissement" of *Recherche de la vérité*, in which Malebranche argues that "the perfections which are in God, which represent created or possible beings, are not all equal, as representative of those beings." The perfections that represent bodies, he goes on, "are not so noble as those which represent minds." After admitting that it is somewhat difficult to conceive exactly how the mind of a perfect being contains perfections that represent beings that are necessarily imperfect—a point John Locke later complained of—Malebranche concludes that "if it is true, then, that God . . . encloses in himself all beings in an intelligible manner, and that all of these intelligible beings . . . are not in every sense equally perfect, it is evident that there will be an immutable and necessary order between them." He adds that "just as there are necessary and eternal truths, because there are *rapports de grandeur* between intelligible beings," so too "there must be an immutable and necessary order, because of the *rapports de perfection* which exist between these same beings." It is thus in virtue of "an immutable order that minds are nobler than bodies, as it is a necessary truth that two times two makes four."[32] Order,

[30] Malebranche, *Entretiens sur la métaphysique*, in *Oeuvres complètes*, vol. 12-13, pp. 190-191.
[31] See A. O. Lovejoy, *The Great Chain of Being* (New York: Harper and Row, 1960), passim.
[32] Malebranche, *Recherche de la vérité*, in *Oeuvres complètes*, vol. 3, pp. 137-

then, requires respect for degree of perfection attained (or at least enjoyed) by every created being in the great chain of being. This is at its clearest in the *Traité de morale*, in which order gives new meaning to Christian charity:

> The charity which justifies [men], or the virtue which renders just and virtuous those who possess it, is properly a ruling love of the immutable order. . . . The immutable order consists of nothing else than the relations of perfection which exist between the intelligible ideas that are enclosed in the substance of the eternal Word. Now one ought to esteem and love nothing but perfection. And therefore our esteem and love should be conformable to order. . . . From this it is evident that charity or the love of God is a consequence of the love of order, and that we ought to esteem and love God, not only more than all things, but infinitely more than all things. . . .
>
> Now there are two principal kinds of love, a love of benevolence, and a love which may be called a love of union. . . . One loves persons of merit through a love of benevolence, for one loves them even though they are not in a condition to do us any good. . . . Now God alone is [truly] good, he alone has the power to act in us . . . thus all love of union ought to incline towards God.[33]

Even in these passages, which stress the notions of charity, order, and perfection, and which seem to have left the general-particular dichotomy far behind, Malebranche finds an occasion for animadversions against *particularisme*. Just as everyone can see that twice two are four, Malebranche urges, so too everyone can see that "one ought to prefer one's friend to one's dog"; the mathematical *rapport*

---

138. For a helpful commentary on this tenth "Eclaircissement," see Henri Gouhier, *La Philosophie de Malebranche et son éxperience religieuse* (Paris: Vrin, 1948), pp. 236-243.

[33] Malebranche, *Traité de morale*, pp. 41-42.

de grandeur and the moral *rapport de perfection* both rest in "a universal reason that enlightens me and all intelligences whatever." This universal reason, which is "co-eternal" and "con-substantial" with God, and which all intelligences "see," is to be strictly distinguished from particular reasons—the not-very-reasonable reasons that a passionate man follows. And the passionate man turns out to be the familiar horse lover: "When a man prefers the life of his horse to that of his coachman, he has his reasons, but they are particular reasons that every reasonable man abhors. They are reasons that fundamentally are not reasonable, because they are not in conformity with the sovereign reason, or the universal reason, that all men consult."[34]

Malebranche, then, will not countenance any *raisons que la raison ne connaît point*. If in this passage he appeals to what is universal and not merely general, he still finds time to lump *des raisons particulières* with "passion" and the "abhorrent." Toward the end of the tenth "Eclaircissement," even the notion of the universal yields, and *le général* makes its way back in; one can finally see, Malebranche urges, "what the immutable order of justice is, and how this order has the force of law through the necessary love that God has for himself." Since men ought to love the order that God loves, "one sees how this law is general for all minds, and for God himself"; one sees that to abandon the idea of eternal and immutable order, common to all intelligences, is to "establish *pyrrhonisme* and to leave room for the belief that the just and the unjust are not at all necessarily such."[35] Thus, even in his treatment of relations of perfection, Malebranche manages to retain his antiparticularism and his equation of generality with justice.

It should be noted in passing that Malebranche fre-

---

[34] Malebranche, *Recherche de la vérité* in *Oeuvres complètes*, vol. 3, p. 131. This passage is treated well in Desmond Connell, *The Vision in God* (Louvain and Paris: Editions Nauwelaerts and Beatrice-Nauwelaerts, 1967), p. 297.

[35] Malebranche, *Recherche de la vérité*, in *Oeuvres complètes*, vol. 3, p. 140.

quently tries to extract or derive rather more moral and political content from "order" and "perfection" than is obviously there. In an important letter of 1706 to the Jesuit Malebranchist Y. M. André, Malebranche begins by conceding that "it is not easy to derive the details of our duties from the immmutable order of divine perfections" and suggests that it is sometimes advisable to fall back on "the written law." Nonetheless, he goes on, we *can* know that, since other men are "of the same nature as we are, united to the same reason," we ought to "esteem them as much as ourselves, and will for them the same perfections which we will for ourselves." This leads him to the conclusion that "we cannot will that we be deceived, for error in itself is not estimable," and that, since all men share the same nature, "we ought not to will to deceive others."[36] This line of thought he pursues in a way that recalls what Plato says about benevolent deception in the *Republic* and anticipates Kant's *On a Supposed Right to Lie from Benevolent Motives*,[37] though Malebranche and Kant come to opposite conclusions:

> Thus it is against immutable order to lie: that is to *will* to deceive. For if it turned out that a little lie [*une legère erreur*] would be useful to a fellow-man, and would deliver him from a greater evil—if for example one told a madman who was looking for a man in order to kill him, that this man was not where he really was—I do not see how this would be contrary to order, since the purpose of him that responds [to the madman's question] is not to deceive, but to preserve a man's life.[38]

This passage leads Malebranche to reflections on social

---

[36] Malebranche, letter to Y. M. André, in *Oeuvres complètes*, vol. 19, p. 742.

[37] Immanuel Kant, *Über ein vermeintes Recht aus menschenliebe zu Lügen*, in *Werke*, ed. W. Weischedel (Wiesbaden: Insel Verlag, 1956), vol. 4, pp. 637-643.

[38] Malebranche, letter to André, pp. 742-743.

life that are certainly interesting but that seem to have a somewhat tenuous connection with order and perfection. In the letter to André, he goes on to say that the murderous madman whom one rightly deceives has gone against "the laws of society for which keeping one's word was invented," and that the madman "no longer has any right to the [correct] signification of terms." The notion that rights turn on *mutuality* is far from odd; still, in Malebranche it seems ill-grounded. In any case, Malebranche goes on to say that he is not at all sure that it is contrary to order to deceive a madman, or to "give him a wooden sword." If the purpose of one's will is deception itself then this is "always a disorder," but if the purpose of the deception is the good of the deceived or of society generally, then deception is "in conformity to order."[39] Here Malebranche insists on perfectly reasonable moral distinctions; all that one can doubt is that order and perfection *yield* these distinctions.

What, finally, is the relation between these relations of size and perfection (the latter constituting order) and the rule of divine general will in the realms of nature and grace? One cannot simply say that nature is to *rapports de grandeur* as grace is to *rapports de perfection*, because the created world is not "orderly"; it contains monsters and hardened hearts. "The present world is a neglected work," Malebranche insists. "Man . . . inhabits ruins, and the world which he cultivates is only the *débris* of a more perfect world."[40] The main passage in which Malebranche tries to relate relations to the general will is to be found in the *Méditations chrétiennes et métaphysiques*—this time in the seventh *méditation*: "God has two kinds of laws which rule him in his conduct. The one is eternal and necessary, and this is order; the others are arbitrary, and these are the general laws of na-

[39] Ibid., p. 743.
[40] Malebranche, *Méditations chrétiennes*, p. 73.

ture and of grace. But God established the latter only because order required that he act in that way."[41]

This works, of course, only if order entails the simplicity (of divine action) that makes general laws better than a multiplicity of particular ones. In any case, the formulation of the seventh *méditation* contains a great tension: order or perfection is eternal and necessary, while the *volontés générales* that govern nature and grace are arbitrary. But the burden of *Nature et grâce* is to show that *volontés générales*, unlike *volontés particulières*, are precisely *not* arbitrary but wise, constant and just. "Arbitrary" calls to mind Malebranche's characterization of the *volonté particulière* of some earthly sovereigns: "une volonté aveugle, bizarre et impérieuse."[42] However, the word may simply mean "not necessary" and "not eternal"; after all, the world itself is neither necessary nor eternal[43] (this would be a Spinozistic denial of creation, in Malebranche's view), and, therefore, the general wills that govern the world's realms, nature and grace, cannot be necessary or eternal either.

Even if, however, the "arbitrariness" of *volonté générale* simply means non-eternity and non-necessity, one can still ask: Why, if *volonté générale* and *loix générales* are inferior to "order" and to *rapports de perfection*—as must be the case— should God have "realized" a world that can have nothing more than a shadow of a "relation" to order and perfection (or perhaps *no* intelligible relation, unless order generates simplicity, and simplicity, generality)? Malebranche himself asks this radical question at the very beginning of *Nature et grâce*; he concludes that there *is* no relation between God and the world, between infinity and finitude.[44] He re-

---

[41] Ibid., p. 76.

[42] Malebranche, *Nature et grâce*, in *Oeuvres complètes*, vol. 5, p. 189.

[43] Ibid., p. 18: "Si vous demeurez d'accord que le Monde ne peut être une émanation nécessaire de la Divinité; vous verrez bien qu'il ne falloit pas qu'il fut éternel. . . . L'éternité est le caractère de l'indépendance; il falloit donc que le Monde commencat."

[44] Ibid., p. 11: ". . . le Monde n'est pas digne de Dieu: il n'a même avec Dieu aucune proportion, car il n'y a nul rapport entre l'infini et le fini."

alizes throughout *Nature et grâce* that he must show that it is in some sense better that a world disordered by sin, now governed by *volontés générales* that permit monsters and grace falling uselessly on hardened hearts, exist rather than never have been. His "solution" is peculiarly Christian: the ruined world as *redeemed* by Christ is of greater worth than the nonexistence (or never-existence) of that world. Since the Incarnation constitutes philosophical "salvation" for Malebranche, quite literally saves his system, and gives a perfect being a motive for creating a ruined world, a great deal—indeed, everything—turns on the advent of Christ. For Malebranche, *culpa* is not simply *felix*, but essential.[45] "The world as saved by Jesus Christ," he insists in the *Entretiens sur la métaphysique*,

> is of greater worth than the same universe as at first constructed, otherwise God would never have allowed his work to become corrupted. Man . . . is a sinner, he is not such as God made him. God, then, has allowed his work to become corrupt. Harmonize this with his wisdom, and his power, save yourself from the difficulty without the aid of the man-God, without admitting a mediator, without granting that God has had mainly in view the incarnation of his son. I defy you to do it even with the principles of the best philosophy.[46]

It is in view of this that Malebranche can insist that, while it is true that "everything is in disorder," this is the consequence of sin; "order itself requires disorder to punish the sinner."[47] This, then, would be the relation between *rapports de perfection* and a very imperfect (though still generally governed) world: order necessitates disorder, so mere general will is justifiable. Even so, one can ask, Is disorder the unintended, unwanted, and unwilled *upshot* of God's simplicity and generality of operation (as *Nature et grâce* in-

[45] See Gouhier, *Experience religieuse*, pp. 97-103.
[46] Malebranche, *Entretiens*, p. 207.
[47] Malebranche, *Méditations chrétiennes*, p. 39.

sists), or is it the intended, wanted, and willed divine punishment of human sin? Or is it precisely human sin—divinely previewed—that justifies God in creating a disordered world that can be no more than simple and general? This final version, in which Cartesian generality is fused with something much more specifically Christian, might seem to be the most comprehensive and adequate one; for, particularly in the *Méditations chrétiennes*, Malebranche suggests that the (generally governed but) ruined world symbolizes human depravity. He makes this suggestion in a wonderfully imaginative descriptive passage:

> The present world is a neglected work. It is the abode of sinners, and it was necessary that disorder appear in it. Man is not such as God made him: thus he has to inhabit ruins, and the earth he cultivates can be nothing more than the debris of a more perfect world. . . . It was necessary that the irregularity of the seasons shorten the life of those who no longer think of anything but evil, and that the earth be ruined and submerged by the waters, that it bear until the end of all centuries visible marks of divine vengeance.[48]

Though divine wisdom does not appear in the ruined world "in itself," Malebranche adds, in relation to both simplicity and the punishment of sinners the world is such that only an "infinite wisdom" could comprehend all of its "beauties."[49]

At least this argument, whatever its implausibilies, is more successful than Leibniz's demi-Christian one—demi-Christian in the sense that Leibniz insists that "universal justice" for God and men alike consists in the "charity of the wise [*caritas sapientis*]" but then is hard-pressed to explain why a "charitable" God would create a necessarily imperfect world that can be (at best) "best" (the "best of all

[48] Ibid., p. 73.
[49] Ibid.

possible worlds"), though not good (absolutely). In explaining God's decision to create, Leibniz stresses God's "glory" and the notion that the world "mirrors" that glory; here, however, charity has vanished altogether.[50] At least Malebranche's deployment of Christ as redeemer—of both men and Malebranchism—does not attempt, *per impossibile*, to combine "charity" and "glory."

One can still ask, of course, why an *être parfait* would see as a manifestation of "order" an historical drama in which fallen and corrupt beings are redeemed through the sacrifice of Christ qua "perfect victim."[51] This, however, would be to question Christianity more closely than Malebranche was ever prepared to do. As early as 1687, Fénelon complained that, whether one considers it theologically or scripturally, Malebranche's version of the Incarnation is radically problematical. From a theologian's perspective, Fénelon argues that, "if one examines exactly what glory is truly added by the Incarnation" to the "infinite and essential glory" of God, one finds that it "only adds an accidental and limited glory." What Christ suffered, though "infinite in price," is "not at all something infinitely perfect, which can be really distinguished from the perfection of the divine person." Scripturally, according to Fénelon, the Oratorian is no better off; Malebranche argues that "it would be unworthy of God to love the world, if this work were not inseparable from his son," Fénelon suggests, but "Jesus Christ teaches us, on the contrary, that 'God so loved the world, that he gave it his only son.' "[52]

Indeed, Malebranchism seems to suffer from a great difficulty: Malebranche wants to operate only with an *être parfait* and imagine what such a perfect being *would* do—leav-

---

[50] See the Introduction to *Political Writings of Leibniz*, pp. 16-17.

[51] Malebranche, *Entretiens*, p. 97.

[52] F. Fénelon, *Réfutation du système du Père Malebranche*, in *Oeuvres de Fénelon* (Paris: Chez Lefevre, 1835), vol. 2, p. 284. Fénelon is thinking, of course, of the gospel according to St. John 3:16. Fénelon's *Réfutation* is misdated c. 1682-1684 in Hink Hillenaar's otherwise valuable *Fénelon et les jesuites* (The Hague: Martinus Nijhoff, 1967), p. 48.

ing out all scriptural "anthropology." But the idea of an *être parfait* acting uniformly through general laws leads to deism, not to Christianity;[53] the concept of a perfect being does not yield a son of God who, qua "perfect victim" redeems a ruined and sin-disordered world. Anthropological Scripture does indeed yield Christ and his earthly works, but anthropology is a concession to weakness and anthropomorphism. Only Christ saves Malebranche's system and gives the Father a motive for creating a world unworthy of him, but Christ is not and cannot be spun out of the bare idea of perfection. Malebranche thus needs historical Christianity, even as he claims to rely solely on the concept of *l'être parfait*. It is this need that drives him to the astonishing claim (in the *Traité de morale*) that God the Father "never had a more agreeable sight than that of his only son fastened to the cross to re-establish order in the universe."[54]

If, finally, order and relations of perfection seem to have toppled mere general will from the high place it occupies in *Nature et grâce*, one can still recall that God, who "encloses" all perfection and order, is referred to by Malebranche as *le bien général*, while mere earthly goods are called *les biens particuliers*. Even here, then, generality recovers some of its lost lustre; it is preserved even as it is canceled. As Malebranche has "the Word" itself say to a *dévot* in the *Méditations chrétiennes*, "God inclines you invincibly to love *le bien en général*, but he does not incline you invincibly to love *les biens particuliers*."[55] If *généralité* does not shape the whole of what is right in Malebranche, at least *particularisme* is constantly and uniformly condemned.

---

[53] See the excellent remarks in Alquié, *Cartésianisme de Malebranche*, pp. 445, 485-486.
[54] Malebranche, *Traité de morale*, p. 41.
[55] Malebranche, *Méditations chrétiennnes*, p. 65.

Even if what Malebranche says about order and *rapports de perfection* deprives general will of much of the importance it seemed to have in *Nature et grâce*, that *volonté générale* is still the regulator of the realms of nature and grace and thus remains quite significant. But what is the relation (perhaps the key Malebranchian notion) between the general will and the "occasionalism" for which Malebranche is celebrated? That there must be some such *rapport* is evident in *Nature et grâce* itself; Malebranche opens the *Second Discours* by observing that, "since God alone acts immediately and by himself in minds, and produces in them all the different modifications of which they are capable, it is only he who diffuses light in us, and inspires in us certain feelings which determine our different volitions." Adding that God alone is the "true cause," Malebranche concludes that "since the general cause [God] acts by laws or by *volontés générales*, and since his action is lawful, constant and uniform, it is absolutely necessary that there be some occasional cause which determines the efficacy of these laws, and which serves to establish them."[56] If occasional or second causes—for example, human beings—did not act *particularly*, then there would be no relation between general laws and particular actions. Indeed, in one of his defenses of *Nature et grâce*, Malebranche even insists that God cannot act by the simplest means or by general laws until there are occasional causes that determine the efficacy of divine *volontés générales*.[57] Obviously, these causes must be established by creative divine *volontés particulières*; but, since such willings are "base" and "servile," God abandons them as soon as generality and simplicity become available.[58]

[56] Malebranche, *Nature et grâce*, in *Oeuvres complètes*, vol. 5, pp. 66-67. On Malebranche's occasionalism, see Ginette Dreyfus, *La Volonté selon Malebranche* (Paris: Vrin, 1958), chapter 6 ("Dieu seule cause éfficace"), and Robinet, *Système et éxistence*, pp. 27ff. ("passage de la philosophie de l'occasion au système occasionaliste").

[57] Malebranche, *Réponse au livre I* des Réflexions philosophiques, in *Oeuvres complètes*, vol. 8-9, p. 780.

[58] Cited in Dreyfus, *Volonté selon Malebranche*, p. 105.

What, then, is the role of occasionalism in relation to general will? Originally—that is, in orthodox Cartesianism—occasionalism was only a theory of perception and of will: if the essence of body is extension and the essence of mind is thought, then mind and body cannot modify each other, since thought is not a modification of extension and extension is not a modification of thought.[59] Given a strict mind-body dualism, the obvious question is, How can minds "perceive," if perception is viewed as a physical modification of the eye or the ear, as motion "in" a sense organ (as in Hobbes's bawdy insistence that "there is no conception in a man's mind, which hath not . . . been begotten upon the organs of sense"),[60] and how can minds "move" bodies—through "volition"—if thought cannot modify extended substances? The obvious answer for an occasionalist must be that so-called "perception" is not *really* a modification of mind by sensed matter, and that volition is not *really* efficacious; instead, God presents to the mind the *idea* of the thing "seen" on the *occasion* of its being "seen," just as he moves bodies (for us, as it were) on the occasion of our willing. This occasionalism does not, of course, require a constantly intervening *Deus ex machina* who scurries about the universe giving efficacy to occasional causes. Indeed, Malebranche's theory of *general* law means that God has established a permanent, general relation between mind and body, so that these naturally unrelated substances operate in constant conjunction. Thus, for Malebranche, whenever one wills to move his arm, it moves—

---

[59] See the excellent notes on Cartesianism by Pierre Costabel that accompany Malebranche, *Oeuvres complètes*, vol. 17-1, pp. 30-37, 199-236. See also Alquié, *Cartésianisme de Malebranche*, pp. 243ff., who shows that Descartes himself cannot be called an orthodox occasionalist. Nonetheless, there are intimations of occasionalism in Descartes' thought; for these see Pierre Clair, "Louis de La Forge et les origines de l'occasionnalisme," in *Recherches sur le XVIIème siècle* (Paris: CNRS, 1976), vol. 1, pp. 63-72.

[60] Thomas Hobbes, *Leviathan*, ed. M. Oakeshott (Oxford: Basil Blackwell, 1957), p. 7. One can wonder how moral "conceptions" are conceivable at all on this view.

thanks to a constant, general (though non-natural) conjunction between mind and body, which God has established by a general will. "It is only God," he insists in the
Conversations chrétiennes, "who can act in the [human] soul
. . . through his general will which makes the natural order."[61]

It was not simply in order to be a Cartesian that Malebranche was an occasionalist; indeed, his motivation was as
much theological as philosophical. Malebranche's view was
that the attribution of independent causal efficacy to non-
divine beings is *impious*; to make that clear, he employed
the political idea of "sovereignty." "The idea of a sovereign
power is the idea of a sovereign divinity," Malebranche
urges in *De la recherche de la vérité*, "and the idea of a subordinate power is the idea of an inferior divinity. . . . Thus
one admits something divine in all the bodies that surround
us, when one admits . . . real beings capable of producing
certain effects by the [causal] force of their nature; and one
thus enters insensibly into the sentiment of the pagans." It
is true, he adds, that "faith corrects us" by reminding us of
the Pauline notion that *in God* we "move" and "have our
being"; nonetheless, if one reads too much Aristotle, "the
mind is pagan" even if "the heart is Christian." This is why
one must prefer St. Augustine, "this great saint [who] recognized that the body cannot act upon the soul, and that
nothing can be above the soul, except God."[62] It is no wonder that Malebranche read Descartes as an Augustinian,
and the Aristotle-loving Scholastics as thinly veiled pagans.

One of the best brief and nontechnical accounts of occasionalism is offered by Malebranche in the *Traité de morale*:

> The [human] mind can be immediately related to God
> alone . . . for mind cannot be related to body, except by
> being united to God himself. It is certain for a thousand

---

[61] Malebranche, *Conversations chrétiennes*, in *Oeuvres complètes*, vol. 4, p. 83.
[62] Cited in Alquié, *Malebranche* (Paris: Seghers, 1977), pp. 116, 117.

reasons that when I suffer, for example, the pain of being pricked, it is God who acts in me, in consequence nonetheless of laws of the union of soul and body. . . . But the body itself cannot be united to the mind, nor the mind to the body. They have no relation between them, nor any creature [a relation] to any other: I mean a relation of [true] causality. . . . It is God who does everything. His will is the link of all unions.[63]

All of this, of course, is merely an elaboration of Malebranche's first statement of occasionalist doctrine in book 6 of *Recherche de la vérité*:

There is only one true God, and one cause who is truly a cause: and one must not imagine that what precedes an effect is the true cause of it. God cannot communicate his power to creatures, if we follow the light of reason: there cannot be [many] true causes, there cannot be gods. But even if he could do this, we cannot conceive that he would will it. Bodies, minds, pure intelligences—none of these can do anything. It is he who has made minds that enlightens and moves them. . . . It is, finally, the author of our being who executes our wills.[64]

Like the Cartesians, Malebranche begins by viewing occasionalism as a theory of perception and of volition. In the end, however, occasionalism serves a huge range of functions, some of them non-Cartesian. As a theory of knowledge and perception, Malebranchian occasionalism leads to the famous idea that "we see all things in God";[65] as a the-

---

[63] Malebranche, *Traité de morale*, p. 117.

[64] Malebranche, *Recherche de la vérité* in *Oeuvres complètes*, vol. 2, p. 318.

[65] See particularly Gouhier, *Experience religieuse*, pp. 211-243. Gouhier properly lays great weight on the following line from the "Dixième Eclaircissement" of the *Recherche*: "This principle that it is only God who enlightens us, and that he only enlightens us through the manifestation of an immutable and necessary reason or wisdom, seems to me . . . so absolutely necessary to give to any truth whatsoever a certain and unshakable foundation, that I believe myself indispensably obliged to explain it and to sustain it as far as it is possible for me" (p. 237).

ory of volition, it holds that God "moves our arm" ("it seems to me quite certain that the will of minds is not capable of moving the smallest body that there is in the world");[66] as part of the theory of grace, it maintains that the "human soul" of Jesus Christ is the occasional cause of the distribution of grace to particular persons.[67] (It is this last element that is non-Cartesian, or at least extra-Cartesian, since Descartes was politic enough to say next to nothing about grace.)[68] Since these three main facets of occasionalism have important moral and political implications in Malebranche and even have a *rapport* with Montesquieu, who appropriates and transforms Malebranche's notion of *causes générales* determining second or occasional *causes particulières*,[69] one must find an occasion to treat perception, volition, and the (particular) distribution of grace in Malebranche's philosophy.

One can begin, as does Malebranche himself, with knowledge and perception. The most important passage in which he treats the moral-political significance of the notion that

[66] Malebranche, *Recherche de la vérité*, in *Oeuvres complètes*, vol. 2, pp. 318, 315.

[67] Malebranche, *Nature et grâce*, in *Oeuvres complètes*, vol. 5, pp. 65-99.

[68] See Alquié, *Cartésianisme de Malebranche*, p. 429: "Le *Traité de la nature et de la grâce* ramène la conduite divine à une action physicienne. Jamais les cartésiens n'avaient osé étendre si loin les principes du mécanisme . . . [In Malebranche] . . . l'ordre de la grâce est soumis aux principes de l'occasionalisme et de la simplicité des voies." As for Descartes himself, he is carefully orthodox (and a little vague) in his letter to Père Mersenne (March 1642): "Pelagius said that one could do good works and merit eternal life without grace, which was condemned by the Church; as for me, I say that one can know by natural reason that God exists, but I do not therefore say that this natural knowledge merits in itself, and without grace, the supernatural glory that we expect in heaven. For, on the contrary, it is evident that, this glory being supernatural, it requires more than natural powers to merit it" (in Descartes, *Oeuvres et lettres*, ed. André Bridoux [Paris: Pléiade, 1953], p. 1144). By naturalizing the distribution of grace—by making the realm of grace operate through general, simple, uniform, quasi-physical laws—Malebranche does indeed, as Alquié says, "extend" the principles of mechanism in a non-Cartesian way.

[69] See Shackleton, *Montesquieu*, pp. 168-169.

we see all things in God is a remarkable commentary on St. Augustine in yet another of his defenses of *Nature et grâce* against Antoine Arnauld—this time, the *Trois Lettres* of 1685. Malebranche begins by allowing that St. Augustine himself did not claim to find *all* things in God: "I realized," he grants, "that this Father spoke only of truths and of eternal laws, of the objects of the sciences, such as arithmetic, geometry, morality; and that he did not urge that one saw in God things which are corruptible and subject to change, as are all the things that surround us." Malebranche himself does not claim that one sees corruptible and changing things in God; "to speak exactly, one sees in God only the essences" of things, and those essences or *ideas* of things alone are "immutable, necessary and eternal." One sees in God only "that which represents these things to the mind, . . . that which renders them intelligible."[70] As Malebranche put the matter in his correspondence of 1714 with Dortous de Mairan (later Montesquieu's ally in the Bordeaux Academy), "I see immediately [in God] only the idea, and not the *ideatum*, and I am persuaded that the idea has been for an eternity, without [any] *ideatum*."[71] Corruptible things are problematical because they change, though their essence does not, but incorruptible, unchanging things one sees *simply* in God. "One can see only in an immutable nature, and in eternal wisdom, all the truths which, by their nature, are immutable and eternal." It would not be difficult to prove, as St. Augustine did, that "there would no longer be any certain science, any demonstrated truths, any assured difference between the just and the unjust—in a word, truths and laws which are nec-

[70] Malebranche, *Trois Lettres touchant la défense de M. Arnauld*, in *Oeuvres complètes*, vol. 6-7, pp. 199-200. Malebranche says in a footnote that he is relying particularly on Augustine's *De libero arbitrio* and *De trinitate*; Arnauld, by contrast, builds *his* "Augustinianism" on the late, proto-Jansenist *De correptione et gratia*.

[71] In Malebranche, *Oeuvres complètes*, vol. 19, p. 910.

essary and common to all minds—if that which all intelligences contemplate were not . . . by its nature absolutely immutable, eternal and necessary."[72] All of this, of course, simply reinforces the already examined view that God and men see the same *rapports de grandeur* and the same *rapports de perfection*, view the same speculative and practical truths.

Malebranche maintained this view of the moral importance of a "vision" in which nothing is seen, which is not a modification of mind by body, to the end of his philosophical career. In the fragmentary remains of a letter of 1713 to Fénelon, he argues that "if the mind forms its ideas by a vital act," and if "our ideas as distinguished from our perceptions are only chimeras," then Pyrrhonism will be established. If *all* ideas are simply mind modified by matter, then "Hobbes and Locke, authors greatly esteemed by many men, will be right."[73] And if they *are* right, "there will be no more true, nor false, immutably such; neither just, nor unjust, neither science nor morality." If empirical notions of perception and knowledge carry the day, "St. Augustine will pass for a fanatical Platonist" who has taught his "subtle atheism" to Malebranche himself. In Malebranche's view, Hobbes and Locke simply extend the theory of Aristotle (and of his "impious commentator" Averroës) that "seeing objects is accomplished by means of impressed species . . . by the power of an active intellect which presents [ideas] to a passive intellect." But this, Malebranche insists, is a "fiction of men who wanted to discuss what they did not understand."[74]

Locke, for his part, thought Malebranche's "vision in God" just as impious as Malebranche thought Locke's

---

[72] Malebranche, *Trois Lettres*, p. 199.

[73] Malebranche, letter to Fénelon, in *Oeuvres complètes*, vol. 19, pp. 842-843. The circumstances surrounding the composition of this letter are given in Yves Marie André, *La Vie du R. P. Malebranche*, pub. Ingold (Geneva: Slatkine, 1970), pp. 355ff.

[74] Malebranche, letter to Fénelon, pp. 842-843.

"sense perception." In his "Examination of Père Malebranche's Opinion of Seeing All Things in God" Locke argues, "God has given me an understanding of my own; and
I should think it presumptuous in me to suppose I appre-
hended anything by God's understanding, saw with his
eyes, or shared of his knowledge." He goes on to ask (and
this bears directly on Malebranche's notion that we see
moral *rapports de perfection* in God), "In which of the perfections of God does a man see the essence of a horse or an ass,
of a serpent or a dove, of hemlock or parsley?" Locke con-
fesses that he himself cannot see the essence of any of these
things "in any of the perfections of God." It is perfectly
true, he goes on, that "the perfections that are in God are
necessary and unchangeable." However, it is not true that
"the ideas that are . . . in the understanding of God . . . can
be seen by us"; it is still less true that "the perfections that
are in God represent to us the essences of things that are out
of God."[75] Here Locke strikes on a real difficulty in Malebranchism—namely, that Malebranche calls a "perfection"
in God what he ought to have called a mere *idea* in God
(since it is hard to see how a perfection can "represent" an
imperfect thing, though an *idea* of an imperfect thing remains quite conceivable).

In another criticism of Malebranche, Locke adds that the
Malebranchian notion that God cannot communicate to
creatures the powers of real perception and real volition
sets "very narrow bounds to the power of God, and, by pre-
tending to extend it, takes it away." He concludes his assault on occasionalism with a moral objection:

The creatures cannnot produce any idea, any thought
in man. How then comes he to perceive or think? God
upon the occasion of some motion in the optic nerve,

[75] Locke, "An Examination of P. Malebranche's Opinion of Seeing All
Things in God," in *The Works of John Locke* (London: Otridge & Son et al.,
1812), vol. 9, pp. 211-255. For a fine commentary on this work, see Mc-
Cracken, *Malebranche and British Philosophy*, pp. 119ff. See also J. Yolton,
John Locke (Oxford: Clarendon Press, 1956), p. 98.

exhibits the colour of a marygold or a rose to his mind. How came that motion in his optic nerve? On occasion of the motion of some particles of light striking on the retina, God producing it, and so on. And so whatever a man thinks, God produces the thought: let it be infidelity, murmuring or blasphemy.[76]

For Locke, then, *tout en Dieu* is a moral enormity; for Malebranche it is a moral necessity. For Malebranche, as for Kant a century later, mere sense perception of a natural world can never explain the possibility of the idea of moral necessity, since that idea does not arise in perception. Kant argues in his *Critique of Pure Reason* that " 'ought' expresses a kind of necessity . . . which is found nowhere in the whole of nature,"[77] and Malebranche would have wholly agreed. Nor are other interesting Malebranche-Kant relations lacking; both, though on different grounds, deny the possibility of "seeing" things-in-themselves. To be sure, Kant was harshly critical of all forms of neo-Platonic idealism, whether Malebranchian or Berkeleian; nevertheless, this does not destroy all Malebranche-Kant *rapports*.[78]

Before leaving *tout en Dieu* behind it should be pointed out that Malebranche sometimes draws moral-political consequences *directly* from his occasionalism. For example, in his *Défense de l'auteur de la recherche de la vérité* (1684) he asserts that "to love even one's father, one's protector, one's friend, as if they were capable of doing us good" is to "render them an honor due only to God." According to Malebranche, this mistake follows from the false supposition that "the bodies which surround us can act as true causes in us." According to the occasionalist doctrine, this must be

[76] Locke, "Remarks upon Some of Mr. Norris's Books, Wherein He Asserts P. Malebranche's Opinion of Our Seeing All Things in God," in vol. 10, p. 255.

[77] Kant, *Critique of Pure Reason*, trans. Kemp Smith (London: Macmillan, 1963), A547/B575, pp. 472-473.

[78] See Alquié, *Cartésianisme de Malebranche*, pp. 491-520 ("Malebranche et Kant").

false; therefore, one "should love his brothers, not as capable of doing us [any] good, but as capable of enjoying with us the true good."[79]

On occasion Malebranche makes occasionalism yield slightly different social consequences. In the relatively late *Entretien d'un philosophe chrétien et d'un philosophe chinois* (1708), he first argues for divine *volonté générale*, then goes on to insist that "it is absolutely necessary for the preservation of the human race and the establishment of societies" that God "act ceaselessly" in terms of the "general laws of the union of the soul and the body"—that, if God did not *constantly* give men the same perceptions through the operation of these general laws, this alone "would destroy society. . . . A father would fail to recognize his child, a friend his friend . . . take away the generality of natural laws [for example, of perception, which permits recognition] and everything collapses in chaos."[80] Here occasionalism and *généralité* fuse to generate a *social* doctrine; even occasionalism, then, leans heavily on the ideas of *Nature et grâce*.

Just as, for Malebranche, there is no empirical perception in the Hobbesian or Lockean sense, so too there is little notion of human will—"little" rather than "no" because of an obvious problem: if men are merely the occasional causes of their own actions, in what sense are they free agents who are accountable for good action, for choosing order or *le bien général* in preference to *amour-propre* and *les biens particuliers*?[81] As Malebranche himself says in *Recherche de la vérité*, "without liberty there are neither good nor bad actions."[82]

[79] Malebranche, *Défense de l'auteur de la Recherche de la vérité*, in *Traité de la nature et de la grâce* (Rotterdam: Chez Reinier Leers, 1684), p. 23.

[80] Malebranche, *Entretien d'un philosophe chrétien et d'un philosophe chinois sur l'éxistence et la nature de Dieu*, in *Oeuvres complètes*, vol. 15, pp. 3-31.

[81] See Dreyfus, *Volonté selon Malebranche*, p. 197.

[82] Malebranche, *Recherche de la vérité*, in *Oeuvres complètes*, vol. 3, p. 225: "If we had no liberty at all, there would be neither future punishments nor

(To be sure, this is not quite the problem for Malebranche that it would be for a moralist like Kant, who holds that a good will is the only *unqualifiedly* good thing on earth.)[83] Still, according to Malebranche, men are free and hence possibly responsible in the sense that they must "consent" to a "motive"; God inclines men through Augustinian-Pascalian *délectation* toward *le bien* or order *en général,* and one must feel this delight before consent is possible.[84] (Or, as Malebranche put it in an untranslatable passage, "il faut sentir . . . avant que de consentir.")[85] Nevertheless, one can suspend one's consent, can be motivated by a *délectation* without being irresistibly or "invincibly" determined by it. Hence, Malebranche's most adequate definition of will, at least in his later work, is "consenting to a motive."[86] The essence of liberty, he argues in *Réflexions sur la prémotion physique,* "consists in a true power . . . which the soul has, to suspend or to give its consent to motives, which naturally follow interesting perceptions."[87] In suspending one's consent to an interesting or even delectable motive, however, one does not actually *cause* anything to happen—as Malebranche is careful to make clear in the first "Eclaircissement" of the *Recherche de la vérité*. If we allow a *délectation* that is *déreglé* (such as "concupiscence") to overwhelm us, and if we fail to suspend our consent to this motive in favor of order or *rapports de perfection,* what do we actually *do*?

Nothing. We love a false good, which God does not

recompenses; for without liberty there are neither good nor bad actions: so that religion would be an illusion and a phantom."

[83] Kant, *Fundamental Principles of the Metaphysic of Morals,* trans. T. K. Abbott (Indianapolis: Library of Liberal Arts, 1949), pp. 11-12.

[84] Malebranche, *Réflexions sur la prémotion physique,* in *Oeuvres complètes,* vol. 16, pp. 3ff.

[85] Ibid., p. 18. Cf. p. 35: "It is agreed that it is in the feelings and in the movements which God produces in us without us [*en nous sans nous*], that the material of sin consists, and that the formal [cause of sin] consists only in the consent that one gives: and all this because it does not depend on us to feel, but it does depend on us to consent."

[86] Ibid., p. 50: "To will is to consent to a motive."

[87] Ibid., p. 47.

make us love by an invincible impression. We cease to look for the true good. . . . The only thing we do is stop ourselves, put ourselves at rest. It is through an act, no doubt, but through an immanent act which produces nothing physical in our substance . . . that is, in a word, through an act which does nothing and which makes the general cause [God] do nothing . . . for the repose of the soul, like that of the body, has no force or physical efficacy.[88]

This somewhat peculiar doctrine, in which human willing is "an act, no doubt," but one that "produces nothing physical," is necessitated by Malebranche's view that God alone is a *true* cause, but that, at the same time, men must in some way be accountable for their volitions.[89] In his last work, the *Réflexions sur la prémotion physique*, Malebranche tries especially hard to make this doctrine plausible by drawing a fine distinction between two different powers or activities in the human soul. He begins by asserting that "the *willing* power of the soul, so to speak, its desire to be happy, its movement toward the good in general" is the first power or activity; but it is a power that is "certainly the effect of the Creator's will." This power, then, is "only the action of God" *in* the soul; it is therefore "like that of created bodies in motion . . . whose moving force . . . depends on the action of God." It is a power *in* us, indeed, but it is not "ours"; it is, to recall a favorite Malebranchism, *en nous sans nous*.[90]

---

[88] Malebranche, *Recherche de la vérité*, in *Oeuvres complètes*, vol. 3, pp. 24-25.

[89] In *Prémotion physique*, p. 45, Malebranche explains the relation between human will and divine general will by urging that "the immanent acts of the [human] will are inefficacious by themselves . . . they do not produce the slightest physical change in the soul, and . . . are only occasional causes, which determine the efficacy . . . of the *volontés générales* of the all-powerful."

[90] Malebranche, *Prémotion physique*, pp. 46-47. The best commentary on

For Malebranche, it is the second power of the soul that is more interesting with regard to human moral responsibility, because it is really ours: "The second power or activity of the soul . . . which constitutes the essence of liberty . . . consists in a true power, not to produce in itself, through its own efficacity, any new modifications; but it consists in a true power which the soul has, to suspend or give its consent to motives, which naturally follow interesting perceptions."[91] Will, then, understood as "consent to a motive," consists in passively permitting that motive to operate.

Even if one can perhaps characterize this passive consent as involving "rien de physic," can one say the same of suspending a motive (such as concupiscence) while one searches for order and *rapports de perfection*? Do "suspending" and "searching" involve *rien de physic*? Malebranche seems to be caught between God as the only true cause and the wish to avoid a Spinozistic determinism in which men are unfree "modes" of the divine substance, and will is therefore an illusion; hence his account of will as both passive and active (or perhaps suspended on a line between the passive and the active). Malebranche thought that he was avoiding one of the chief errors of Jansenism—namely, viewing the *délectation* of "efficacious" grace as irresistible. An irresistible motive, which one cannot suspend or resist without contradiction, truly destroys the possibility of freely loving order and *le bien général* and of meritoriously abandoning *les biens particuliers*, such as the pleasures of the body, which has no natural *rapport* with the mind.[92]

Locke thought Malebranche's attenuated notion of "will" even more impious, if possible, than the notion of "vision in God": "A man cannot move his arm or his tongue; he has

---

this part of Malebranche's thought is Dreyfus's *Volonté selon Malebranche*, pp. 274-283.

[91] Malebranche, *Prémotion physique*, p. 47.

[92] Ibid., pp. 8-22.

no power; only upon occasion, the man willing it, God moves it. . . . This is the hypothesis that clears doubts, and brings us at last to the religion of Hobbes and Spinoza, by resolving all, even the thoughts and will of men, into an irresistible fatal necessity."[93] It is ironic, of course, that in the second edition (1694) of his *Essay Concerning Human Understanding* Locke himself defines human liberty as the capacity to "suspend" any "particular" desire while one searches for happiness "in general," for the true good.[94] Here there is a strong Locke-Malebranche "relation"—strong enough to make one wonder whether, despite Locke's general hostility to Malebranchism, that doctrine did not (particularly) affect the Lockean notions of liberty and will. This *rapport* is at its clearest in the account of the alterations to the 1694 edition of the *Essay* that Locke provided in a letter to his friend Molyneux, the Dublin *savant*, in August 1693: "All that we desire is only to be happy. But though this general desire of happiness operates constantly and invariably in us, yet the satisfaction of any particular desire can be suspended from determining the will to any subservient action, till we have maturely examined whether the particular apparent good we then desire make a part of our real happiness."[95]

Like Malebranche, Locke speaks of a "general" desire for happiness; this general desire operates "constantly and invariably" (like all Malebranchian general laws). Moreover, all "particular" desires can be "suspended" (Malebranche's very terms), and "particular" goods may be merely "apparent" and not part of "real" or "general" happiness. In book 2 chapter 28 of the *Essay*, entitled "Of Other Relations,"

[93] Locke, "Remarks upon Some of Mr. Norris's Books," pp. 255-256. For a fuller treatment of Locke's theory of volition, see the author's *Will and Political Legitimacy: A Critical Exposition of Social Contract Theory in Hobbes, Locke, Rousseau, Kant and Hegel* (Cambridge, Mass.: Harvard University Press, 1982), pp. 74-83.

[94] Locke, pp. 343ff.

[95] In Locke, *Correspondence of John Locke*, ed. E. S. de Beer (Oxford: Clarendon Press, 1979), vol. 4, p. 722.

Locke argues that "there is another kind of relation, which is the conformity or disagreement men's voluntary actions have to a rule to which they are referred . . . which, I think, may be called *moral relation*"; he goes on to call three "sorts" of moral relation *laws* (divine, civil and "of reputation").[96] Like Malebranche, then, Locke defines law as a *rapport*. Despite a seemingly strong relation between the two thinkers, however, Locke's final view may well be that Malebranche has no grounds for insisting on the real existence of human "will" and hence is not entitled to speak of "suspension"— even as an "immanent" act which "does nothing," produces *rien de physic*.

Unusual as are Malebranche's notions of knowledge, perception, and will (from a Lockean perspective, not only unusual but impious), perhaps the most peculiar part of his occasionalism is his view that the "human soul" of Jesus Christ is the occasional cause of the distribution of grace. (This particular strand of Malebranchism bears on a study of the general will before Rousseau, because Rousseau himself takes up general and particular grace in *La Nouvelle Héloïse* and denounces particular grace divinely conferred on the "elect" as a wholly unjust "acceptation of persons." Rousseau was no more ready to countenance *particularisme* in God than in a citizen;[97] *généralité* has a general validity.)

Malebranche begins his treatment of Christ as "distributor" of grace by arguing that, "since it is Jesus Christ alone who can merit grace for us, it is also him alone who can furnish occasions for the general laws, according to which it is given to men." The human soul of Jesus Christ

thus having different thoughts successively in relation to the different dispositions of which [men's] souls in

[96] Locke, *Human Understanding*, pp. 471ff.
[97] Emile Bréhier, "Les Lectures malebranchistes de J.-J. Rousseau," *Revue internationale de philosophie* 1 (1938-1939), pp. 113-114.

general are capable, these different thoughts [in
Christ] are accompanied by certain desires in relation
to the sanctification of those souls. Now these desires
being the occasional causes of grace, they must diffuse
it in some persons *en particulier*, whose dispositions are
like those which the soul of Jesus presently thinks.[98]

Since the "different movements of the [human] soul of Jesus Christ" are the occasional causes of grace, one should
not be astonished if grace is sometimes given by Christ to
"great sinners" or to "persons who will not make the slightest use of it." The reason for this is (again) a physicalist one,
resembling Malebranche's treatment of grace as a variety of
rain in *Nature et grâce*: just as the mind of an architect thinks
"in general of square stones" when "those sorts of stones
are actually necessary to his building," so too the soul of Jesus Christ needs "minds of a certain character" to serve as
building-blocks of his church—a "temple of vast extent and
of an infinite beauty"—and hence "diffuses in them the
grace that sanctifies them."[99]

Malebranche's reasoning here seems a bit odd. One can
see why Christ would will *particularly* the gracious sanctification of a former great sinner whom he wants to use as a
stone in his temple, but why would he will particularly the
attempted sanctification of "persons who will not make the
slightest use" of grace? God the Father allows grace to fall
"uselessly" because his operation is *general*, and the generality excuses the uselessness; but if God the Son confers
useless grace particularly, through a desire of his human
soul, does this not lead to the possibility of charging Christ
with "acceptation of persons" and arbitrariness—even as
the Father escapes this charge with his simplicity and uniformity? Certainly it is Malebranche's view that Christ wills
many things particularly: "We have," he urges, "reason to

[98] Malebranche, *Nature et grâce*, in *Oeuvres complètes*, vol. 5, p. 73. For a
helpful commentary on Malebranche's theory of grace, see L. Esquirol,
"Le Mérite et la grâce dan l'oeuvre de Malebranche," in *Archives de philosophie* 14 (1938), pp. 107ff.
[99] Ibid., p. 74.

believe, that the vocation of St. Paul was the effect of the efficacity of a particular desire of Jesus Christ." Not everyone, of course, will be given such a vocation, for the "different desires of the soul of Jesus" do not diffuse grace equally upon all men. Finally, however, perhaps recalling what he had said about the "levity" and inconstancy of *volonté particulière*, Malebranche attempts to distinguish between the particular wills of Christ and what is permanent in his volitions.

> It is by present, passing and particular desires of the soul of Jesus, that grace is diffused to persons who are not prepared for it, and in a way which has something singular and extraordinary about it. But it is by permanent desires that it is given regularly to those who receive the sacraments with the necessary disposition. For the grace which we receive through the sacraments is not at all given to us precisely because of the merit of our action . . . it is because of the merits of Jesus Christ, which are liberally applied to us as a consequence of his permanent desires.[100]

In this passage one notices, apart from the effort to preserve the gratuity of grace, that Malebranche tries to bring the human soul of Christ as *near* to the Father as possible by speaking of *désirs permanens*; these are not quite *volontés générales*, of course, but they are an advance on *des désirs actuels, passagers et particuliers*.[101] This keeps Christ from being charged with any more *particularisme* than is required to explain something as particular as the vocation of St. Paul. Nonetheless, those who say that in Malebranche generality saves the Father and brings down upon Christ reasonable complaints of "inequity" in distributing grace unequally through mere desires of his human soul seem to have a point.[102]

[100] Ibid., pp. 75, 88, 91.
[101] Ibid.
[102] See Sainte-Beuve, *Port-Royal: Le Cours de Lausanne, 1837-1838* (Paris: Librairie Droz, 1937), p. 501: "Malebranche imaginait pourtant ce système

One can hardly say that Malebranche was unaware of this difficulty. In a manuscript from c. 1680-1683 entitled *De la prédestination*, he insists that, while some people imagine that "all desires of Jesus Christ with respect to the distribution of grace are commanded of him in detail and through *volontés particulières* [of the Father]," such a view makes it impossible to "justify divine providence." He ends the manuscript with the unequivocal assertion that "it is thus in Jesus Christ as man that one must seek the reason for the distribution of grace, if one wants to justify the conduct of God in this matter; and this is what I have tried to do in the *Traité de la nature et de la grâce.*"[103] If the blame for all men's not being saved thus falls on Christ's human particularism, *ainsi* (apparently) *soit il*.

The problem, finally, is this: if men *ought* to incline toward God, order, and perfection—toward *le bien général*—and away from *les biens particuliers*, they need grace; to deny this would be a "Pelagian" assertion of perfect human independence. However, since grace is given on the Father's part only by a *loi* or *volonté générale*, and not particularly, is there any *rapport* between those who need grace (in order to love order) and those who get it? The Father cannot attend to this difficulty, since that would turn him into a Calvinist who elects a few and damns all others. Yet Christ's particularism does not always pick out just those persons who need grace; as Malebranche says, Christ may choose "great sinners" for his temple, and not those who want to love order. At the same time, Malebranche wants to avoid the Jansenist "heresy" that "some commandments are not possible for the just."[104] One wonders how completely he escapes this difficulty.

---

pour rendre Dieu plus aimable et adorable; mais on peut remarquer qu'à son insu, il ne met si hors d'atteinte Dieu le Père que pour accumuler les difficultés sur le Fils."

[103] Malebranche, *De la prédestination*, in *Oeuvres complètes*, vol. 17-1, p. 560.

[104] See J. Paquier, *Le Jansénisme* (Paris: Librairie Bloud, 1909), p. 162.

In the end, Malebranchian general will is profoundly modified by order, *rapports de perfection*, and occasionalism. This does not make *volonté générale* unimportant; it simply ceases to be (in Jurieu's phrase) the "sole foundation" of the Malebranchian system. After all, it was not Malebranche who said that "the general will is always right." In the governance of a ruined world it is certainly justifiable, but it is not everything. The significance of Malebranche's contribution is that his occasionalism, his notion of an efficacious divine *cause générale*, later became transformed, especially by Montesquieu, into a social theory of physical and moral *causes générales* that produce the particular characters of various peoples. If Malebranche's *généralité* came out in Rousseau primarily in the shape of civic and secular *volonté générale*, Montesquieu arguably reflected Malebranche's own fusion of "real" causality (God) with *généralité*, yielding the composite notion of *cause générale*. In Malebranche there is one *cause générale*: God; in Montesquieu there is a concatenation of physical and moral *causes générales*. In very different and always limited ways, Malebranchism was the *cause occasionnelle* of some of the principal social ideas of Montesquieu and Rousseau.[105]

[105] See Judith N. Shklar, "General Will," in *Dictionary of the History of Ideas*, ed. Philip P. Weiner (New York: Charles Scribner's Sons, 1973), vol. 2, pp. 275ff.; Alberto Postigliola, "De Malebranche à Rousseau: Les Apories de la volonté générale et la revanche du 'raisonneur violent,' " in *Annales de la Société Jean-Jacques Rousseau* (Geneva: Chez A. Jullien, 1980), vol. 39, pp. 134ff.

FOUR

THE GENERAL WILL SOCIALIZED: THE CONTRIBUTION OF MONTESQUIEU

Even if the gap between Malebranche (who died in 1715) and Rousseau (who first published works on *volonté générale* in the mid-1750s) is narrowed by considering Pierre Bayle's extensive and well-known secularization of *généralité* and *particularité* and by examining the Malebranchian idea of order, which later played a large role in Rousseau's *Emile*,[1] it still seems that something or someone is missing in the translation of general will from a primarily theological notion into a primarily political one—though one should recall that even Descartes occasionally relies on a general-particular dichotomy in treating politics (as when he says, apropos of Machiavelli, that "it is the plan which he had to praise Cesare Borgia, which made him establish general maxims to justify particular actions which are difficult to execute").[2] That missing person would be found if there

[1] See above all André Robinet, "Lexicographie philosophique et paléographie: A propos d'ordre dans la *Profession de foi du vicaire savoyard*," in *Studi filosofici* 1 (1978), pp. 39ff.

[2] René Descartes, letter to Princess Elisabeth of Bohemia (November 1646), in *Descartes: Oeuvres et lettres*, ed. André Bridoux (Paris: Pléiade, 1953), p. 1245. Cf. Descartes' letter to Elisabeth (September 1645), p. 1206, which shows that he agrees to *some* extent with the Pascalian-Malebranchian notion of a "body" to whose general good particular interests must be subordinated:

Although each of us is a person [who is] separated from others, and

were an important writer completely familiar with both Malebranchism and Bayle's secular conversion of that doctrine. That important writer was Montesquieu, and it is a point of no small interest that he received his education from the Oratorians—the religious order the most famous member of which was Malebranche.[3] Thus Montesquieu was early inducted into a body full of *thinking* members.[4]

It was not only Montesquieu's official Oratorian education at the Collège de Juilly that brought him into the Malebranchian orbit. As a young provincial from Bordeaux, Montesquieu was introduced into Parisian literary society by Malebranche's associate Père Demolets, the librarian of the Oratoire who had also published important manuscripts of Pascal (including the *pensée*, omitted from the

whose interests are in consequence to some extent distinct from those of the rest of the world, one must still reflect that one cannot subsist alone, and that one is, indeed, one of the parts of the universe, and still more *particulièrement* one of the parts of this earth, of this society, of this family, to which one is connected by his residence, by his oath, by his birth. And one must always prefer the interests of the whole [*du tout*], of which one is a part, to that of one's own person *en particulier*; nonetheless with measure and discretion, for one would be wrong to expose himself to a great evil, in order to procure only a small good for one's relatives or for one's country; and if a man is worth more, all by himself, than the rest of his city, he would not be right to want to sacrifice himself to save it.

Pascal and Malebranche, of course, would never have added the phrases beginning with, "nonetheless with measure and discretion."

[3] See Robert Shackleton, *Montesquieu* (Oxford: Oxford University Press, 1961), pp. 5-8; Pierre Barrière, *Un Grand Provincial: Charles-Louis de Secondat, Baron de La Brède et de Montesquieu* (Bordeaux: Editions Delmas, 1946), pp. 12-20, esp. p. 16: "[Malebranche's] grand ouvrage est la *Recherche de la vérité*: n'est-ce point une perpétuelle recherche de la vérité historique qui anime Montesquieu . . . ?" See also André Robinet, "L'Attitude politique de Malebranche," in *XVIIe Siècle* 38 (1958), pp. 24-27 ("Précurseurs de Montesquieu"), and H. Roddier, "De la composition de *l'Esprit des lois* de Montesquieu et les oratoriens de l'Académie de Juilly," in *Revue d'histoire littéraire de la France* (October 1952), pp. 347ff.

[4] Including, in addition to Malebranche, Bernard Lamy (so much admired by Rousseau), Richard Simon (the great scriptural scholar), and Fathers Lecointe and Thomassin, *inter alia*. See Barrière, *Un Grand Provincial*, pp. 16-17.

Port-Royal edition, that *le coeur a ses raisons que la raison ne connaît point.*[5] He befriended Cardinal Polignac, who had intervened on Malebranche's behalf (with Fénelon) to rescue the Oratorian from a Jesuitical onslaught in the *Mémoires de Trévoux,*[6] and whose *Anti-Lucrèce* is full of Malebranchian *généralité.* He formed an alliance in the Bordeaux Academy with Dortous de Mairan, Malebranche's ablest philosophical sparring partner during the last decade of his life. He was always close to Fontenelle, who delivered Malebranche's memorial *éloge* in the Académie des Sciences.[7] Montesquieu's Malebranchian education, then, by no means ended with his departure from the Collège de Juilly in 1705; he was surrounded by *malebranchistes* throughout his life.

Of course, Montesquieu should not be seen *merely* as the heir of Malebranche, for this approach necessarily overlooks more familiar facets of his thought. It ignores Durkheim's Montesquieu as father of all modern sociology; it ignores Althusser's Montesquieu as pre-Marxian discoverer of inevitable social laws; it ignores Oakeshott's Montesquieu as advocate of moderation and the rule of "recognized" law; it ignores Berlin's Montesquieu as generous tolerator of diversity; it ignores Shklar's Montesquieu as builder of a misanthropic "liberalism of fear," contrasting with Locke's "liberalism of rights."[8] But these views are

[5] Shackleton, *Montesquieu*, p. 9; Robinet, "L'Attitude politique de Malebranche," pp. 24-25.

[6] Shackleton, *Montesquieu*, pp. 98-99; Hink Hillenaar, *Fénelon et les jésuites* (The Hague: Martinus Nijhoff, 1967), pp. 286-287; A. R. Desautels, *Les Mémoires de Trévoux et le mouvement des idées au XVIIIe siècle* (Rome: Institutum Historicum. 1956), pp. 26-31.

[7] Shackleton, *Montesquieu*, pp. 21-22; N. Malebranche, *Oeuvres complètes de Malebranche*, ed. André Robinet (Paris: Vrin, 1966), vol. 19, pp. 999ff.

[8] See Emile Durkheim, *Montesquieu et Rousseau: Précurseurs de la sociologie* (Paris: M. Rivière, 1953), passim; Louis Althusser, *Montesquieu: La Politique et l'histoire* (Paris: Presses Universitaires de France, 1959), chapter 1 ("Une Révolution dans la méthode"); Michael Oakeshott, *On Human Conduct* (Oxford: Clarendon Press, 1975), pp. 246-251; Isaiah Berlin, "Montesquieu," in *Against the Current*, ed. H. Hardy (New York: Penguin Books, 1982), pp. 130ff.; Judith N. Shklar, *Ordinary Vices* (Cambridge, Mass.: Har-

justly familiar, and there is much to be said for drawing out an unfamiliar side of Montesquieu that is as real as it is little known, which lets him serve as a "bridge" between the seventeenth century and Rousseau. One may think, with Voltaire, that the Malebranchian opening book of *Spirit of the Laws* is a "metaphysical labyrinth," but the fact remains that Montesquieu freely constructed that labyrinth, and that one can find his way out of it only by first granting its existence.

Any attentive reader of *De l'esprit des lois* knows that in book 11, which deals with the separation of powers, particularly in England, Montesquieu uses the terms *volonté générale* and *volonté particulière* in distinguishing legislative and judicial authority; thus his most celebrated "constitutional" idea is couched in Malebranchian theological language. After observing that there is "no liberty" in a state unless "the power of judging is separated from the legislative power," Montesquieu laments that in the republics of Italy the "same body of magistrates" has, "as executor of the laws, all the power which it is given as law-maker." In consequence of this improper union of powers, he complains, the body of magistrates "can ravage the state through its *volontés générales*, and, as it also has the power of judging, it can destroy each citizen through its *volontés particulières*."[9]

It was surely no accident that Montesquieu, who was wholly familiar with the seventeenth-century controversy over the nature of divine will, should have used the ideas of general will and particular will in a substantially new political way. How better defend the importance of general laws than to connect them with a divine mode of operation—or

---

vard University Press, 1984), pp. 197, 217ff., 235ff. (For a fuller appreciation of Shklar's remarkable reading of Montesquieu, see the author's review of *Ordinary Vices* in *American Political Science Review*, June 1985, pp. 610-611.)

[9] Montesquieu, *De l'esprit des lois*, ed. Robert Dérathé (Paris: Editions Garnier, 1973), vol. 1, p. 170. (In his excellent notes, pp. 476ff., Dérathé does not treat this passage at all.)

at least with terminology that reminds one of divinity? (Montesquieu, like Malebranche, defines law in terms of general "relations.")[10] Admittedly, even while using language that could not fail to conjure up quasi-Malebranchian reminiscences, Montesquieu was not exactly following Malebranche: he is not so much praising *volonté générale* and decrying *volonté particulière* as he is deploring their union in the same body of magistrates. What is important here is the fact that Montesquieu was using the language of a controversy over what was once considered the supreme question—the nature of divine justice—in order to dignify and elevate a controversy over the nature of human justice. And this cannot have been inadvertence.

That this choice of language was policy and not inadvertence is clear enough if one looks at the whole body of Montesquieu's work. *De l'esprit des lois* was published in 1748, but as early as 1725—only ten years after the death of Malebranche—one finds Montesquieu urging in his already-mentioned *Traité des devoirs* that justice is not dependent merely on human positive laws, on human dispositions or *volontés particulières*, but that justice is a "general relation" based on "the existence and the sociability of reasonable beings."[11]

To be sure, the *généralité* of the *Traité des devoirs* is more nearly a kind of "universality," for in *Devoirs* he makes particular duties (within some particular polity) yield to a *morale universelle*; a duty may be *général* within a state, but dangerously *particulier* with respect to the entire *genre humain*.

All particular duties [*tous les devoirs particuliers*] cease when one cannot fulfil them without damaging the duties of man. Should one think, for example, of the good of the fatherland [*la Patrie*] when the good of the hu-

---

[10] Ibid., vol. 1, p. 7: "Laws, in the broadest sense, are the necessary relations which arise from the nature of things."

[11] Montesquieu, *Oeuvres complètes* (Paris: Pléiade, 1949), vol. 1, pp. 109-110. Since the *Traité des devoirs* is lost, one must rely on the summary published by the Bordeaux Academy (July 1725); see same source, pp. 108-111.

man race is in question? No; the duty of the citizen is a crime when it makes him forget the duty of man. The impossibility of ranging the universe under a single society has made men strangers to men, but this arrangement has not prescribed against the primary duties, and man, everywhere reasonable, is neither a Roman nor a barbarian.[12]

This is basically Cicero, Montesquieu's early hero, slightly "colored" by Malebranche; it is *De republica* read in the light of *Nature et grâce*.[13] It is a passage that Montesquieu could have repeated in his mature works, but one that Rousseau would have rejected after he had abandoned a reason-ordained *morale universelle* in favor of the general will of the citizen.[14] Nor is Montesquieu's use of quasi-Malebranchian language confined only to the general-particular distinction, or to the idea that laws are general relations; he also speaks, in the *Traité des devoirs*, of princes who have ruled by "the simplest means."[15]

The distinction between the general and the particular, which runs throughout the *Traité des devoirs*, recurs often in Montesquieu, though sometimes only as a stylistic feature rather than a substantive doctrine (as in the *Lettres persanes*, no. 90, in which Montesquieu has Usbek observe that "from this *passion générale* which the French nation has for glory, has arisen in the minds of *particuliers* a certain *je ne*

---

[12] Ibid. p. 110. This passage, at least, is not merely paraphrased but actually quoted from Montesquieu's lost *Traité*.

[13] Cicero, *On the Commonwealth*, trans. G. Sabine (Indianapolis: Library of Liberal Arts, n.d.), p. 216: "[The law] will not lay down one rule at Rome and another at Athens, nor will it be one rule today and another tomorrow. But there will be one law, eternal and unchangeable, binding at all times upon all people. . . ." The Malebranchian contribution comes from *De la recherche de la vérité*, in *Oeuvres complètes*, vol. 1, p. 490: "[If I ask] whether I should prefer riches to virtue . . . I will hear a clear and distinct response . . . because all the world knows it . . . it is neither Greek nor Latin, neither French nor German, and all the nations understand it."

[14] See chapter 5 of the present work.

[15] Montesquieu, *Oeuvres complètes*, Pléiade ed., vol. 1, p. 111.

sais quoi which is called a 'point of honor.' ")[16] More often, however, the distinction involves more than a mere stylistic feature: in the collection of Montesquieu-fragments published under the title *Mes Pensées*, the general-particular dichotomy surfaces over and over again. In a fragment dealing with princes, for example, Montesquieu urges that "it is necessary above all that princes guard against *des affections particulières*: [for] a certain group, certain men, certain habits, certain opinions." Providence, he says, has decreed that princes ought to have *une affection générale* for "great objects." (The notion of *affections particulières* he condemns further by calling them "fantasies,"[17] which is not far from Malebranche's *volontés bizarres*.)

But it is not only a question of princes; indeed, in a passage dealing with republics, Montesquieu comes extraordinarily close to the Rousseauean notion that a genuine *volonté générale* can exist only in a small, simple republic of uncorrupted *moeurs*. "It is essential in republics," he argues, "that there be an *esprit général* which dominates. In proportion as luxury is established, the spirit of *particularisme* is established as well." A "soul corrupted by luxury" is "the enemy of the laws"—laws that are, of course, precisely general rather than particular. Indeed, "the spirit of the citizen is to love the laws, even when there are cases in which they are detrimental to us, and to consider rather the *bien général* which they always do us, than the *mal particulier* which they sometimes do us."[18]

The constant use of a general-particular distinction, of the phrases *volonté générale* and *volonté particulière* in his greatest work, and of Malebranchian catch phrases such as "the simplest means," would seem to indicate a knowledge of Malebranche in particular and of seventeenth-century theology in general; and, in fact, this indication is borne out

[16] Montesquieu, *Lettres persanes*, no. 90, in *Oeuvres complètes*, Pléiade ed., vol. 1, p. 265.

[17] Montesquieu, *Mes pensées*, in *Oeuvres complètes*, Pléiade ed, p. 1163.

[18] Ibid., pp. 1134, 1144.

in Montesquieu's writings. Sometimes Montesquieu's view of Malebranche is not very flattering: Père Malebranche, he says "has built a magnificent palace in the air, which is hidden from our eyes and which is lost in the clouds." Montesquieu does not refrain from criticizing Malebranche, particularly his *De la recherche de la vérité*: "The argument of Père Malebranche proves nothing except that we do not know how we perceive objects."[19] Certainly Montesquieu had no use for the Malebranchian notion that "we see all things in God"; this idea was simply too *recherché* to be a *verité*. But the point here is that Montesquieu *knew* Malebranche's works, not that he approved of all of them; hence, he knew that Malebranche had used the notion of "general will" as a *justifying* notion that could be secularized by "bracketing" God.

Occasionally Montesquieu actually praises Malebranche: at one point, he says that "the four great poets" in the history of Western literature are Plato, Malebranche, Shaftesbury, and Montaigne; at another, he claims that "no visionary ever had more good sense than Père Malebranche." Sometimes one finds him using explicitly Malebranchian arguments—in treating "false miracles," for example. "The idea of false miracles," he says in a passage reminiscent of Malebranche's *Traité de la nature et de la grâce*, "comes from our conceit, which makes us believe that we are an important enough object for the supreme being to upset the whole of nature for us . . . we want God to be a partial being."[20] And partiality, of course, is a form of particularism; it is a manifestation of the *amour-propre* that Pascal and Malebranche had condemned before Montesquieu and that Diderot and, above all, Rousseau, would condemn after him.

---

[19] Ibid., pp. 1177, 1540.
[20] Ibid., pp. 1546, 1548, 1569.

The earliest consequential work of Montesquieu in which traces of Malebranchian *généralité* appear is the *Observations sur l'histoire naturelle* (c. 1719-1721), which concerns itself particularly with the study of plants but concludes its fifth section with general praise of "Cartesian" science. Those who admit a *"Providence particulière* of God" in the production of plants, Montesquieu asserts, are "mitigated Cartesians who have abandoned the rule of their master," while those who correctly account for plant life exclusively in terms of "the general movement of matter" can "pride themselves on being strict Cartesians." (The "great system" of Descartes, he adds, which will be "admired in all ages," magnifies Providence by showing that it acts "with so much simplicity.")[21]

As Shackleton has rightly observed in his fine biography of Montesquieu, this notion of a simple divinity who operates through general movement, and not through *Providence particulière*, is "less the doctrine of Descartes himself . . . than of his successors. . . . It is the illustrious Malebranche who is the author of the opinions adopted by Montesquieu." With as much charm as accuracy, Shackleton adds that "to be a Cartesian, then, for Montesquieu in 1721, is to be a disciple of Malebranche; and a disciple of Malebranche who concentrated on the laws of movement, forgot the spirituality of the soul, and was very far from seeing all things in God."[22]

This notion of a "Cartesian" (really Malebranchian) science, in which all divine "particular Providence" yields to the simplicity of the general movement of matter, turns up again a few years later in the *Lettres persanes*—though in a very different tone. In the ninety-seventh letter, Montesquieu has Usbek write to a Persian dervish that, while Western science has not attained "the peaks of Eastern wisdom," nor "been transported to the throne of light, nor

[21] In Montesquieu, *Oeuvres complètes*, ed. Daniel Oster (Paris: Editions du Seuil, 1964), p. 55.
[22] Shackleton, *Montesquieu*, p. 25.

heard the ineffable words resounding from angelic choirs, nor felt the fearful onset of the divine ecstasy," nonetheless, the Western method of following human reason alone has "put order into chaos" and "explained by simple mechanics the organization of God's architecture."[23] (In Malebranche, of course, order is what God cherishes above all, while Christ operates as "architect" of the Church.)[24]

Beginning with the "Cartesian" observation that "the creator of nature gave movement to matter" and that "that was all that was needed to produce the prodigious variety of phenomena that we can observe in the universe," Usbek goes on to borrow a political comparison of human legislation with divine legislation that had been used by Malebranche in *Nature et grâce* and then by Bayle in *Réponse aux questions d'un provincial*: "It is for ordinary legislators to suggest laws for the regulation of human societies, laws which are as changeable as the minds of the men who invented them or the nations which obey them." By contrast, those Cartesians who uncover divine legislation "tell us only of *des lois générales*, immutable and eternal, which are observed without any exceptions, with infinite regularity, immediacy and orderliness, in the immensity of space." These Malebranchian turns of phrase and thought, which foreshadow the opening book of *De l'esprit des lois* and which treat nature as the model for the moral world, are shorn up by a further Malebranchian intimation: far from divine general laws being so mysterious that one can only admire (but never understand) them, their very "simplicity caused them to be under-estimated for a long time, and it is only after much reflection that their fecundicity and scope have been realized."[25] Malebranche too had stressed simplicity

---

[23] Montesquieu, *Lettres persanes*, no. 97, in *Oeuvres complètes*, ed. Oster, p. 113.

[24] Malebranche, *Traité de la nature et de la grâce*, in *Oeuvres complètes*, vol. 5, pp. 65ff.

[25] Montesquieu, *Lettres persanes*, no. 97, p. 113.

and fecundicity as the chief properties of "general" divine laws in *Nature et grâce*.

Usbek continues to employ the same Malebranchian language in the 129th of the *Lettres persanes*, in which he talks further of defective legislators: "The majority of legislators have been limited men whom chance has placed at the head of others, and who have consulted scarcely anything but their prejudices and their fantasies." (The key terms—"limited," "prejudice," "fantasy"—are favorite Malebranchisms.) Legislators have "misunderstood the greatness and the dignity of their work"; they have "thrown themselves into useless details." Worst of all, "they have ruled [*donné*] in particular cases, which shows a limited intelligence that only sees things in parts and embraces nothing of a general view." Even where they have inherited good laws, they have needlessly abolished them, and have thereby "thrown [their] peoples into the disorders that are inseparable from changes."[26] All of this—limited intelligence, indulging in particular cases, lack of a general view, disorder arising from inconstancy and change—is a political translation, or transposition, of *Nature et grâce*. Here Montesquieu's bad legislators are acting just like Malebranche's "pagan divinities."[27]

Montesquieu offers a striking example of just such a bad legislator, who embraces no *vue générale*, in chapter 14 of *Considerations on the Greatness and Decline of the Romans*, which deals with Tiberius. After describing at length Tiberius's debasement of and contempt for the Senate, Montesquieu adds that

> nonetheless, it does not seem at all that Tiberius wanted to debase the Senate: he complained of nothing so much as the penchant of this body for servitude. . . . But he was like the majority of men, and wanted contradictory things: his *politique générale* was not in

[26] Ibid., no. 129, p. 130.
[27] Malebranche, *Nature et grâce*, pp. 148ff.

agreement with his *passions particulières*. He would have desired a free Senate, capable of respecting his government; but he also wanted a Senate which satisfied, at every moment, his fears, his jealousies, his hates. In fine, the statesman yielded continually to the man.[28]

One should notice the perfectly Malebranchian groupings of terms: it is passion that is *particulière* (there was, evidently, no "silence" of Tiberius's passions) and that is satisfied by "fear," "jealousy," and "hate"; it is *politique générale* that would have yielded a "free" Senate capable of "respect." Here is another instance of Montesquieuean secular transformation of the language of *Nature et grâce*. Tiberius's *particularisme*, indeed, leads to something resembling Malebranche's description of the gods of antiquity: "sovereignly powerful," but also "cruel, adulterous, voluptuous."[29] (If one can look backward to Malebranche, one can also look forward to Rousseau. When, in Montesquieu's version of Tiberius, "the statesman yielded continually to the man," *le général* yielded to *le particulier*; this is very close to Rousseau's notion that the general will is the will that one has "as a citizen"—precisely *not* as a mere "man."[30])

If the *Considerations on the Romans* both reflect Malebranche and foreshadow Rousseau, they also, on occasion, remind one of Pascal's notion of a body governed by the spirit of *généralité*. In chapter 9 of *Considerations*, entitled "Two Causes of Rome's Ruin," Montesquieu laments that, once Rome "had subjugated the whole world," the civic unity of the Roman republic was shattered; a single *esprit général* no longer sustained a single *corps politique*: "Rome was no longer a city whose people had but a single spirit, a single love of liberty, a single hatred of tyranny. . . . Once

---

[28] Montesquieu, *Considérations sur les causes de la grandeur des romains et de leur décadence*, in *Oeuvres complètes*, ed. Oster, p. 462.

[29] Malebranche, *Recherche de la vérité*, in *Oeuvres complètes* vol. 3, p. 86.

[30] Jean-Jacques Rousseau, *Du contrat social*, in *Political Writings*, ed. C. E. Vaughan (Oxford: Basil Blackwell, 1962), vol. 2, p. 35.

the peoples of Italy became its citizens, each city brought to Rome its genius, its particular interests [*ses interêts particuliers*], and its dependence on some great protector. The distracted city no longer formed a complete whole."[31]

What Rome had lost forever, in Montesquieu's view, was "what is called union in a body politic [*un corps politique*]." "True" political union, he goes on, "is a union of harmony, whereby all the parts . . . cooperate for the general good [*le bien général*] of society." To be sure, he adds, there is another kind of general "concord": the false "peace" generated by oriental despotism. Anticipating *De l'esprit des lois*, and echoing Pascal, Montesquieu says that "if we see any union" in "Asiatic despotism," it is "not citizens who are united but dead bodies [*des corps morts*] buried one next to the other."[32] Here there is assuredly no "body full of thinking members"; there are bodies, but all of them are dead. (Once again, the groupings of terms reflect a [now secularized] French theological inheritance; *interêts particuliers* are associated with "tyranny" and "distraction," while *le bien général* consorts with "unity" and "concord.")

Montesquieu's familiarity with seventeenth-century theological controversies is clear in all his writings, but especially in the careful *Réponses et explications pour la faculté de théologie*, which he wrote in 1750 in an effort to head off the Sorbonne's condemning *De l'esprit des lois*.[33] Here he adheres to an essentially Malebranchian line—general laws of nature, few miracles—while conceding just enough particular divine interventions to satisfy, or at least placate, the Sorbonne. The last of the seventeen propositions questioned by the Sorbonne was one from *Spirit of the Laws*, book 9, chapter 2: "The Canaanites were destroyed because they were small monarchies, which were not confederated, and which did not defend themselves in common." The Sorbonne evidently wanted Montesquieu to say, since he had

---

[31] Montesquieu, *Considérations sur les romains*, p. 453.
[32] Ibid.
[33] Shackleton, *Montesquieu*, pp. 368ff.

had the temerity to use a biblical example, that God, rather than federalism, might have saved the Canaanites; in his response Montesquieu tried to affirm both positions at once: "Eh bien! God willed that they not be confederated."[34]

Montesquieu begins his *Réponses* by saying that God "does not always bring about his marvels in the same way. Sometimes he acts directly: 'Let there be light! And there was light.' Sometimes he employs second causes: 'I have sustained thee to show my power through thee, so that my name will be manifested throughout the world.' Sometimes God even wills to submit himself to second causes: 'If you had knocked five times, etc.' " Here Malebranchian language is used to make a non-Malebranchian point: Scripture, Montesquieu says, is "full of the diverse ways of God," not just full of his simple or general ways.[35]

Soon, however, the "diverse ways" begin to yield to a more authentically Malebranchian simplicity and generality. The Jews were a particularly chosen people, Montesquieu concedes, but, "in the extraordinary way that God took, everything was not extraordinary." God, he insists, "did not change the course of nature except when the course of nature did not enter into his plans"; he performed miracles, but only "when wisdom demanded them." Finally, Malebranchian general law and prudent particularist orthodoxy are carefully balanced: "If one posed me the question, 'Why did the Israelites enter into Jericho?,' I would say that it was because God caused the walls to fall down. But, if Jericho had been open, I would respond to the question by saying that the city was without defense. I would not say that it was because of a *voie particulière* of God, because, in this case, there would not have been any *volonté particulière* at all."[36]

This is the only reasonable view, Montesquieu adds, un-

[34] Montesquieu, *Réponses et explications pour la faculté de théologie*, in *Oeuvres complètes*, ed. Oster, p. 829.
[35] Ibid.
[36] Ibid., p. 830.

less one asserts that "God does everything," even by doing nothing. He declines further comment on this point by saying that he was not asked about *la cause générale*, but only about *les causes sécondes*.[37] Without denying miracles altogether, but restricting them to *explicit* scriptural assurances, Montesquieu's *Réponses* reinforce the Malebranchian view that God acts most often by laws and *volontés générales*, and only rarely through *volontés particulières*.

Since, despite the *Réponses* for the Sorbonne's theology faculty, Montesquieu was no theologian (as he himself insisted), one could perhaps doubt the theological *provenance* of the general-particular dichotomy in Montesquieu's thought, as well as of the distinction between general and second causes, were it not for the fact that on occasion he lets this origin stand out in high relief. One instance is in the *Spicilège*, that collection of facts and aphorisms that, appropriately enough, had been started for Montesquieu by Père Desmolets, the librarian of the Oratoire.[38] "If it is true that we cannot save ourselves except by an efficacious *grâce particulière*, then one must say that the plan of God is *not* to save all men *en général*."[39] Here, precisely, is a commentary on the very text of St. Paul that set in motion the whole controversy over general will, the same text treated by Pascal, Arnauld, and Malebranche. This shows that the notion of *généralité* was not just in the air, but in Montesquieu's mind.

So well established was the general-particular distinction in Montesquieu's thought that on occasion he even made it the foundation of a joke. In a fragment from *Mes pensées* dealing with marriage, he says: "A man consulted me about

[37] Ibid.

[38] Shackleton, *Montesquieu*, pp. 9-10; Robinet, "L'Attitude politique de Malebranche," pp. 24-25.

[39] Montesquieu, *Spicilège*, in *Oeuvres complètes*, ed. Oster, p. 391. It is worth noting, however, that Montesquieu himself did not take any of his main ideas to be theological: "My book [*De l'esprit des lois*] is not, either in fact or in intention, a book of theology; I teach nothing about theology . . . I only give reasons for the political and civil laws of the various peoples of the earth" (letter to the Duc de Nivernais [January 1750], in *Correspondance de Montesquieu* [Paris: Librairie Champion, 1914], vol. 2, p. 250).

a marriage. I told him: 'Men, *en général*, have decided that you would be committing folly; the majority of men, *en particulier*, have decided that you would not.' "[40]

A more elaborate general-particular joke, but one that sports with a subject Montesquieu actually took very seriously, appears in the *Lettre persane* no. 24. This letter opens with a wonderfully malicious characterization of Louis XIV's ruinous adventurism:

> He has no gold mines, like the King of Spain, his cousin; but he has greater riches than him, because he draws them from the vanity of his subjects, which is more inexhaustible than the mines. He has been seen undertaking great wars, having no other funds than honorific titles to sell, and, by a prodigy of human pride, his troops have been paid, his fortunes supplied, and his fleets equipped. . . . This king is a great magician.[41]

If Louis's efforts at universal monarchy met with some success abroad, though at a disastrous price, he was less fortunate at home. Within his own kingdom he was "surrounded by countless invisible enemies," and, though he "searched for them for more than thirty years, he didn't find a single one." Montesquieu describes these invisible enemies in language that borrows Malebranche's general-particular distinction, seemingly fusing it with Pascal's distinction between a body and its members: "They live with him: they are at his court, in his capital, in his troops, in his tribunals; and nonetheless it is said that he will have the unhappiness to die without having found them. It is said that they exist *en général*, but that they are nothing *en particulier*; that there is a body, but no members."[42]

---

[40] Montesquieu, *Mes pensées* in *Oeuvres complètes*, Plèiade ed., vol. 1, p. 1463.

[41] Montesquieu, *Lettres persanes*, no. 24, in *Oeuvres complètes*, ed. Oster, p. 75.

[42] Ibid.

No doubt, Montesquieu has his letter writer Rica conclude, heaven is punishing Louis "for not having been modest enough towards his vanquished enemies" by surrounding him with invisible ones whose genius and destiny are above the king's own.[43] In this letter, received theological terms are tossed in the air, turned into a *jeu d'esprit*, but with a serious purpose.

If Montesquieu could base jokes about marriage and the schemes of Louis XIV on the general-particular dichotomy, so too could he have fun with Malebranchian occasionalism. In the relatively late *Défense de l'Esprit des lois* (1750), he plays with an unintelligent critic who had insisted that *De l'esprit des lois* was "one of those irregular productions" that have "multiplied since the arrival of the [anti-Jansenist] Bull *Unigenitus*." Here Montesquieu had an opportunity to make light of Malebranchism, papal authority, and outraged piety in a single stroke: "To make the *Spirit of the Laws* appear because of the arrival of the constitution *Unigenitus*—isn't this laughable? The Bull *Unigenitus* is not at all the occasional cause of the book *Spirit of the Laws*; but the Bull *Unigenitus* and the book *Spirit of the Laws* [taken together] were the occasional causes which have led this critic to such puerile reasoning."[44]

In Montesquieu it is not only the constant use of the general-particular dichotomy that is reminiscent of Malebranche. Just as, on careful inspection, Malebranchism rests on more than *volonté générale* and *volonté particulière* (if one gives due weight to occasionalism and to eternal relations of perfection), so too the Malebranchian influence on

[43] Ibid.

[44] Montesquieu, *Défense de l'esprit des lois,* in *Oeuvres complètes,* ed. Oster, p. 812. At the very end of his life Montesquieu was still trying to calm the religious quarrels occasioned by *Unigenitus*'s attack on Jansenism; see his late *Mémoire sur la constitution* (1753), in *Oeuvres complètes,* ed. Oster, pp. 843-844.

Montesquieu derives from all three strands of Malebranchism, not just from *généralité*. In Montesquieu, indeed, it is almost as if several strands of Malebranchism, distinct enough in Malebranche himself, were run together; it is almost as if Montesquieu had conflated Malebranche's general-particular dichotomy with the Malebranchian distinction between "true" and "occasional" causes (yielding the composite terms *cause générale* and *cause particulière*) and then transferred this synthesis from philosophy to social science.[45] This is most clear in Montesquieu's remarkable essay, *Sur les causes qui peuvent affecter les esprits et les caractères*: "There is, in each nation, a *caractère général*, which each *particulier* bears, more or less. It is produced in two ways, by physical causes, which depend on climate . . . and by moral causes, which are the combination of laws, of religion, of *moeurs* and of manners."[46]

Here the terms *général* and *particulier* are grafted onto a theory of social causality; the Malebranchian idea of general laws regularly producing all particular effects is translated from physics and metaphysics into social science. But there are more "layers" of causality in Montesquieu than in Malebranche, because the Oratorian needs to draw only the primary distinction between God as sole true or efficacious cause and all other occasional causes, while Montesquieu must work backwards from the *caractère particulier* of an individual to the *caractère général* of that individual's nation, and from that national *caractère général* to the *causes générales* (physical and moral) that have produced that character, and, finally, from the *causes générales* to the *cause générale*: God ("*il y a un effet, donc il y a une cause*").[47] Even so, when Shackleton asserts that Montesquieu solves "for the historian the problem of determinism as it had been solved for

---

[45] Shackleton, *Montesquieu*, pp. 168-169.

[46] Montesquieu, *Sur les causes qui peuvent affecter les esprits et les caractères*, in *Oeuvres complètes*, ed. Oster, p. 492.

[47] Montesquieu, *Mes pensées*, in *Oeuvres complètes de Montesquieu*, ed. A. Masson (Paris: Nagel, 1950), vol. 2, p. 641.

the metaphysician by Malebranche," and that "the distinction between the First Cause and occasional causes which was made by the author of *De la recherche de la vérité* has been carried into history by Montesquieu,"[48] he is essentially right. After all, in the single most celebrated passage from his *Considerations on the Romans*, Montesquieu insists—paraphrasing Bossuet's *Histoire universelle* even as he undermines its providentialist *particularisme*—that

> it is not fortune that rules the world. . . . There are *des causes générales*, be they moral, be they physical, which act in each monarchy, raise it, maintain it, or hurl it down; all accidents are subject to these causes, and, if the chance of a battle, that is, of a *cause particulière*, has ruined a state, there was a general cause which decreed that this state should perish through a single battle: in a word, the principal attraction carries with it all *accidents particuliers*.[49]

Here one sees Malebranchian strands intertwined and then historicized: *le général* and true or efficacious cause fuse to become *cause générale*, while *le particulier* and occasional causes blend and become *cause particulière*. Two strands of theology turn into a single method of understanding history and society. Once one sees this, certain passages from Malebranche's *Nature et grâce* seem to "intimate" Montesquieu: "In order that the general cause act through laws or through *volontés générales*, and that its action be regular, constant and uniform, it is absolutely necessary that there be some occasional cause which determines the efficacy of these laws, and which serves to establish them."[50] If one substitutes "general causes" for

---

[48] Cited in Shackleton, *Montesquieu*, pp. 167-169.
[49] Montesquieu, *Considérations sur les romains*, p. 472. On the Montesquieu-Bossuet *rapport*, see the excellent remarks in Mark Hulliung, *Montesquieu and the Old Regime* (Berkeley: University of California Press, 1976), pp. 168-171.
[50] Cited in Ferdinand Alquié, *Malebranche* (Paris: Seghers, 1977), pp. 138-139.

"general cause," the language is abstract enough to fit nearly as well into Montesquieu's *Sur les causes* as into Malebranche's *Nature et grâce.*

Confirmation of all this is to be found mainly in Malebranche's last book, the only important one he published while Montesquieu was an adult. In finding a *rapport* between Malebranche and Montesquieu, no work matters more than the *Réflexions sur la prémotion physique,* a copy of which was in Montesquieu's personal library.[51] It is in the *Réflexions* that one finds what appears to be the embryonic and still-theological form of Montesquieu's doctrine, adumbrated in *Sur les causes* and in book 19 of *De l'esprit des lois,* that there are social *causes générales*—both physical (climate) and moral (education)—that produce the *caractères particuliers* of individuals. To be sure, Malebranche speaks of nature and grace, while Montesquieu speaks of the physical and the moral, but is not the second pair a secularized version of the first? Malebranche himself, without waiting for Montesquieu, converts *nature et grâce* into *la physique* and *la morale* in the *Méditations chrétiennes,* in which he urges that something right and just on a truly grand scale—Noah's Flood, for instance—arose out of a divine *proportioning* of the moral to the physical. In the seventh *méditation,* a *dévot* praises God's wisdom in having "so combined the physical with the moral that the universal deluge and other considerable events were the necessary consequences of natural laws." How much more justice and foresight there is, the *dévot* goes on, "in having established [general] laws which . . . should have ravaged the earth just at the time that corruption was general" than in making the waters rise through "*des volontes particulières et miraculeuses.*"[52] The

---

[51] See L. Desgraves, *Catalogue de la bibliothèque de Montesquieu* (Paris: Droz, 1954). Montesquieu clearly knew Malebranche's *Prémotion physique,* since he paraphrases the book in one of his *pensées*; see *Mes pensées,* in *Oeuvres complètes,* Pléiade ed., vol. 1, p. 1548.

[52] Malebranche, *Méditations chrétiennes et métaphysiques,* in *Oeuvres complètes,* vol. 10, p. 79.

point here, beyond Malebranche's usual and familiar diminution of the miraculous, is the notion that God as *cause efficace* combines the physical and the moral in general laws that produce "just" particular events. Diminish or "bracket" God, and one has the substance of Montesquieu.

In the *Réflexions sur la prémotion physique* Malebranche urges that

> the continual variety of thoughts and of movements which modify the soul, in consequence of the general laws of nature and grace, contribute to the variety of our acts of consent. . . . All of this produces different modifications in us: not, again, through the efficacy of our wills, but . . . through the general laws of nature and grace—laws which he [God] has established . . . to fix a constant order between natural causes and their effects.[53]

Of course, when Malebranche thinks of these general laws, he is also thinking of "the efficacy of the *volontés pratiques* of the creator, who does everything in all things,"[54] whereas Montesquieu is thinking of the efficacy of a concatenation of physical and moral causes, not of God in the first instance. Yet, for both Malebranche and Montesquieu there is a *general* causality, operating both physically and morally, which produces *les choses particulières*, even though both affirm a measure of freedom ("consent") and both deny having fallen into a Spinozistic determinism.[55] Indeed, can it be wholly accidental that both Malebranche and Montesquieu fell afoul of the same Spinoza-hating Jesuit, Father Tournemine, editor of the *Mémoires de Trévoux*—Malebranche near

---

[53] Malebranche, *Réflexions sur la prémotion physique*, in *Oeuvres complètes*, vol. 16, pp. 48-49.

[54] Ibid., p. 49.

[55] See Malebranche's self-defense against Dortous de Mairan's assertion that Malebranchism is finally reducible to Spinozism, in *Oeuvres complètes*, vol. 19, pp. 852ff.; for Montesquieu's self-defense against the same changes, see Shackleton, *Montesquieu*, pp. 261-264.

the end of his career, Montesquieu near the beginning of his? Did Tournemine think to see Spinoza alive and well in the Oratoire—Malebranche's home and Montesquieu's school?[56]

Montesquieu's notion of *causes générales* producing an *esprit* or *caractère général* (which in turn gives rise to the *esprits particuliers* of individuals) receives its definitive summing-up in chapter 4 of the rightly famous book 19 of *De l'esprit des lois* (characterized by Shackleton as "perhaps the most significant chapter of the whole work.")[57]

> Several things govern men: climate, religion, laws, maxims of government, examples of past things, *moeurs*, manners—from which arises a resulting *esprit général*.
>
> In proportion as, in each nation, one of these causes acts with more force, the others yield to it. Nature and climate almost alone dominate savages; manners govern the Chinese; laws tyrannize Japan; *moeurs* used to set the tone in Sparta; maxims of government and ancient *mores* did so in Rome.[58]

Thus, as Shackleton correctly insists, it is only a caricature of Montesquieu to view him as a climatological determinist, since he offers a variety of determining *causes gé-*

---

[56] Malebranche was accused of Spinozism in Père Tournemine's Preface to Fénelon's *De l'éxistence de Dieu*; after Malebranche complained to the Archbishop of Cambrai—who had never authorized the Preface—Tournemine publicly apologized to Malebranche in the pages of the *Mémoires de Trévoux*. Père André, Malebranche's disciple and biographer, described Tournemine as an "homme d'un scavoir assez mediocre, mais d'une hardiesse qui supplée à tout." See the documents in Malebranche, *Oeuvres complètes*, vol. 19, pp. 836-850; see also Henri Gouhier, *Fénelon philosophe* (Paris: Vrin, 1977), pp. 201-202. For Montesquieu's encounters with Père Tournemine, see Shackleton, *Montesquieu*, pp. 62-63. Montesquieu would certainly have agreed with Voltaire's verses:

> C'est notre Père Tournemine,
> Qui croit tout ce qu'il imagine.

[57] Shackleton, *Montesquieu*, pp. 316-317.

[58] Montesquieu, *De l'esprit des lois*, in *Oeuvres complètes*, ed. Oster, p. 641.

nérales. This is especially plain in a *pensée* dating from the 1730s: "I beg," Montesquieu pleads, "that I not be accused of attributing to moral causes the things which depend on climate alone." (He need not have worried; he was actually accused of giving too *little* weight to moral causes.) It is true, he goes on, that, "if moral causes do not interrupt physical ones," the latter will "operate to their full extent." Even if physical causes "have the power to operate by themselves (as when people inhabit inaccessible mountains)," moral causality need not be wholly destroyed, for often a "physical cause needs a moral cause in order to operate."[59]

All of this is plainer still in *Sur les causes qui peuvent affecter les esprits et les caractères*, in which Montesquieu asserts, after granting that "the complication of causes which form the *caractère général* of a people is very great," that nonetheless "moral causes do more to form the *caractère général* of a nation, and decide more the quality of its *esprit*, than physical causes." He insists that one finds a "great proof" of this in the case of the Jews, who, physically "dispersed all over the earth, cropping up in all ages, born in all countries," have nevertheless produced a number of writers, "of whom one can name scarcely two who have had any common sense." The *cause morale* (in this case education) that worked to unify Jewish writers in a general lack of common sense was that rabbinical writers, born into generations of slavery, had a superstitious reverence for the "early and miserable" works of their ancestors, which recorded "great marvels that God had worked on behalf of their fathers." In eternally imitating these works as if they were "perfect models," Jewish writers kept up a consistently bad taste wherever and whenever they found themselves.[60] Thus, for Montesquieu, constantly refurbished tastelessness took precedence over every *cause physique*.

Montesquieu's notion of "taste," of course, is as com-

---

[59] Montesquieu, *Mes pensées*, in *Oeuvres complètes*, ed. Oster, p. 996.
[60] Montesquieu, *Sur les causes*, pp. 492-493.

pletely dominated by a general-particular dichotomy as is any of his theories. The distinction does much to shape his last important work, the *Essai sur le goût*, written in the 1750s for the *Encyclopédie* and published only after Montesquieu's death. In this essay he insists that "all works of art have *des règles générales*, which are guides that must never be lost sight of." Since Montesquieu has let art be shaped, quasi-legally, by general rules, he next permits himself a reflection *on* rules, noting that, "since laws are always just in their *être général*, but almost always unjust in their application," in the arts one must permit taste, which is individual or particular, to depart from the tyranny of the law's unbending generality. (How odd it is to find this neo-Aristotelian argument in the usually Malebranchian Montesquieu!) On this point Montesquieu draws in the distinction between *causes générales* and *causes particulières* that had been the foundation of *Sur les causes*: "Although each effect [in a work of art] depends on a general cause, this is mixed with so many particular causes that each effect has, in some sense, a cause to itself." Art then, "gives rules, and taste the exceptions"; sometimes one must submit, sometimes the other.[61] Even in a discussion of aesthetics, the language of law, of rules, of *causes générales* and *causes particulières* is marshalled.

Shackleton is surely right in believing that Montesquieu believed "firmly in the concomitance of moral and physical causes."[62] A strict physical determinism would have been obviously incompatible with his assertion, in book 1 of *De l'esprit des lois*, that the institutions of each nation are only the *cas particulier* of a perfectly general *raison humaine* (*la raison* being, of course, a moral cause).[63] Thus Montesquieu can honestly say, in book 19, that none of his efforts to

[61] Montesquieu, *Essai sur le goût*, in *Oeuvres complètes*, ed. Oster, p. 851.
[62] Shackleton, *Montesquieu*, p. 317.
[63] Montesquieu, *De l'esprit des lois*, in *Oeuvres complètes*, ed. Oster, p. 532: "La loi, en général, est la raison humaine . . . ; et les lois politiques et civiles de chaque nation ne doivent être que les cas particuliers ou s'applique cette raison humaine."

show the relation between institutions and their physical and moral causes is designed to "diminish any of the infinite distance that there is between vices and virtues," and that it is only by granting that "all political vices are not moral vices" that one can urge that no particular nation make laws that shock its own peculiar *esprit général*.[64]

Montesquieu's emphasis on the relation between social institutions and their causes serves to remind one that the Malebranchian idea of *rapports*, like the notions of *généralité* and occasionalism, turned up in Montesquieu in a transformed state. The Malebranchian idea that moral laws are relations of perfection—relations as eternal as the *rapports de grandeur* of mathematics—comes out most clearly in two especially important works of Montesquieu: the eighty-third *Lettre persane*, and the opening book of *De l'esprit des lois*.

In *Lettre persane* no. 83, Usbek says that God is necessarily just—that, were he not, he would be "the most imperfect of all beings" because omnipotently unjust—then moves on quickly to define justice itself. Justice is, Usbek asserts, a "rapport de convenance" (the very phrase of *Recherche de la vérité*), a relation of suitability that is "always the same, whatever being considers it, be it God, be it an angel, or, finally, be it a man."[65] The notion that God and men "see" and "follow" the same *rapports*, whether of perfection or of size, is, of course, central in Malebranche. As a recent study has suggested, Montesquieu's mentioning of angels is a good indication of Malebranchian influence, since Montesquieu personally had no use for an angelic layer of intelligent beings lying between God and man and could only have mentioned them out of the wish to reproduce Malebranche's argument that *all* minds see the same *rapports*.[66]

---

[64] Ibid., p. 643.

[65] Montesquieu, *Lettres persanes*, no. 83, in *Oeuvres complètes*, ed. Oster, p. 106.

[66] See Charles Jacques Beyer, "Montesquieu et la philosophie de

Even when men see this *rapport de convenance*, Usbek continues, they frequently prefer their own interest to it; justice has difficulty making herself heard "in the tumult of passions." (Plainly, a Malebranchian "silence of the passions" is needed for justice's weak voice to be heard.) Where passions remain tumultuous, men will prefer their own satisfaction to that of others. Still, there is no *pointless* malice: "No one is evil gratuitously . . . there must be a determining reason, and that reason is always one of [self-]interest."[67] This is not far from Malebranche's belief that men pursue false or inadequate *biens particuliers* because of a misguided but "invincible" wish for happiness; wholly "disinterested" evil is not more conceivable than wholly disinterested or quietistic love.[68] The same is true for Montesquieu.

Since God has no tumultuous passions to silence, Usbek continues, it is not possible that he ever do anything unjust. As soon as he sees justice—in himself, obviously—"it follows necessarily that he follow it." This anti-Hobbesian truth is true because, since God "needs nothing" and is totally self-sufficient, he would be "the most evil of all beings" if he acted wrongly, for "he would be without interest."[69] The first half of this assertion (God's self-sufficiency) is in perfect accord with Malebranche; the second half goes beyond what Malebranche would have ventured, for Malebranche would never have treated a disinterested but evil God, even hypothetically, as "the most evil of all beings."

Next, Usbek passes on to claims that Malebranche would have disputed: "If there were no God, we should still have to love justice: that is, strive to resemble that being of whom we have so fine an idea, and who, if he existed, would nec-

l'ordre," in *Studies on Voltaire and the 18th Century* (Banbury: Voltaire Foundation, 1972), vol. 87, pp. 145-166.
    [67] Montesquieu, *Lettres persanes*, no. 83, p. 106.
    [68] See Malebranche, *Traité de l'amour de Dieu*, in *Oeuvres complètes*, vol. 14, passim.
    [69] Montesquieu, *Lettres persanes*, no. 83, p. 106.

essarily be just." Even if we were free of "the yoke of religion," he adds, we would not be free of that of equity.[70]
Malebranche would certainly claim here that an initially
correct position has been overstated to the point of falsity:
one need not say that, simply because God does not create
rapports de convenance (or *de perfection*), they are wholly independent of him and subsist even without him. Malebranche's view is that the eternal verities are coeternal and
consubstantial with God—that, to borrow Leibniz's language, God is the "ground" of those truths, though not
their cause. Here Malebranche would surely have agreed
with Leibniz's insistence that "even if we concede that the
essence of things cannot be conceived without God . . . it
does not follow that God is the cause of the essence of
things; . . . for a circle cannot be conceived without a center, a line without a point, but the center is not the cause of
the circle nor the point the cause of the line."[71] This makes
God necessary for, though not the cause of, the truth of the
eternal verities; it is just what Malebranche himself has in
mind in calling *rapports* coeternal and consubstantial with
God.[72] Just because Descartes was wrong in viewing truth,
including moral truth, as *created, ex nihilo*,[73] one need not
eliminate all relation between *rapports* and God.

Usbek returns to Malebranchian orthodoxy, however, in
the very next paragraph: "Justice is eternal and depends
not at all on human conventions." This is a *précis* of the neo-
Augustinian, anti-Hobbesian argument of the *Réflexions sur
la prémotion physique*. Nevertheless, Usbek adds (possibly
for the accommodation of skeptics) that even if justice *were*
merely human and conventional, this would be a "terrible
truth which one would have to hide from himself."[74]

---

[70] Ibid.

[71] G. W. Leibniz, "Notes on Spinoza's *Ethics*," in *The Philosophical Works
of Leibniz*, 2d ed., ed. G. M. Duncan (New Haven: Yale University Press,
1908), pp. 21-22.

[72] Malebranche, *Prémotion physique*, pp. 98ff.

[73] See Ferdinand Alquié, *Le Cartésianisme de Malebranche* (Paris: Vrin,
1974), pp. 226ff.

[74] Montesquieu, *Lettres persanes*, no. 83, p. 106.

Usbek finally passes on to the cheering (and largely Malebranchian) thought that, even though we are "surrounded by men who are stronger than us" and who might harm us with "impunity," there is relief to be found in the thought that an inner principle of justice in all men "fights in our favor." Without that inner principle, he continues, borrowing a favorite Malebranchian image, "we would walk among men as if before lions." In the penultimate paragraph of *Lettre persane* no. 83, Malebranchian ideas and images dominate completely. All of his thoughts about those *rapports de convenance* that keep men from being lions, Usbek says, "animate" him against those who "represent God as a being who undertakes a tyrannical exercise of his power" and who "make him act in a way in which we would not wish to act ourselves."[75] This is the very language of *Prémotion physique*, a reflection of Malebranche's polemic against Boursier's quasi-Hobbesian divine sovereignty. "Reflection," however, is the strongest allowable word; as Mason points out in her fine study of Montesquieu's theory of justice, the "soaring metaphysical vision" of *Lettre persane* no. 83 is not developed or followed up but exists in splendid isolation.[76] *Lettre* no. 82 deals quite irreverently with a sharp contrast between the eternally silent Carthusians, and society wits who have the art of "knowing how to talk without saying anything"; while *Lettre* no. 84 treats with consummate nastiness a scene at the Hôtel des Invalides in which tottering old soldiers cling to religious consolations ("what could be more admirable than to see these enfeebled warriors observing discipline in their place of retirement, as strictly as if they were forced to do so by the presence of an enemy, seeking a last satisfaction in

---

[75] Ibid., p. 107.

[76] Mason, *Idea of Justice*, pp. 143ff., esp. p. 157: "In Letter 83 . . . there is little in the way of coherent metaphysical theory linking the moral and the theological elements of the argument together, and placing the definition of justice [as *rapport*] with its geometric structural undertones in the context of a unified cosmological theory. . . . We must acknowledge Montesquieu's debt to Malebranche, but nevertheless, the precise ontological significance of his definition of justice remains unclear."

this imitation of war, and dividing their hearts and minds between the duties of religion and those of military skill").[77] It is true, perhaps, that the Malebranchian *Lettre* no. 83 stands out in higher relief for being surrounded by satirical accounts of religious and military folly; but Mason is right in saying that the letter is more a remembrance than an argument.

The idea of law as a relation comes far closer to being *argued* for in the opening sections of *De l'esprit des lois*. As in *Lettre persane* no. 83, a number of Malebranchian ideas resurface here. For example, book 1 itself is called "Of Laws *en général*," and its first section is entitled "Of Laws, in Their *Rapport* with the Various Beings." That section opens with a celebrated but much maligned claim: "Laws, in the largest sense, are the necessary relations [*les rapports nécessaires*] which arise from the nature of things: and in this sense all beings have their laws; the Divinity has his laws, the material world has its laws, the intelligences superior to men have their laws, the beasts have their laws, man has his laws."[78]

The notion that the Creation, all creatures, and even the Creator are governed by law and that all these legal connections are *rapports* is perfectly Malebranchian, as was seen in Montesquieu's own time by David Hume. Indeed, in his *Enquiry Concerning the Principles of Morals*, Hume insists on

[77] Montesquieu, *Lettres persanes*, nos. 82 and 84, in *Oeuvres complètes*, pp. 106-107.

[78] Montesquieu, *De l'esprit des lois*, in *Oeuvres complètes*, ed. Oster, p. 530. For a view of Montesquieu's legal theory that stresses not Malebranchian traditionalism but radical innovation, see Louis Althusser, *Montesquieu: La Politique et l'histoire* (Paris: Presses Universitaires de France, 1959), pp. 22ff. Perhaps the finest short appreciation of Montesquieu's devotion to law is to be found in Oakeshott, *Human Conduct*, pp. 246-251, esp. p. 249: "Law [for Montesquieu] . . . is a system of conditions . . . to be subscribed to and used by persons in making their own choices of what to do or to say in contingent situations, and the associates are joined solely in recognition of the authority of these conditions." Since this corresponds exactly to Oakeshott's own theory of the "civil condition" (pp. 146-147), it is no wonder that he cherishes Montesquieu.

this relation between Malebranche and Montesquieu, if only to deplore it. Even after calling Montesquieu an "author of genius as well as learning," whose *De l'esprit des lois* "abounds in ingenious and brilliant thoughts," Hume complains that

> this illustrious writer . . . supposes all right to be founded on certain *rapports* or relations; which is a system that, in my opinion, never will be reconciled with true philosophy. Father Malebranche, as far as I can learn, was the first that started this abstract theory of morals . . . and as it excludes all sentiment and pretends to found everything on reason, it has not wanted followers in this philosophic age.[79]

Even the contemptuous last clause is not as hostile as Voltaire's characterization of book 1 of *Lois* as a "metaphysical labyrinth";[80] but if the contempt is lifted out it seems that Hume is essentially right—the weight of Malebranchism in book 1 is very great. Nor was Hume's knowledge of Malebranche's practical thought limited to the notion of law as *rapport*; he was equally familiar with the distinction between general and particular will. In the same *Enquiry* he declares that he will "examine the *particular* laws by which justice is directed" (emphasis in original) and goes on to say that if there were "a creature, possessed of reason but unacquainted with human nature," who tried to decide "what rules of justice or property would best promote the public interest," such a creature would hit upon the obvious thought of assigning "the largest possessions to the most extensive virtue" and of giving "every one the power of doing good, proportioned to his inclination." Such a crea-

[79] David Hume, *An Enquiry Concerning the Principles of Morals*, in *Hume's Moral and Political Philosophy*, ed. H. D. Aiken (New York: Hafner, 1948), pp. 195-196.

[80] Voltaire, "Commentaire sur l'esprit des lois," in *Oeuvres complètes de Voltaire* (n.p.: Société Littéraire-Typographique, 1785), vol. 29, p. 354: "Ne nous jouons point dans les subtilités de cette métaphysique; gardons nous d'entrer dans ce labyrinthe."

ture would have to be omniscient in order to know exactly what is merited. "In a perfect theocracy," Hume argues, "where a being, infinitely intelligent, governs by particular volitions, this rule would certainly have place." However, infinitely intelligent beings do not rule on earth; the uncertainty and obscurity of merit, coupled with the "self-conceit of each individual," leads *not* to "perfect theocracy" governed by particular volitions but to "the total dissolution of society."[81] All of this lends support to Hume's conclusion in book 3 of *A Treatise of Human Nature* that society must be directed not through theocracy or merit but through a shared *sentiment* of the advantage of general, standing rules and practices: "It is only when a character [or an action] is considered in general, without reference to our particular interest, that it causes such a feeling or sentiment as denominates it morally good or evil."[82] Hence, as in Pascal, Malebranche, Montesquieu, and Rousseau, generality is good, while particularity is evil. Where Hume gets this principle is not clear, but it *is* clear that he substitutes general utility for particular providence in a "perfect theocracy."[83] Since this sort of language does not arise in the British tradition of Hobbes and Locke, and since Hume mentions Malebranche, Montesquieu, and even Bayle, there is reason to believe that French practical thought had some influence on him.[84]

Nothing less than Hume's authority, then, points to a Malebranchian *provenance* of Montesquieu's legal theory. Montesquieu himself begins to develop the notion of law as relation after dismissing the "absurd" idea that "a blind fa-

[81] Hume, *Principles of Morals*, pp. 192-193.
[82] Hume, *A Treatise of Human Nature*, in *Hume: Theory of Politics*, ed. F. Watkins (Edinburgh: Nelson, 1951), p. 20.
[83] See the author's comments on *généralité* in Hume in his *Kant's Political Philosophy* (Totowa, N.J.: Rowman and Littlefield, 1983), pp. 22-23.
[84] See Charles J. McCracken, *Malebranche and British Philosophy* (Oxford: Clarendon Press, 1983), pp. 254ff., esp. p. 290, which quotes Dr. Johnson's complaint about Hume: "Why, Sir, his style is not English, the structure of his sentences is French!"

tality" has produced the world. Insisting upon an "original reason" accounting for the existence of intelligent beings, he goes on to say that laws are the relations that exist between this *raison primitive* and "the different beings," and that laws are also "the relations of these diverse beings between themselves."[85]

If this is a bit vague, though plainly Malebranchian, Montesquieu moves quickly in the direction of a more concrete illumination of these various *rapports*. He sets out, as would Malebranche, with God. God, he begins, "has a relation to the universe, as creator and as conservator; the laws according to which he has created it are those according to which he conserves it."[86] This is reminiscent of Malebranche's assertion, in one of his defenses of *Nature et grâce*, that "it may absolutely be that God formed successively heaven, earth, and the rest, following the same natural laws which he still observes today."[87] Montesquieu goes on to say that God operates according to his laws "because he made them," adding that he made them because "they have a relation to his wisdom and his power."[88] Malebranche would agree that the general laws of nature are divinely made and therefore arbitrary, but he would also specify that they are dictated by wisdom.

Book 1 of *De l'esprit des lois* moves on to a further "Cartesian" thought, namely, that the world is formed by "the movement of matter." Furthermore, since the world "subsists always," it must be the case that "its movements have invariable laws." Even if there were another world, it would still have to operate through constant rules, or else be destroyed. This is a perfectly Malebranchian physics, but without Malebranche's doubts about the actual existence of bodies. The creation, Montesquieu adds, supposes

---

[85] Montesquieu, *De l'esprit des lois*, in *Oeuvres complètes*, ed. Oster, p. 530.
[86] Ibid.
[87] Malebranche, *Réponse au livre I des Réflexions philosophiques*, in *Oeuvres complètes*, vol. 8-9, p. 780.
[88] Montesquieu, *De l'esprit des lois*, in *Oeuvres complètes*, ed. Oster, p. 530.

"rules as invariable as the fatality of the atheists." In enlarging on this idea, further notions from "Cartesian" physics are drawn in; the laws of nature, he insists, are "a constantly established relation." Between moved bodies, it is "according to the relations of mass and of speed that all the movements are received, increased, diminished, lost; all diversity is uniformity, each change is constancy."[89]

Leaving a uniform and constant physics behind, Montesquieu goes on to consider moral relations. According to book 1, human beings ("les êtres particuliers intelligents") may have some laws that they have made, but they also have some that they have not made. Since essence precedes existence, intelligent beings were possible even before there were any; thus, "they had possible relations, and as a consequence possible laws." Before there were any positive laws, there were "relations of possible justice [*des rapports de justice possibles*]." To say, with Hobbes, that there is nothing just or unjust except what the positive laws "ordain or forbid" is to say that "before a circle is drawn, all the radii were not equal."[90] This assimilation of moral-legal relations to relations of size in mathematics and geometry is entirely Malebranchian (as well as Platonic, Augustinian, and Leibnizian): it is Malebranche who asserts, in his *Entretiens sur la métaphysique*, that relations of perfection cannot be clearly known unless they are expressed in terms of relations of size.[91] The hostility to Hobbesian legal positivism is equally Malebranchian. In any case, Montesquieu insists, one must grant the existence of "relations of equity which are anterior to the positive law," *rapports* that demand that "if human societies existed, it would be right to conform to their laws."[92]

In his splendid biography of Montesquieu, Robert Shack-

---

[89] Ibid.

[90] Ibid.

[91] Malebranche, *Entretiens sur la métaphysique*, in *Oeuvres complètes*, vol. 12-13, pp. 190-191.

[92] Montesquieu, *De l'esprit des lois*, in *Oeuvres complètes*, ed. Oster, p. 530.

leton, quoting Hume on the *provenance* of Montesquieu's legal theory and giving full (perhaps excessive) weight to Malebranche's influence, claims that Malebranche "makes no express definition of a law as a relationship."[93] This is true of Malebranche's *Traité de morale*, which alone Shackleton quotes, but it is not true of *Réflexions sur la prémotion physique*, which Montesquieu knew well enough to paraphrase in *Mes pensées*.[94] In the *Réflexions* Malebranche asserts something very close to Montesquieu's famous claim that laws are "necessary relations," that those *rapports* resemble geometrical and mathematical truths, and that Hobbesian power adds nothing to eternally just relationships. Moral relations or *rapports de perfection*, he insists,

are not simple *truths*, but . . . also have the force of *laws*; for one must esteem all things in proportion as they are estimable and lovable; in proportion as they participate in the divine perfections. And since the nature of God is immutable and necessary, and since God can neither see nor will that two times two be equal to five, how can it fail to be perceived that God can neither see nor will that the idea of man which he has participate less in his perfections than that of the beast? that, as a consequence, he can neither see nor will that it be just to prefer, or rather will to prefer, one's horse to one's coachman, simply because one can or wants to? Power or will adds nothing to the eternal law, to the relations of perfection which subsist between the eternal and immutable ideas.[95]

There is very little in the opening book of *De l'esprit des lois*, including the polemic against Hobbesian sovereignty, that is not a slightly secularized reworking of this passage.

Passing over Montesquieu's treatment of animals—stop-

[93] Shackleton, *Montesquieu*, p. 246.
[94] Montesquieu, *Mes pensées*, in *Oeuvres complètes*, Pléiade ed., vol. 1, p. 1548.
[95] Malebranche, *Prémotion physique*, p. 99.

ping, however, to notice his uncertainty whether "beasts are governed by general laws of movement, or by particular motion"—one arrives at the rest of his account of humans and their *rapports*. Man as a physical being, he asserts, is, like all bodies, governed by invariable laws. As an intelligent being, however, man "violates ceaselessly the laws that God has established and changes those that he himself establishes." This is because human "intelligence" is not wholly intelligent; it is "finite" and "weak," and subject to "a thousand passions." (All of this is thoroughly Malebranchian.) Since such a finite intelligent being might "forget his Creator," God has supplied the laws of religion; since he might "forget himself," philosophy has provided the laws of morality. Since men, though "made to live in society," might nonetheless "forget others," legislators have brought him back to his duty through political and civil laws. Man as limited intelligence is hemmed in by these various *rapports*.[96]

Following an interesting excursus on the state of nature, in which Hobbes is shown to have attributed to "natural" men before the establishment of societies that which "can happen only after that establishment" (a point much enlarged by Rousseau), Montesquieu returns to law as a relation. First, however, he discusses particularism in a way that recalls Pascal and Malebranche and anticipates Rousseau: after societies are established, he asserts, each *société particulière* "begins to feel its power," which produces "a state of war between nation and nation." Similarly, within each *société particulière* individuals (*les particuliers*) begin to feel their power, which leads to an internal state of war. These two states of war, internal and external, are largely blocked by law ("la force générale.") It is Malebranchism at its purest that *société particulière* and the strivings of *les particuliers* lead to power and war, while a moderating govern-

[96] Montesquieu, *De l'esprit des lois*, in *Oeuvres complètes*, ed. Oster, pp. 530–531.

ment and law are precisely *la force générale*. Montesquieu again uses the general-particular distinction as a bridge from law as *force générale* back to the idea of relations: "Law *en général*," he insists, is "human reason" insofar as it governs all the peoples of the earth; and the civil and political laws of each nation "should be only the particular cases" to which that law *en général* is applied. Since the case of each nation is particular, it is only by chance that the laws of one nation "can suit another"; thus, the laws of each nation, while maintaining some *rapport* with *la raison humaine*, must be relative to a number of things. Offering a remarkable one-paragraph précis of *De l'esprit des lois*, Montesquieu insists that the laws

> must relate to the nature and to the principle of the government which is established. . . . They must be relative to the climate [*la physique*] of the country . . . to the quality of its soil, to its situation, to its size; to the way of life of peoples, [whether] laborers, hunters or farmers; they must relate to the degree of liberty that the constitution can permit; to the religion of the inhabitants, to their inclinations, to their riches, to their number, to their commerce, to their *moeurs*, to their manners. . . .[97]

The rest of *De l'esprit des lois* can reasonably be viewed as the systematic examination of all of these relations, the fleshing out of this précis. Montesquieu himself immediately declares that "this is what I shall undertake to do in this work. I shall examine all these *rapports*: they form, taken together, that which is called *the spirit of the laws*."[98] He does not stop with law as a Malebranchian relation of perfection; that Malebranchian notion informs mainly the opening book of *Lois*. (In Malebranche, after all, *rapports de perfection* turn out to constitute a "great chain of being" in

[97] Ibid., pp. 531–532.
[98] Ibid.

which those beings nearest to God are worthiest of divine [and human] love; therefore, *rapports* have the force of "law" in the sense that we *ought* to love beings in proportion to their degree of perfection.)

For Montesquieu it is mainly other *rapports* that matter; he is concerned with law as it relates to various physical and moral *causes générales*, such as climate and education. Thus it is no accident that most of the chapter titles in *De l'esprit des lois* contain the term *rapport*. To take three or four at random, one finds that book 9 is called "Of Laws, in the *Rapport* Which They Have with Defensive Force," book 11 (the most celebrated of all) is "Of the Laws Which Constitute Political Liberty, in Its *Rapport* with the Constitution, and book 13 is "Of the *Rapports* Which the Raising of Tributes and the Size of Public Revenues Have with Liberty." What Montesquieu means, of course, is that law is relative to— perhaps even the product of—many physical and moral causes. This is clear in book 5, entitled "That the Laws Which the Legislator Gives Must Be Relative to the Principle of Government, and in book 4, called "That the Laws of Education Must Be Relative to the Principles of Government."[99] Montesquieu, then, is indeed a "relativist" in the special sense just indicated. Thus the allegedly rambling and formless structure of *De l'esprit des lois*[100] is in fact held together, as Montesquieu himself insisted, by the notion of law as *rapport*, as something relative to various general *causes physiques* (climate, geography) and *causes morales* (religion, *moeurs*). To be sure, nine-tenths of *De l'esprit des lois* is taken up with these *causes générales* and not with the concept of *rapport*. Nonetheless, the opening book of *Lois* is not, *pace* Voltaire, a "metaphysical labyrinth" having no es-

[99] Ibid., pp. 540, 544, 577, 585, 608.
[100] Franz Neumann, Introduction to *The Spirit of the Laws*, trans. Nugent (New York: Hafner, 1949), p. xxix: "It is generally agreed that the arrangement of *The Spirit of the Laws* is difficult to perceive, if a systematic arrangement can be said to exist in it at all." (Most of this introduction is excellent, however.)

sential *rapport* with the rest of the work; it is related by the notion of relation itself.

It may be that the continuous use of the term *rapport* throughout *De l'esprit des lois* conceals real discontinuity in Montesquieu's thought, that the signification of "relation" changes permanently after the Malebranchian opening book. So much is suggested by Isaiah Berlin in his brilliant essay, "Montesquieu."

> Montesquieu's . . . whole aim is to show that laws are . . . the expression of the changing moral habits, beliefs, general attitudes of a particular society, at a particular time, on a particular portion of the earth's surface, played upon by the physical and spiritual influences to which their place and period expose human beings. It is difficult to see how this doctrine . . . can be reconciled with belief in universal, unvarying, everlasting rules, equally valid for all men in all places at all times—rules discovered by the faculty of reason as conceived by Descartes or Leibniz, that is, as nonnatural means of perceiving eternal verities.[101]

Even Berlin, however, passes from the early assertion that "there is obviously a genuine disparity of attitude," a "contradiction . . . evidently present in [Montesquieu's] own thought," to the final conclusion that "there is a kind of continuous dialectic in all Montesquieu's writings between absolute values which seem to correspond to the permanent interests of men as such, and those which depend upon time and place in a concrete situation." And none of his criticisms keep Sir Isaiah from concluding that Montesquieu left behind him "an understanding of what men, or, at any rate, human societies, live by, unparalleled since Aristotle."[102]

---

[101] Isaiah Berlin, "Montesquieu," pp. 153-154.
[102] Ibid., pp. 155-161.

Looking back at Montesquieu as the heir of Malebranche, one finds a number of Malebranchian notions "canceled and preserved." The Oratorian's idea of law as a *rapport* is retained, but Montesquieu is less concerned, beyond the opening book of *Lois*, with quasi-mathematical eternal relations than with the relations of various social institutions to equally various physical and moral *causes générales*. Malebranchian occasionalism is kept, though subtly transformed, with a divine *cause générale* expanding into a multiplicity of *causes générales*. The general will continues to hold an important place—a place now occupied not by God but by "magistrates" who ought not to combine general and particular, legislative and judicial, authority. Indeed, Montesquieu says that the legislative power can and should be given to *des corps permanents*, which merely enunciate "the general will of the state [*la volonté générale de l'Etat*]," while the power of judging, which is "so terrible among men" because it deals with *des particuliers*, ought to be given temporarily to nonprofessional judges drawn from the body of the people, so that that power will become *invisible et nulle*.[103] What Montesquieu had called Père Malebranche's "magnificent palace in the air" has been pulled down onto solid ground and readied for imminent occupation by Rousseau.

Though the provenance of *volonté générale* and *volonté particulière* seems to be traceable mainly to a constellation of primarily French seventeenth-century theologians, one important modern Rousseau scholar, C. W. Hendel, argues in *Jean-Jacques Rousseau, Moralist* that, while Malebranche et al. indeed had some influence on Rousseau (perhaps via Montesquieu), the notion of the "general will" actually reached

[103] Montesquieu, *De l'esprit des lois*, ed. R. Derathé (Paris: Editions Garnier, 1973), vol. 1, pp. 170-171.

him primarily through the purely political thought of Bodin, Hobbes, and, above all, the German Hobbesian Samuel Pufendorf.[104] Hobbes, of course, does speak of the "will" of the state, which he ordinarily identifies with the will of a sovereign "representative person," most commonly a monarch, who deliberates, wills, and acts on behalf of all those who, by covenant, have alienated the exercise of their own natural rights to the beneficiary of that agreement.[105] But Hobbes never speaks of a "general will." Neither, however, does Pufendorf, who in his *De officio hominis et civis* (1682) argues in quasi-Hobbesian fashion that "the wills of many men can be united in no other way, than if each subjects his will to the will of one man, or one council, so that henceforth whatever such a one shall will concerning things necessary to the common security, must be accounted the will of all, collectively and singly."[106] This is simply a restatement of the Hobbesian notion of a sovereign, representative will; but it has very little connection with Montesquieu—who was not overly fond of sovereignty theory—and still less with Rousseau, who certainly never identified general will with the will of a ruler, the supposed representative of the will of all. Indeed, Rousseau always argued that will cannot be represented, and that the will of all is not the same as *volonté générale*.[107] How,

---

[104] C. W. Hendel, *Jean-Jacques Rousseau, Moralist* (Oxford: Clarendon Press, 1934), vol. 1, pp. 100ff. In general, Hendel's book is a remarkable and useful one; it is only when he deals particularly with *volonté générale* that one can question his judgment.

[105] See the author's *Will and Political Legitimacy: A Critical Exposition of Social Contract Theory in Hobbes, Locke, Rousseau, Kant and Hegel* (Cambridge, Mass.: Harvard University Press, 1982), chapter 2.

[106] S. Pufendorf, *De officio hominis et civis* (Cambridge, Eng., 1682), cited here in the English translation of F. G. Moore (New York: Carnegie Endowment, 1927), p. 107.

[107] Rousseau, *Du contrat social*, p. 42: "There is often a good deal of difference between the will of all and the general will: the latter considers only the common interest; the former considers private interest, and is only a sum of *volontés particulières*."

then, can Hendel have imagined that "general will" descends through Hobbes and Pufendorf to Montesquieu, and finally to Rousseau?

The answer appears to be that Hendel was misled by Barbeyrac's French translation of Pufendorf into believing that the notions of *volonté générale* and *volonté particulière* are really in *De officio hominis*; but Pufendorf, in turn, was an avowed Hobbesian; *ergo*. . . . What is unmistakably plain is that Hendel cites Pufendorf neither in the original Latin nor in an accurate English translation but only in a paraphrase of Barbeyrac's French version of *De officio hominis*, published in 1718 as *Les Devoirs de l'homme et du citoyen*.[108] Barbeyrac, who was amply familiar with seventeenth-century theological controversies, as his *Traité de la morale des Pères de l'Eglise* (1728) clearly shows,[109] used the notions of *volonté générale* and *volonté particulière* in rendering *De officio hominis* into French; his version is more a transmogrification than a mere translation. Pufendorf's plain phrase "if each subjects his will" becomes in Barbeyrac "if each subjects his *volonté particulière*"; the former's straightforward "the will of all, collectively and singly" becomes in the latter "the positive *volonté* of all *en général* and of each *en particulier*."[110] A Hobbesian doctrine of representative will (on the part of a sovereign) is thus transformed into something that *looks* pre-Montesquieuean and pre-Rousseauean—but only in French.

The fact that Barbeyrac has Pufendorf speak in Malebranchian tones does not mean, of course, that Barbeyrac was himself any sort of Malebranchian. Indeed, in the *Traité de la morale des Pères de l'Eglise* it emerges, however obliquely, that Barbeyrac was rather hostile to Male-

[108] Pufendorf, *Les Devoirs de l'homme et du citoyen*, trans. J. Barbeyrac (Amsterdam, 1718), title page.

[109] J. Barbeyrac, *Traité de la morale des Pères de l'Eglise* (Amsterdam, 1728), passim.

[110] Pufendorf, *Devoirs de l'homme*, p. 328.

branche's *généralité*. The Oratorian's name does not appear anywhere in Barbeyrac's *Traité*; still, by attacking a quasi-Malebranchian passage from Ceillier's *Apologie de la morale des Pères de l'Eglise* (1718), he makes it clear that he is no partisan of Père Malebranche. In the *Apologie* Ceillier had asserted that God transferred to the angels "the care of things here below," reserving for himself nothing more than a *Providence générale*;[111] this is not far from Malebranche's assertion in the fourth "Eclaircissement" of *Nature et grâce* that God has left particular earthly operations to beings such as the Archangel Michael, thereby preserving his own simplicity and generality.[112] Barbeyrac clearly will not have this: Ceillier's quasi-Malebranchian *généralité* "leaves" to God "only" a *Providence générale*, and it "abandons" all *Providence particulière* to the angels. (The choice of the quoted terms makes Barbeyrac's attitude plain enough.) The notion that God abandons *particularité*, Barbeyrac complains, "directly shocks Holy Scripture, which makes us regard the Providence of God as extending to the least things." Barbeyrac likes this generality no better when it is extended to politics: "It will be useless for my critic [Ceillier] to parade passages from Scripture where tutelary angels are spoken of, who take charge of nations, or even of each person."[113] One cannot say, then, that Barbeyrac was himself a personal partisan of *généralité*.

It is quite revealing, though not revelatory of what Hendel imagines, that Barbeyrac should have used the Malebranchian terms that he actually used. His tranformation of Pufendorf shows just how current were the ideas of *volonté générale* and *volonté particulière* at the beginning of the eighteenth century—current mainly in a theological tradition, the terms of which Barbeyrac carried over into politics (though in connection with a mere translation, and not in Montesquieu's large-scale and re-creative fashion). Of

---

[111] Cited in Barbeyrac, *Pères de l'Eglise*, p. 26.
[112] Malebranche, *Nature et grâce*, pp. 197ff.
[113] Barbeyrac, *Pères de l'Eglise*, p. 27.

course, one should suspect on other grounds the notion that either a Montesquieuean or Rousseauean general will is traceable to Hobbes or to a Hobbesian like Pufendorf, given Montesquieu's wholehearted and Rousseau's substantial aversion to Hobbes.[114] But it seems that Hendel notices neither this "internal" evidence nor the fact that Barbeyrac's *Les Devoirs de l'homme* is not so much a translation of Pufendorf's actual words as it is a recasting of Pufendorf in a quasi-Malebranchian mold. So even if Rousseau relied on Pufendorf as heavily as Hendel suggests—which is doubtful—he was relying on a French "translation" that made Pufendorf resemble, or appear to resemble, the great seventeenth-century theologians of *volonté générale*.

[114] Cf. Montesquieu's remarks on Hobbes in *Mes pensées*: "A great genius [Hobbes] has promised me that I shall die like an insect. . . . This same philosopher wants, as a favor to me, to destroy liberty in me. . . . He deprives me of the motive for all my actions and relieves me of all morality" (in *Oeuvres complètes*, Pléiade ed., vol. 1, pp. 1138-1139). Rousseau had a rather more favorable opinion of Hobbes—at least as the greatest describer of modern corruption.

F I V E

THE GENERAL WILL COMPLETED: ROUSSEAU AND THE *VOLONTÉ GÉNÉRALE* OF THE CITIZEN

Did Rousseau, then—who tells us in the *Confessions* of his reading of the great seventeenth-century theologians of general will[1]—use the notions of *volonté générale* and *volonté particulière* simply out of historical piety, simply because the notions were "there" (as he is sometimes said to have used social contract theory simply because it was a "venerable fiction" in his time)?[2] Is it simply a question of the influence of Pascal, Malebranche, Bayle, and Montesquieu on Rousseau? By no means. Judith Shklar has argued persuasively that the notion of general will "conveys everything he most wanted to say," that it is "a transposition of the most essential individual moral faculty to the realm of public experience."[3] This means that Rousseau's reasons for using *volonté générale* were essentially philosophical, however ready-made for his purposes the old theological notion may

[1] Jean-Jacques Rousseau, *Les Confessions*, ed. B. Gagnebin and M. Raymond, in *Oeuvres complètes de Jean-Jacques Rousseau* (Paris: Pléiade, 1959), vol. 1, p. 237: "Je commencois par quelque livre de philosophie, comme *la Logique* de Port-royal, *l'Essai* de Locke, Malebranche, Leibnitz, Descartes, etc."

[2] C. E. Vaughan, Introduction to Rousseau, *Political Writings* (Oxford: Basil Blackwell, 1962), vol. 1, pp. 71ff.

[3] Judith N. Shklar, *Men and Citizens: A Study of Rousseau's Social Theory* (Cambridge: Cambridge University Press, 1969), p. 184.

have been. After all, the two terms of *volonté générale*—
"will" and "generality"—represent two main strands in
Rousseau's thought. "Generality" stands, *inter alia*, for the
rule of law, for civic education that draws us out of ourselves and toward the general (or common) good, for the
non-particularist citizen virtues of Sparta and republican
Rome.[4] "Will" stands for Rousseau's conviction that "civil
association is the most voluntary act in the world," that "to
deprive your will of all freedom is to deprive your actions of
all morality."[5] And if one could "generalize" the will, so
that it "elects" only law, citizenship, and the common
good, and avoids willful self-love, then one would have a
general will in Rousseau's special sense. The *volonté générale*
and *volonté particulière* of Pascal, Malebranche, and Leibniz
corresponded closely to these moral aims; hence, why not
employ terms already rendered politically usable by writers
as important as Bayle and Montesquieu?

One could see plainly enough, even without considering
the *Confessions*, that Rousseau had read the most important
seventeenth-century French theologians of general will—
especially Malebranche and Fénelon—simply by looking at
the "Profession of Faith of the Savoyard Vicar" (from *Emile*), at the *Letter to Voltaire on Providence*, at the third and
fifth of the *Lettres écrites de la montagne* (1764), and, above all,
at book 6 of *La Nouvelle Héloïse*. All of these are replete with
Malebranchian reminiscences.

The most important evidence is to be found in the sixth
and seventh letters from book 6 of Rousseau's novel. In the
sixth letter, Julie de Wolmar, advising her former lover St.
Preux on religious matters, warns him to take care that human pride not mix any "low ideas" of God with "the sublime ideas of the great being which you formulate for yourself." Stressing human dependence on a divine father
("slaves by our weakness, we are free through prayer"),

---

[4] See particularly Rousseau's *Gouvernement de Pologne*, in *Political Writings*, vol. 2, pp. 424ff.
[5] Rousseau, *Du contrat social*, in *Political Writings*, vol. 2, pp. 105, 28.

she makes it clear that the low ideas that she fears are precisely Malebranchian. She cautions St. Preux against believing that the simple "means which help our weakness" are also "suitable to the divine power" and that God "has need of art, like us, to generalize things in order to treat them more easily." It seems to St. Preux, she goes on, that "it would be an embarrassment" for God to have to look after each particular person. Perhaps St. Preux fears that a "divided and continual attention" would fatigue God; perhaps this is the reason for his believing it "finer" that God "do everything by general laws," doubtless because these would cost him less care. "O great philosophers!" Julie ends mockingly, "how obliged God is to you for having furnished him with these convenient methods and to have saved him so much work!"[6]

To this "railery" (as Emile Bréhier has called it) St. Preux responds "en bon Malebranchiste":[7] all "analogies," he tells Julie, "are in favor of these general laws which you seem to reject." Reason itself, together with "the soundest ideas" we can form of the supreme being, are "very favorable" to (Malebranchian) generality, for, while God's omnipotence "has no need of method to abridge work," it is nonetheless "worthy of his wisdom" to prefer the simplest means.[8]

Following an eloquent anti-Spinozist excursus on freedom ("a reasoner proves to me in vain that I am not free, because an inner feeling, stronger than all his arguments, refutes them ceaselessly"), St. Preux returns to Malebranchian themes in connection with a discussion of grace. On this subject, his *generalism* is more rigorous than Male-

---

[6] Rousseau, *Julie ou La Nouvelle Héloïse*, ed. René Pomeau (Paris: Garnier Frères, 1960), p. 660. For a splendid commentary, see Jean Starobinski, *Jean-Jacques Rousseau: La Transparence et l'obstacle* (Paris: Gallimard, 1971), pp. 102ff.

[7] Emile Bréhier, "Les Lectures malebranchistes de Jean-Jacques Rousseau," in *Etudes de philosophie moderne* (Paris: Presses Universitaires de France, 1965), p. 95.

[8] Rousseau, *La Nouvelle Héloïse*, p. 671.

branche's own; for St. Preux, it is precisely on Malebranchian grounds that one must deny the reality of any
particular, special grace. "I do not believe," he insists, that
God "gives to one [person] sooner than to another" any
"extraordinary help" at all. Grace conferred particularly
and unequally would constitute "acceptation of persons"
and would be "injurious to divine justice."[9] Here the principles of *Du contrat social* are divinized: what is not permis-
sible in earthly law cannot be right in God's governance
either. That this was Rousseau's view as early as 1756 is
clear in the *Letter to Voltaire on Providence*, in which he urges
that, just as a wise king who wills that "everyone live happily within his estates" need not concern himself to discover "whether the taverns are good," so too "particular
events are nothing in the eyes of the master of the universe," whose providence is *universelle* or *générale*.[10]

Even if the "hard and discouraging doctrine" of particularly conferred grace were "deduced from Scripture itself,"
St. Preux continues, "is it not my first duty to honor God?"
On this point, exactly as in Malebranche, the *idea* of what
God would do takes precedence over Scripture; justice matters more than anthropology. Whatever respect one owes
to the "sacred text," St. Preux insists, one owes still more to
its author: "I would rather believe the Bible falsified or un-
intelligible, than God unjust or evil-doing." If the notion of
"grace" means anything for St. Preux, it refers simply to
nonsupernatural gifts that God has given equally to all: "He
has given us reason to know the good, conscience to love it,
and liberty to choose it. It is in these sublime gifts that di-

[9] Ibid., pp. 671, 672.
[10] Rousseau, *Letter to Voltaire on Providence* (1756), in *Religious Writings*,
ed. R. Grimsley (Oxford: Clarendon Press, 1970), p. 44. *Universelle* is the
term used by Rousseau in the text of the *Letter* actually sent to Voltaire; *générale* is a manuscript-variant made by Rousseau in his letter-book. See
R. A. Leigh, "Rousseau's Letter to Voltaire on Optimism," in *Studies on
Voltaire and the 18th Century* (Geneva: Institut et Musée Voltaire, 1964), vol.
30, p. 287 n. 70.

vine grace consists." And he adds pointedly that "we have all received them."[11]

At this point Rousseau may well be arguing against Fénelon—whom, in general, he greatly admired.[12] In one of his letters of 1708 to the Benedictine Father François Lami on grace and predestination (published in 1718, and therefore fully available to Rousseau) Fénelon had begun his treatment of divine justice by saying that

God could limit himself to giving to all men, without predestining any of them, the same grace, fully sufficient for all. He could say to himself: I shall give my heavenly reward to all those who by their free will answer to this [divine] help, and I shall deprive of this reward all those who, being in a position to merit it, do not will to make themselves worthy of it. On this supposition, could you accuse God of injustice? Not the slightest inequality would appear; not the slightest favoritism [*prédilection*]; not the slightest preference; everything would be general [*tout serait général*], effective, proportional to [human] need, and abundant on

[11] Rousseau, *La Nouvelle Héloïse*, pp. 672, 671.

[12] Particularly in his earlier works; see above all Rousseau, *Chronologie universelle, ou Histoire générale des temps* (c. 1737), in *Annales de la Société Jean-Jacques Rousseau* (Geneva: Chez A. Jullien, 1905), vol. 1, pp. 213ff., esp. pp. 214-215:

Nous sommes tous frères; notre prochain doit nous être aussi cher que nous-mêmes. "J'aime le genre humain plus que ma patrie," disoit l'illustre M. de Fénelon, "ma patrie plus que ma famille et ma famille plus que moi-même." Des sentiments si pleins d'humanité devroient être communs à tous les hommes. . . . L'univers est une grand famille dont nous sommes tous membres; nous sommes donc obligez d'en connoitre aussi la situation et les intérêts. Quelque peu loin que s'étende la puissance d'un particulier, il est toujours en état de se rendre utile par quelque endroit au grand corps dont il fait partie.

Later in his career, of course, Rousseau would abandon the *universelle* in favor of the *générale*, would exchange a Fénelonian *respublica christiana* for more modest republics: Sparta, Rome, Geneva. Indeed, Rousseau's great struggle with Diderot in the *Première Version du contrat social* rests precisely on his rejection of a reason-ordained *morale universelle*.

God's part. There would be no inequality except on the part of men: all inequality would come from their [wrongly used] free will.[13]

This language would certainly have interested Rousseau, for it virtually equates justice with generality, equality, and the absence of favoritism—the very things that shape the meaning of justice in *Du contrat social*. However, Rousseau could never have countenanced Fénelon's next move, for, while the Archbishop of Cambrai begins by equating justice and *généralité*, he wants to be able to justify special divine grace given to the predestined or elect; therefore, a little later in his letter to Lami, he says that

> the special goodness of [divine] favoritism for the few, in no way diminishes the general goodness for all the others. The superabundance of aid for the elect, diminishes not at all the quite sufficient aid that all the others receive. . . . Does the superabundance of [God's] goodness for another destroy the exact justice, the gratuitous and liberal goodness that he has for you, and the quite sufficient aid that he gives you?[14]

To deny this superadded, extra goodness that God gratuitously heaps upon the elect, according to Fénelon, is to deny Augustinian predestination altogether, which is a heresy.

Now it is obvious that the totality of men cannot be included in this special decree, and that this favoring cannot embrace the whole human race. Favor would no longer be favor, but a general love, if it extended generally to all men. The special will [of God] would be confused with the *volonté générale*. Election would be

---

[13] F. Fénelon, *Oeuvres spirituelles* (n.p., 1751 [orig. ed. 1718]), vol. 4, p. 290. For a good commentary see Henri Gouhier, *Fénelon philosophe* (Paris: Vrin, 1977), pp. 55ff.
[14] Ibid., p. 294.

no more particular [*n'aurait rien de plus particulier*] than simple vocation.[15]

From a Rousseauean perspective, Fénelon begins well by *imagining* a God who links up justice, generality and equality (although later, to save the dogma of predestination, he severs the tie between *généralité* and justice, trying to justify God's particularistic favoritism by appealing to Scripture— "many are called, but few are chosen").[16] But at least Fénelon starts at the right point; indeed he (at first) relates *généralité* and *égalité* to each other more strongly than had any figure before Rousseau himself.[17] Indeed, in Fénelon's initial account of a nonpredestining God one might almost be reading *Du contrat social*: "Not the slightest inequality would appear; not the slightest favoritism; not the slightest preference; everything would be general, effective, proportioned to need. . . ." Might not Rousseau's city be an imitation of what God *could* have done had he wished to dispense with all particular grace? For then *vox populi* would be (almost) *vox dei*.[18]

Rousseau's hostility to any Fénelonian notion of non-universal grace, of divine favoritism, carries over into the *Lettres écrites de la montagne* in a way that shows Rousseau knew perfectly well that arguments over particular grace had had (mainly unfortunate) political effects in the seven-

[15] Ibid., p. 321.

[16] Ibid., pp. 320-321.

[17] Though Malebranche says in part 2, chapter 11 of the *Traité de morale* that, while men are "naturally" equal, force and ambition have brought them to abandon "universal reason, their inviolable law," in favor of "visible protectors." In this passage natural equality and universality (not simple generality) go hand in hand. See *Traité de morale*, in N. Malebranche, *Oeuvres complètes de Malebranche*, ed. André Robinet (Paris: Vrin, 1966), vol. 11, pp. 242-243.

[18] Alberto Postigliola, in his excellent "De Malebranche à Rousseau: Les Apories de la volonté générale et la revanche du 'raisonneur violent,' " in *Annales de la Société Jean-Jacques Rousseau* (Geneva: Chez A. Jullien, 1980), vol. 39, pp. 136-137, argues persuasively that Rousseau erroneously attributed to the *volonté générale* of a sovereign people the "infinite" qualities that can attach only to a Malebranchian *divine* general will.

teenth century. In the *Cinquième Lettre* he argues that *Emile* and *Du contrat social* have been illegally condemned by the Genevan authorities, and he appeals to the authority of the neo-Pascalian moralist Vauvenargues ("whoever is more severe than the laws is a tyrant"). He claims that he knows of only one comparable instance of legal oppression in Genevan history; "this was in the great quarrel of 1669 over particular grace." Following the inability of *les professeurs* to decide the truth about divine grace, the Council of Two Hundred rendered a judgment: "The important question at issue was to know whether Jesus had died only for the salvation of the elect, or whether he had also died for the salvation of the damned." After many sessions and "ripe deliberations," Rousseau adds sarcastically, the "magnificent" Council of Two Hundred "declared that Jesus had died only for the salvation of the elect." For Rousseau, this was a merely political decision, in the worst sense of "political": "Jesus would have died for the damned, if Professor Tronchin had had more credit than his adversary." Rousseau brands the whole affair as "fort ridicule," adding that civil authorities should "appease quarrels without pronouncing on doctrine."[19]

In the original (unpublished) manuscript of *Montagne*, Rousseau offers an analogy that only makes clearer his knowledge of seventeenth-century theological disputes: "What ridicule would the Parlement of Paris not have drawn on itself if it had wanted to decide, on its own authority [*de son chef*], whether the five propositions were or were not in the book [*Augustinus*] of Jansenius!" Since the Jansenists disputed even Rome's right to judge the *Augustinus*, "How could they have recognized [this right] in a secular tribunal?"[20] The published version of the *Cinquième*

---

[19] Rousseau, *Lettres écrites de la montagne* (Amsterdam: Rey, 1764), pp. 170n-171n.

[20] Rousseau, "Manuscrit autographe" of the *Lettres écrites de la montagne*, ed. J. S. Spink, in *Annales de la Société Jean-Jacques Rousseau* (Geneva: Chez A. Jullien, 1932), vol. 21, p. 13n.

Lettre, together with the unpublished passage on Jansenism, make it plain that Rousseau knew perfectly the *provenance* of the controversy over *volonté générale*: if he knew the
five propositions, he knew that the last of them dealt with
the scriptural assertion that "God wills that all men be
saved."

Rousseau's reference to the "great quarrel of 1669 over
particular grace" merits a slightly fuller examination; since
he did a great deal of research on Genevan history before
writing the *Lettres écrites de la montagne,* he knew perfectly
well what the great quarrel had involved.[21] In 1669 the
Council of Two Hundred—moved to act by Calvinist con-
servatives who had been alarmed by the theological inno-
vations of a newly arrived Cartesian philosopher—required
that all Genevans deny the universality of grace (as something given generally to all men); this decree was simply a
brief reaffirmation of a 1659 policy. That earlier policy, in
turn, was nothing but a watered-down version of a 1649
"profession of faith" drawn up by the Genevan church,
some of the articles of which seem to color Rousseau's sarcastic pronouncements about Jesus' having died "only for
the salvation of the elect." The 1649 document had rejected
a series of theological "errors": it denied the notion "that Jesus Christ died for each and every individual [*pour tous et un
chacun des particuliers*]"; it denied that "there is a vocation of
universal salvation for all men, and that they can all, if they
will, believe and be saved"; it denied that "by his revealed
will God wills to save all men." All of these errors were rejected, together with the additional mistake of believing
that God "has some desire . . . or universal conditional
grace, to save each individual, if he believes in Jesus

[21] This is particularly clear in the "Manuscrit autographe" (see note 20,
above). The Cartesian philosopher whose arrival in Geneva occasioned so
much consternation was Jean-Robert Chouet; for a thorough study of his
thought see Michael Heyd, *Between Orthodoxy and Enlightenment: Jean-Robert Chouet and the Introduction of Cartesian Science in the Academy of Geneva*
(The Hague: Martinus Nijhoff, 1982), passim.

Christ." One article of the document explicitly added that St. Paul's letter to Timothy asserting that "God wills that all men be saved" must be explained in the light of these errors: "General expressions from Scripture must not be understood [as applying] to each and every man, but to the universality of the body of Jesus Christ."[22] Since the great quarrel of 1669 recapitulated a quarrel of 1659, which in turn recapitulated one of 1649, Rousseau certainly knew all of this. It is all reflected in the language of *Montagne*.

Whatever may have been the facts of the great quarrel of 1669, the whole controversy over *la grâce particulière* is, in Rousseau's final judgment, one of those questions "that interest nobody and that no one whomsoever understands." That being so, it should be "always left to the theologians."[23] This is what one would expect Rousseau to say, given his view in *La Nouvelle Héloïse* that "all" have received the only *real* grace. (It is an irony worth noticing that Rousseau, in appealing to the authority of the neo-Pascalian Vauvenargues, condemns as "quite ridiculous" the very controversy over *grâce particulière* which Pascal himself had treated with utter seriousness in the *Ecrits sur la grâce*.[24] The citing of Vauvenargues at least shows that Rousseau knew the thought of this eighteenth-century Pascalian: hence, that he might well have been familiar with Vauvenargues' *Pensées*-inspired thought that "a body which subsists by the union of many members and confounds the particular interest in the general interest . . . is the foundation of all morality."[25] And this would establish an important link be-

---

[22] Jean Pierre Gaberel, *Histoire de l'église de Génève* (Geneva: Jullien Frères, 1862), pp. 121-123.

[23] Rousseau, *Lettres écrites de la montagne*, 1764 ed., p. 171.

[24] Blaise Pascal, *Ecrits sur la grâce*, in *Oeuvres de Blaise Pascal*, ed. L. Brunschvicg (Paris: Librairie Hachette, 1914), vol. 11, pp. 133ff.

[25] Vauvenargues, *Introduction à la connaissance de l'esprit humain*, in *Oeuvres complètes de Vauvenargues*, ed. H. Bonnier (Paris: Hachette, 1968), vol. 1, p. 241. On the following page Vauvenargues adds a passage that could have been approved equally by Pascal and Rousseau: "La préférence de l'intérêt général au personnel est la seule définition qui soit digne de la

tween Pascal and Rousseau, carrying Pascal's "body full of thinking members" into Rousseau's own time.)

If, for St. Preux in *La Nouvelle Héloïse*, God is a Malebranchian who operates through *des loix générales* and avoids an unjust "acceptation of persons," of what use is prayer, which asks precisely for *grâce particulière*? Here St. Preux, though careful in his language, is strict: "In seeking grace, one renounces reason. . . . Who are we to want to force God to perform a miracle" on our behalf? Prayer has the good effect of elevating us to God and of "raising us above ourselves," but this does not mean that our prayers will be answered by God: "It is not he who changes us; it is we who change by raising ourselves to him."[26]

These quasi-Malebranchian passages—which seem to confirm Bossuet's fear that, if Malebranchian *généralité* is carried far enough, grace vanishes altogether—got Rousseau into great difficulty with the French censorship. In a remarkable letter to the censor Malesherbes (March 1761) Rousseau says that, if he has made St. Preux a "Molinist" (mainly by affirming freedom and minimizing grace to the vanishing point), he has done so in order to avoid making him a "Manichean": if equal and general human liberty is not the cause of evil, then an evil spirit, equal to God, must be. However, he adds, if St. Preux "wants to be a heretic on grace, that is his affair." As for the censor's charge that St. Preux is the leader of "a revolt against the authority of Scripture," Rousseau says, he would sooner call it a "submission to the authority of God and of reason," for God and reason must "go before" the Bible and serve as its "foundation"—a perfectly Malebranchian sentiment.[27] This letter, together with other passages from *La Nouvelle Héloïse* treating Fénelon and quietism, make it clear that Rous-

---

vertu et qui doive en fixer l'idée; au contraire, le sacrifice mercenaire du bonheur public à l'intérêt propre est le sceau éternel du vice."

[26] Rousseau, *La Nouvelle Héloïse*, p. 673.

[27] Rousseau, letter to Malesherbes (March 1761), in *Lettres philosophiques*, ed. Henri Gouhier (Paris: Vrin, 1974), pp. 58-59.

seau's knowledge of the history of French theology was rather extensive and that, at the same time, God's case must be judged by the Rousseauean concept of general justice, which cannot countenance any *particularisme* at all. For St. Preux, as for Malebranche, one must never trade an idea for an anthropology.

———

Part of St. Preux's objection to prayer turns on the notion that no one is entitled to demand a miracle on his own behalf; this serves to remind that Rousseau was just as unsympathetic to miracles as Malebranche had been. Indeed, Rousseau's treatment of miracles, both in the *Profession de foi du vicaire savoyard* and in the *Lettres écrites de la montagne*, is so Malebranchian that it is sometimes a veritable transcription of *Nature et grâce*.

In the third *Lettre* Rousseau defines the miraculous in Malebranche's very language: "A miracle is, in a particular fact, an immediate act of the divine power, a real and visible exception to her laws." (Malebranchisms are piled up here: "particular," "order," "nature," "laws.") Once one knows what a miracle is (or rather, would be), Rousseau urges, there are two remaining questions. The first is, Can God perform miracles? That is certainly no problem: "This question, treated seriously, would be impious if it were not absurd." According to Rousseau, the only interesting question is, "Does God will to perform any miracles?"[28] Does he actually do what he obviously could do? Here Rousseau is quite clear: the (allegedly) miraculous adds nothing to "the glory of God" and only favors human "pride" (Malebranche had said "conceit").[29] In any case, we shall never

[28] Rousseau, *Lettres écrites de la montagne*, cited in *Religious Writings*, p. 356.

[29] Malebranche, *Méditations chrétiennes et métaphysiques*, in *Oeuvres complètes*, vol. 10, pp. 88-89: "Que les hommes sont vains, et ridicules de s'imaginer, que Dieu troublera sans raison l'ordre et la simplicité de ses voies pour s'accommoder à leur fantaisie . . . [le] commun des hommes

really *know* for certain whether there are any miracles, thanks to the very definition of the miraculous:

> Since a miracle is an exception to the laws of nature, in order to judge it one would have to know these laws. . . . Thus he who announces that such-and-such an act is miraculous declares that he knows all the laws of nature, and that he knows that this act is an exception to them.
>
> But where is this mortal who knows all the laws of nature? Newton did not pride himself on knowing them. . . . All that one can say of him who prides himself on performing miracles, is that he does quite extraordinary things: but who is denying that quite extraordinary things happen? I have seen some of these things myself, and I have even done some of them.[30]

As an example of the "quite extraordinary things" that he himself has done, Rousseau says that when he was secretary to the French ambassador in Venice in 1743 he performed a number of "new" and "strange" magic tricks involving the mysterious appearance of writing on blank paper. Finally, he adds, as a deliberate provocation, "I contented myself with being a sorcerer because I was modest, but if I had had the ambition of being a prophet, who could have stopped me from being one?"[31] With a defiantly personal "confessional" touch, then, Rousseau appropriates Malebranche's notion that human conceit, allied with magic, is at the root of most "miraculous" happenings. Ironically, Rousseau's argument is Antoine Arnauld's inverted; both appeal to the *limitations* of human knowledge—Rousseau to defend a Malebranchian nature ruled

---

. . . pleins d'un orgueil insupportable, et de l'amour d'eux-mêmes, s'attendent que Dieu pense à leurs affaires."

[30] Rousseau, *Lettres écrites de la montagne*, cited in *Religious Writings*, p. 357.

[31] Ibid., p. 358n.

by general laws, Arnauld to defend God's particular providence.[32]

Rousseau's Malebranchian distaste for miracles is at its clearest (in the *Lettres écrites de la montagne*) in his attempt to reduce the miraculous elements of Christ's mission to near-nothingness. He begins by insisting that Christ himself started his earthly work "not by miracles but by preaching" in the temple at the age of twelve. According to Rousseau, what mattered to Christ was not miracles but *la Parole*; Malebranche had said *le Verbe*, but the general idea is the same.[33] When Christ finally undertook a few miracles, it was "most often" (*le plus souvent*, Malebranche's term) on *des occasions particulières*, such as the wedding feast at Cana—and even here Christ's purpose was not at all to "manifest his power" but simply to "prolong the gaiety of the feast." This last observation is closely connected to Rousseau's view that what makes Christ "lovable" is that he "had a sensitive heart" and was an "homme de bonne société." Rousseau adds pointedly that Jansenists in particular try to make Christ and Christianity "tiresomely austere"; in a footnote, he tells an amusing story of a Jansenist *curé* who said of Christ's participation in the wedding feast at Cana, "Ce n'est pas ce qu'il fit de mieux." Complaining that Jansenism makes Christianity a "terrible and displeas-

---

[32] Antoine Arnauld, *Réflexions philosophiques et théologiques*, in *Oeuvres de Messire Antoine Arnauld* (Brussels: Culture et Civilisation, 1967), vol. 39, p. 177. "If one considers a particular effect," Arnauld begins, "and if one finds nothing but conformity to general laws of nature, one has reason to say that God has acted, with respect to this effect, according to general laws." However, since this particular effect has many "remote causes," one would have to be "assured" that there has never been a particular or miraculous divine intervention in this causal sequence, before one could say "absolutely" that any particular effect was "*only* a consequence of the general laws of nature." One would have, in short, to be omniscient. Who, Arnauld asks triumphantly, can "assure us of this, without a prodigious temerity, and without ruining the faith we have in Providence?" Both Arnauld and Rousseau rely on human ignorance, but to make opposite points.

[33] Rousseau, *Lettres écrites de la montagne*, 1764 ed., p. 85; cf. Malebranche, *Méditations chrétiennes*, passim.

ing" religion subverting the "agreeable" and "sweet" "véritable loi de Jesus-Christ," Rousseau ends the third *Lettre* with a general assault on "fanatics" who have "disfigured and dishonored" Christianity, thereby lumping Jansenism with partisanship for the miraculous.[34]

Miraculous deviations from *généralité* are treated with equal reverence in Rousseau's single most important religious statement, the *Profession de foi du vicaire savoyard*. Following countless Malebranchian insistences that "God's goodness is the love of order" and that it is through order that he "links each part of the whole," Rousseau has the vicar say withering things about the "miraculous" missions of self-appointed divine agents: "Let us suppose that divine majesty deigns to abase itself far enough to make a man the organ of its sacred *volontés*: is it reasonable, is it just, to demand that the whole human race obey the voice of this minister?"[35]

Rousseau has the vicar continue in a Malebranchian language that has been given a slightly nasty edge: "Is there any equity," the vicar asks, in having to accept as evidence of a miraculous mission nothing better than "quelques petits miracles particuliers," performed before "a few obscure people" known to the rest of the world only by hearsay? If one had to accept as authentically miraculous the "prodigies" that "les simples" (Malebranche's term) find astonishing, there would soon be "more prodigies than natural events." It is not "quelques petits miracles particuliers," the vicar insists, but "the unalterable order of nature" that best reveals the Supreme Being; if there were many exceptions to order, law, and generality one would no longer know what to think. "For myself," he concludes, "I believe too much in God to believe in so many miracles [that are] so little worthy of him."[36] (Again a Malebranchian distinction:

---

[34] Rousseau, *Lettres écrites de la montagne*, 1764 ed., pp. 131-132.
[35] Rousseau, *Emile*, cited in *Religious Writings*, pp. 152, 173.
[36] Ibid.

it is not a question of what God can do, but of what is "worthy" of him.)

The same partisanship for an orderly, general nature, coupled with the same hostility to *miracles particuliers*, recurs in Rousseau's *Lettre à Christophe de Beaumont*—his main defense of *Emile* (including the *Profession de foi*) after its condemnation. In some fragments of this letter—fragments left out of the final version because they were dangerously sarcastic—Rousseau says that those who depict God as a miracle worker must imagine that he "amuses himself" with nature-defying "sleight of hand" because he is "at loose ends" for something to do. He adds a further sarcasm, in which Malebranchism takes an uncharitable turn: miracle lovers represent God "as a bad workman [*un mauvais ouvrier*] who is forced at every moment to re-touch his machine for want of knowing how to make it run from the very beginning." And in an adjoining sentence that colors the whole passage, Rousseau insists that "there are liars who say 'believe,' and imbeciles who believe that they believe."[37]

When Rousseau says, in the *Confessions*, that he supplemented the social education he was receiving from Mme. de Warens at Les Charmettes with a very different sort of education ("I began with some book of philosophy, such as the Port-Royal *Logic*, the *Essay* of Locke, Malebranche, Leibniz, Descartes, etc.,"[38] one can well believe that the book of Malebranche that he pitched upon may have been the *Traité de la nature et de la grâce*, without which St. Preux's defense of *généralité* in *La Nouvelle Héloïse* and the arguments against *grâce particulière* in the *Lettres écrites de la montagne* have no traceable *provenance*. And if Rousseau's early poem *Le Verger des Charmettes* is indeed bad verse, it at least reveals good

[37] Rousseau, *Lettre à Christophe de Beaumont*, in *Oeuvres complètes*, Pléiade ed., pp. 1023-1024.
[38] Same as note 1.

reading—reading that establishes a *rapport* between Rousseau and the seventeenth century:

Tantot avec Leibniz, Malebranche et Newton,
Je monte ma raison sur un sublime ton,
J'examine les lois des corps et des pensées,
Avec Locke je fais l'histoire des idées.[39]

If Rousseau's reason attains sublimity partly through Malebranche's aid, it is still receiving Oratorian assistance in *Le Persifleur*—written for Diderot the year before Rousseau became Rousseau by publishing the *Discourse on the Arts and Sciences* (1750). *Le Persifleur*, a prospectus for a literary magazine that never materialized, is cast in a *galant*, studiedly mercurial manner, but Rousseau takes care to advise potential readers that he will sometimes alternate *une saillie extravagante* with *la plus profonde métaphysique*, that of "Plato, Locke or Mallebranche [sic]."[40] Rousseau may have misspelled "Malebranche," but it is clear that he did not misread him. And it is of the greatest significance that Rousseau is willing to rank Malebranche with his own usual candidates for greatest ancient and greatest modern philosopher.

———————

Sometimes Rousseau, despite a clear echoing of Malebranche, has doubts about a central Malebranchian notion—even "order" itself. To be sure, in *Emile* Rousseau has the Savoyard vicar urge that "general evil [*le mal général*] can only be [found] in disorder, and I see in the system of the world an order that cannot be doubted."[41] That sentence could be invisibly blended into the texture of Malebranche's *Traité de morale*.[42] However, later in *Emile* doubts about the

[39] Cited in Bréhier, "Les Lectures malebranchistes," p. 85.
[40] Rousseau, *Le Persifleur*, in *Les Confessions*, Pléiade ed., p 1111.
[41] Rousseau, *Emile* (Paris: Pléiade, 1959), p. 588.
[42] See Ferdinand Alquié, *Le Cartésianisme de Malebranche* (Paris: Vrin, 1974), p. 29: "Et nous voici, avec la notion d'ordre, parvenus au principe

sheer abstractness of order creep in: "One wishes in vain to establish virtue by reason alone. . . . Virtue, they say, is the love of order; but can and should this love outweigh in me that of my [own] well-being?" When Rousseau has the vicar speak of what "they" say about virtue as reason-given order, he is clearly thinking of Malebranche's argument in the *Traité de morale* that "the love of order . . . is the only virtue";[43] he evidently thinks, however, that Malebranchism stands in need of *précision*.

> At bottom their [the Malebranchians'] pretended principle is a pure playing with words; for I myself say that vice is also the love of order, taken in a different sense. There is some moral order everywhere that there is feeling and intelligence. The difference is that the good person orders himself [*s'ordonne*] in relation [*par rapport*] to the whole, and that the evil person orders the whole in relation to himself. The latter makes himself the center of all things; the other measures his radius and holds himself at the circumference. Thus he [the good person] is ordered in relation to the common center who is God, and by relation to all the concentric circles who are the creatures.[44]

If Rousseau were speaking purely in his own voice, he might make the city (rather than God) the common center that the good person embraces. Even so, he has assembled a collection of authentically Malebranchian fragments—the notions of "order" and "relation," the use of Platonic-Augustinian geometrical analogies to moral truths—only to reorder them in a new *rapport*. Rousseau gives the abstract notion of order a more precise moral-political sense by relating good to a general "whole," and evil to a quite particular "self." This passage from *Emile* is *malebranchisme* given

---

fondamental de toutes les explications que Malebranche propose de la Création, du monde et de l'homme."

[43] Malebranche, *Traité de morale*, p. 28.
[44] Rousseau, *Emile*, Pléiade ed., p. 602.

a more social and less mathematical content. Since it makes moral order center on *le tout* and moral disorder revolve around *soi-même*, it is a pascalization of Malebranche. Alternatively, one could say that it is a correction of Malebranche (the *Traité de morale*'s notion of order) *by* Malebranche (the *Traité de la nature et de la grâce*'s notion of *généralité*).

Moreover, the reservations about Malebranche's rationalism ("one wishes in vain to establish virtue by reason alone") lead Rousseau, slightly later in *Emile*, to doubt Malebranche's clear preference for reason over faith ("faith passes away, but reason subsists eternally") in the *Traité de morale*.[45] In Rousseau's thought, the distinction between reason and faith becomes that between philosophy and religion; in order to elevate religion and denigrate philosophy, Rousseau turns to a consideration of Bayle's early and hyper-Malebranchian *Pensées diverses sur la comète*, into which he weaves a phrase or two from Montesquieu's *Considerations on the Greatness and Decline of the Romans* and onto which he grafts an obscure reference to Pascal.

Rousseau begins by seeming to approve the central argument of the *Pensées diverses*: "Bayle has proved very well that fanaticism is more pernicious than atheism, and that is incontestable." In the next clause, however, Rousseau contests the "incontestable," urging that "it is no less true that fanaticism, while bloody and cruel, is nonetheless a great and strong passion which elevates the heart of man, which makes him contemptuous of death, which gives him a prodigious energy, and which only needs to be better-directed in order to produce the most sublime virtues." Certainly "good fanaticism" is better, according to Rousseau, than "irreligion and generally the reasoning and philosophical spirit," which "attaches [men] to life, effeminizes, debases souls, concentrates all passions in the baseness of particular interest [*l'interest particulier*], in the vileness of the *moi humain*, and thus quietly saps the true foundations of all soci-

[45] Malebranche, *Traité de morale*, p. 34.

ety: for what particular interests have in common is so inconsequential that it will never counterbalance what they have in opposition."[46] Thus Rousseau uses one half of Pierre Bayle—the devotion to *généralité*, the subordination of the selfishly *particulier*—against the other half: the "enlightenment" half that, at least in its early, Malebranchian phase, preferred philosophy to faith.

In the next paragraph, Bayle's "incontestable" preference for atheism to fanaticism is further undermined as Rousseau notes contemptuously that, "if atheism does not spill human blood, it is less out of love for peace than through indifference to the good." The principles of atheism "do not kill men, but they prevent them from being born by destroying the *moeurs* which multiply them, by detaching them from their species, by reducing all their affections to a secret egoism [that is] as destructive to population as to virtue."[47] Simultaneously paraphrasing and transforming Montesquieu's *Considérations*, chapter 9 ("if we see any union" in "Asiatic despotism," it is "not citizens who are united but dead bodies buried one next to the other"),[48] Rousseau urges that "philosophical indifference resembles the tranquility of the state under despotism; it is the tranquility of death; it is more destructive than war itself." It remains to be seen, he adds, "whether philosophy, at its ease and on the throne, would rule over vain-glory, over interest, over ambition, over the little passions of man, and if it would practice this so-sweet humanity which it vaunts with pen in hand." Insisting that "philosophy cannot do any good which religion cannot do better"—at least "in principle," though in practice "c'est autre chose"—Rousseau ends with a cryptic reference to Pascal.[49]

In these passages from *Emile* one sees a Rousseau so fa-

---

[46] Rousseau, *Emile*, Pléiade ed., pp. 632n-633n.
[47] Ibid., p. 633n.
[48] Montesquieu, *Considérations sur les romains*, in *Oeuvres complètes*, ed. Daniel Oster (Paris: Editions du Seuil, 1964), p. 453.
[49] Rousseau, *Emile*, Pléiade ed., pp. 633n-634n.

miliar with his predecessors that he can inherit and disinherit within the compass of a paragraph; his readers, equally brought up on Pascal, Malebranche, Bayle, and Montesquieu, would have known just where he was valuing, where transvaluing. It is clear that, for Rousseau, the mere philosophical appreciation of order is not enough; if injustice and self-love are to be avoided, one must love God, who is more than just orderly. The young person who is being educated to virtue, Rousseau says (now speaking in his own voice and no longer in that of the vicar), must be taught "not only . . . the love of order, to which each always prefers the love of self," but, more importantly, "love for the author of his being, a love that mixes itself with that same love of self, in order finally to be able to enjoy that lasting happiness of a good conscience and the contemplation of that supreme Being promising him another life, after having spent this one well." If one abandons all this, Rousseau warns, "I no longer see anything but injustice, hypocrisy and lying among men," as particular interest teaches each "to hide vice under the mask of virtue." Every "unbeliever who reasons" is quite content that everything relate to himself and that "the whole *genre humain* die, if need be, in pain and misery" in order to spare that same *incrédule* "a moment of pain."[50]

Rousseau's devotion to Malebranchian order, then, is quite genuine; as Robinet has shown, the word *ordre* appears at least forty times in the *Profession de foi* alone.[51] But

---

[50] Ibid., p. 636.

[51] André Robinet, "A propos d'ordre dans la *Profession de foi du vicaire savoyard*," in *Studi filosofici* 1 (1978), pp. 39ff. On p. 51 Robinet reproduces an argument from the "Favre" manuscript of *Emile*—omitted by Rousseau in the definitive version—that makes Rousseau an exceedingly orthodox Malebranchian: "It follows that the human mind cannot raise itself to the contemplation of the universe and of the admirable order which one sees ruling it, except after a long examination of the structure of the parts and the concurrence of the relations [*rapports*] which give birth to the total system united by a single idea." Cf. the words that Rousseau places in the mouth of M. de Wolmar in *La Nouvelle Héloïse*: "Mon seul principe actif est le goût naturel de l'ordre" (cited by Pierre-Maurice Masson in his Intro-

for Rousseau order needs to be *precisé*: if Malebranche viewed order through one Platonic lens—the *Phaedo*'s notion of an eternal, quasi-mathematical moral order[52]—Rousseau viewed it through another—the *Republic*'s notion of a social order in which all the members *feel* the common good together.[53] For this reason, Bayle's final fideism would be more congenial to Rousseau than the early, hyper-Malebranchian rationalism.

If Rousseau's doubts about Malebranche's rationalism led him to some revision of the Oratorian's idea of order, the same doubts about the social efficacy of pure reason led him to certain worries about Malebranchian *volonté générale*. He expressed these worries in a commentary on Diderot's neo-Malebranchian *Encyclopédie* article, "Droit naturel." This commentary, written roughly concurrently with *Emile*, is now called *Première Version du contrat social* or "Geneva MS." It is a piece that Rousseau himself suppressed, not because it was ineffective, but because it was so extremely effective that it cast nearly fatal doubt on the possibility of a social contract ("this pretended social treaty") and even on

---

duction to *La Profession de foi du vicaire savoyard de Jean-Jacques Rousseau* (Fribourg: Librairie de l'Université, 1914), p. 281.

[52] Plato, *Phaedo*, in *Plato: The Collected Dialogues*, ed. E. Hamilton and H. Cairns (New York: Bollingen, 1961), 75A-E, p. 58: "We must have had some previous knowledge . . . [of] . . . absolute beauty, goodness, uprightness, holiness, and, as I maintain, all those characteristics which we designate in our discussion by the term 'absolute'. . . . We had knowledge . . . not only of equality and of relative magnitudes, but of all absolute standards." It is this side of Plato, filtered through St. Augustine, that affected Malebranche.

[53] Plato, *The Republic*, in *Collected Dialogues*, 462A-E, p. 701: "Do we know of any greater evil for a state than the thing that distracts it and makes it many instead of one, or a greater good than that which binds it together and makes it one? . . . The best-governed state resembles an organism . . . [in which], when anyone of the citizens suffers aught of good or evil, [each] will be most likely to speak of the part that suffers as its own and will share the pleasure or the pain as a whole." That passage is surely echoed in 1 Corinthians 12, and in Pascal and Rousseau; the only thing that keeps Plato from anticipating later writers even more is that, while he has a notion of *généralité*, he seems to lack a notion of *volonté*—or so Aristotle argues in his critique of *Protagoras*.

the possibility of the general will itself. Book 1, chapter 2 of the *Première Version* is called "De la société générale du genre humain" (originally, "Qu'il n'y a point naturellement de société générale entre les hommes").[54] Both of these titles foreshadow what the text bears out—namely, that this chapter is a refutation of Diderot's notion that there is a universal *volonté générale* of and for the entire human race. And since Diderot argues, closely paraphrasing *De la recherche de la vérité*, that this general will can be found by anyone who reasons in "the silence of the passions,"[55] Rousseau's commentary on Diderot is an oblique treatment of Malebranche as well.

In "Droit naturel" Diderot had argued that, "if we deprive the individual of the right to decide about the nature of the just and the unjust," we must take "this great question . . . before the human race," for "the good of all" is the "sole passion" that this most inclusive group has. Echoing Malebranche and anticipating Rousseau, Diderot goes on to say that "*volontés particulières* are suspect," for they can be indifferently "good or wicked," but that "the general will is always good," since it has never "deceived" and never will.[56] (In another *Encyclopédie* article on the ancient Greeks, Diderot adds: "The laws, the laws; there is the sole barrier that one can erect against the passions of men; it is the general will that one must oppose to particular wills. . . .")[57]

It is to this always good, never deceiving *volonté générale* "that the individual must address himself," Diderot insists, "in order to know how far he must be a citizen, a subject, a

[54] Rousseau, *Première Version du contrat social*, in *Political Writings*, vol. 1, p. 447.
[55] Malebranche, *De la recherche de la vérité*, in *Oeuvres complètes*, vol. 1, p. 490.
[56] D. Diderot, "Droit naturel," in Rousseau, *Political Writings*, vol. 1, p. 431.
[57] Cited in Robert Wokler, "The Influence of Diderot on Rousseau," in *Studies on Voltaire and the 18th Century* (Banbury: Voltaire Foundation, 1975), vol. 132, p. 68n.

father, a child, and when it is suitable for him to live or to die." It is for the general will "to fix the limits of all duties." So far, no great gap has opened up between Diderot and Rousseau; however, when Diderot begins to indicate where the general will is "deposited," he moves in the direction of a universalism that is usually foreign to Rousseau. The general will can be "consulted," he urges, "in the principles of the written law of all civilized nations; in the social actions of primitive and barbarous peoples; in the tacit conventions of the enemies of the human race between themselves; and even in indignation and resentment, those two passions that nature seems to have placed even in animals, to supply the defect of social laws and of public vengeance." Diderot's nominal *généralité* is in fact a *morale universelle* (to use his own term); it relates to the whole *genre humain*, and seems to extend to "honor among thieves" and even to animals.[58] Rousseau's *volonté générale*—of Rome, of Sparta, of Geneva—is a great deal more *particulière*; indeed, in the *Gouvernement de Pologne* Rousseau insists on the importance of national peculiarities and particularities that should not be submerged in cosmopolitan universalism.[59] For Diderot, then, the general will is to be found almost everywhere, whereas Rousseau doubts that it has ever been fully realized anywhere. Shklar certainly does not exaggerate when she says that Rousseau's general will was "neither a plan for revolution nor a design to say anything about actual societies except that they were irremediably unjust."[60]

The fact that Rousseau's general will is more particular and more purely political than Diderot's emerges even more clearly in Diderot's final paragraph of "Droit naturel." Having begun with a sentiment that Rousseau could have largely approved ("the man who listens only to his *volonté*

[58] Diderot, "Droit naturel," pp. 431-432.
[59] Rousseau, *Gouvernement de Pologne*, chapters 1-4.
[60] Judith N. Shklar, "General Will," in *Dictionary of the History of Ideas*, ed. Philip P. Wiener (New York: Charles Scribner's Sons, 1973), vol. 2, p. 278.

particulière is the enemy of the human race"), Diderot goes on to urge that "the general will is, in each individual, a pure act of the understanding, which reasons in the silence of the passions about what a man can demand of his fellow-man and about what his fellow-man has the right to demand of him."[61] In this passage Diderot comes very close to book 3 of Malebranche's *Recherche de la vérité*: if, Malebranche says, he turns inward and asks himself what he should do, "in the silence of my senses and of my passions," he will hear a "clear and distinct" (obviously Cartesian!) answer. Moreover, it will be an answer that has eternal value and that everyone knows; "all the nations" are familiar with it, and it is written "neither in Greek, nor in Latin, nor in French, nor in German." The "inner man" who conceives this universal law will "smile at the visions of his imagination" and will "follow the path that leads to all perfection."[62] Plainly, Diderot had this celebrated passage in mind.[63]

At this very point Diderot begins to be separated from Rousseau. The *citoyen de Génève*, as he styled himself, would have stressed precisely "citizenship" and "Geneva," not "fellow-men"; and Rousseau would not have urged that *volonté générale* is immediately dictated by understanding and reason (as distinguished from, say, civic education). Had Rousseau thought that, the passions being "silent," understanding and reason could alone dictate what is right, he would never have made his famous claim that "the general will is always right" but "the judgment which guides it is not always enlightened." If reason alone dictated right, Rousseauean men would have no need of a

---

[61] Diderot, "Droit naturel," p. 432.

[62] Malebranche, *Recherche de la vérité*, p. 490.

[63] Wokler, then, is probably incorrect in insisting that "there is no evidence to suggest that either Diderot or Rousseau took any notice of the expression [general will] in one of its earlier formulations." Since Diderot paraphrases Malebranche almost verbatim, and Rousseau cites Diderot's words, this cannot be right. See Wokler, "Influence of Diderot," pp. 70-71.

Numa or a Moses to help effect a "union of will and understanding."[64]

Diderot ends "Droit naturel" with a series of points that are more Malebranchian than Rousseauean. After the initial presentation of his conception of the general will, he goes on to shore up the universalism of his *volonté générale de l'espèce* by calling it not only "the rule of conduct between one individual [*particulier*] and another in the same society" but also the rule of conduct between different societies, so that for Diderot *volonté générale* becomes virtually an *ius gentium*. Indeed, he asserts, a universal "general will of the species" is "the link between all societies, without excepting even those that have been formed by crime." Laws that are not just general but universal "must be made for all, and not for one," for "the general will never errs." Finally, the general will is the "common desire" of "*l'espèce entière*."[65]

Book 1, chapter 2 of Rousseau's *Première Version du contrat social* is a refutation of Diderot's universalism and rationalism. At one time, Rousseau had stressed a roughly comparable *morale universelle*; in an early, unpublished manuscript called *Chronologie universelle, ou Histoire générale du temps* (c. 1737) he had appealed to Fénelon's notion of a universal Christian republic, while summoning up a recollection of Pascal's "body full of thinking members" (or at least of 1 Corinthians 12):

> We are all brothers; our neighbors ought to be as dear to us as ourselves. 'I love the human race more than my country,' said the illustrious M. de Fénelon, 'my country more than my family and my family more than myself.' Sentiments so full of humanity ought to be shared by all men. . . . The universe is a great family of which we are all members. . . . However extensive may be the power of an individual [*d'un particulier*], he is always in a position to make himself useful . . . to the

[64] See Rousseau, *Du contrat social*, pp. 48-54.
[65] Diderot, "Droit naturel," pp. 432-433.

great body of which he is a part. If he can [do this], he indispensably ought to. . . .[66]

Later, of course, most clearly of all in the *Première Version*, Rousseau would abandon the *universelle* in favor of the *générale* and exchange the *respublica christiana* for more modest republics (Sparta, Geneva). Indeed, his great difference from Diderot, as the *Première Version* makes clear, rests precisely on the difference between the *universelle*—known to all by reason alone, in the "silence of the passions"—and the *générale*—known to citizens of a particular republic through a civic education supplied by Numa or Moses or Lycurgus.

That Rousseau is not going to argue for a reason-ordained *morale universelle* valid for the entire human race is evident in the opening sentence of the *Première Version*'s "De la société générale du genre humain": "Let us begin by inquiring why the necessity for political institutions arises."[67] If a passion-silencing reason spoke to and governed all men, no mere particular political institutions would arise at all (as Locke had already shown in section 128 of the "Second Treatise," saying that only a "corrupt" rejection of reason keeps a unitary, unified mankind from being perfectly governed by natural law).[68] Rousseau is struck by the beauty of a Malebranchian-Diderotian *morale universelle*: "No one will *deny* that the general will in each individual is a pure act of the understanding, which reasons

[66] Rousseau, *Chronologie universelle*, pp. 214-215. For a fine appreciation of Rousseau's respect for Fénelon, see Shklar, *Men and Citizens*, pp. 4-5: "Fénelon was one of the few authors of whom one can say with some assurance that Rousseau had read him. Certainly he admired him." Shklar goes on to offer valuable comments on utopianism in the thought of both writers.

[67] Rousseau, *Première Version du contrat social*, in *On the Social Contract*, ed. R. Masters (New York: St. Martin's Press, 1978), p. 157.

[68] John Locke, 'Second Treatise,' section 128, *Two Treatises*; see the author's *Will and Political Legitimacy: A Critical Exposition of Social Contract Theory in Hobbes, Locke, Rousseau, Kant and Hegel* (Cambridge, Mass.: Harvard University Press, 1982), chapter 3.

in the silence of the passions about what man can demand of his fellow-man and what his fellow-man has the right to demand of him." But where, Rousseau immediately and characteristically asks, "is the man who can be so objective about himself; and if concern for his self-preservation is nature's first precept, can he be forced to look in this manner at the species in general in order to impose on himself duties whose connection with his particular constitution is not evident to him?" If reason is not directly morally efficacious (as it cannot be, if great legislators are to have the important formative function that is assigned to them in *The Social Contract*), and if natural law is scarcely natural at all (as *Inequality* tries to prove), then the natural man who fails to find his particular good in the general good will become instead the enemy of the *genre humain*, allying himself with the strong and the unjust to despoil the weak.

> It is false that in the state of independence, reason leads us to cooperate for the common good out of a perception of our own interest. Far from there being an alliance between private interest and the general good, they are mutually exclusive in the natural order of things, and social laws are a yoke that each wants to impose on the other without having to bear himself. "I am aware that I bring horror and confusion to the human species," says the independent man who is stifled by the wise man, "but either I must be unhappy or I must cause others to be so, and no one is dearer to me than myself. . . . Either give me guarantees against all unjust undertakings or do not expect me to refrain from them in turn . . . [failing these guarantees] it will be my business to get the strong on my side, by sharing with them the spoils from the weak."[69]

So strongly does this current of thought sweep Rousseau along that he mounts a brief assault on *généralité* that would

---

[69] Rousseau, *Première Version* in *On the Social Contract*, pp. 161, 160.

be fatal not just to Diderot and Malebranche but to his own political aims as well: "If the general society did exist somewhere other than in the systems of philosophers, it would be . . . a moral being with qualities separate and distinct from those of the particular beings constituting it, somewhat like chemical compounds which have properties that do not belong to any of the elements composing them." In such a *société générale* "there would be a universal language which nature would teach all men and which would be their first means of communication"; there would also be "a kind of central nervous system which would connect all the parts." Finally, "the public good or ill would not be merely the sum of private goods and ills as in a simple aggregation, but would lie in the liaison uniting them. It would be greater than this sum, and public felicity, far from being based on the happiness of private individuals [*des particuliers*], would itself be the source of this happiness."[70]

Plainly, this argument goes too far, since Rousseau himself wants to argue for a general good that is more than a mere sum or aggregation of private goods and ills; it is no wonder that Rousseau suppressed the *Première Version*. Nevertheless, the dilemma remains that a general society cannot be produced by passion-silencing reason alone.[71] The only way out of that dilemma, according to Rousseau, is through denatured, non-natural "new associations" (Sparta, Rome, Geneva) that take the place of well-meant but imaginary reason-governed *sociétés générales* and that, through rigorous civic education, draw natural beings out of their equally natural egocentrism, bringing them to think of themselves as parts of a greater whole—a whole less extensive, but more realizable, than a *respublica christiana* or a *genre humain*. The particular social remedies designed to

[70] Ibid., pp. 159-160.
[71] Rousseau, *Du contrat social*, p. 48: "That which is good and in conformity to order is such by the nature of things. . . . All justice comes from God, who alone is its source; but if we knew how to receive it from on high, we would have need of neither government nor laws."

overcome *particularité* and self-preference at the end of "De la société générale du genre humain" are rather abstractly, even vaguely, characterized ("new associations," "new insights," "perfected art"),[72] but one knows from other works such as the *Economie politique* and the *Gouvernement de Pologne* how Rousseau proposes to produce, through educative shaping, a civic *esprit général* that is certainly no cosmopolitan *esprit universel*.[73] And in the first of the *Lettres écrites de la montagne* Rousseau shows very clearly that his concern is to produce a general will that is peculiar to some particular nation, not a universal will for the good of the whole human race—even if this entails abandoning Christianity as a universal religion.

> All the ancient religions, not excepting that of the Jews, were national in their origin, appropriated to, and incorporated in, the state; forming the basis, or at least making a part, of the legislative system.
>
> Christianity, on the contrary, is in its principles a universal religion, having nothing exclusive, nothing local, nothing peculiar to one country any more than to another. Its divine author, embracing all mankind in his boundless charity, came to remove those barriers that separated the nations from each other, and to unite all mankind in a people of brethren. . . .
>
> National religions are useful to a state . . . but they are hurtful to mankind in general. . . . Christianity, on the contrary, by making men just, moderate and peaceable is very advantageous to society in general, but it weakens the force of the political spring [and] . . . breaks the unity of the moral body.[74]

---

[72] Rousseau, *Première Version*, in *On the Social Contract*, pp. 162-163.

[73] See particularly Rousseau, *Gouvernement de Pologne*, chapters 2-4, esp. p. 437: "Tout vrai republicain . . . ne voit que la patrie, il ne vit que pour elle. . . ."

[74] Rousseau, *Lettres écrites de la montagne*, 1764 ed., pp. 34-37. Later in the same letter (p. 40), Rousseau recalls and transforms St. Paul's "God wills that all men be saved": "The science of salvation and that of government

Rousseau ends the passage with a radical claim that proves how little he finally favored Christian universalism: "Christianity . . . inspires humanity rather than patriotism, and tends rather to the forming of men than citizens."[75] In the end, for Rousseau, no *morale universelle*—either a Christian one based on charity or a Diderotian one based on passion-silencing reason—can help in the transformation of natural men into denatured citizens. The *générale* must be somewhat *particulière*.

Admittedly, in the *Economie politique*, a comparatively early, transitional work, Rousseau seems to vacillate between *universalité* and *généralité*. Perhaps this is simply because the work was written to order for Diderot's *Encyclopédie*[76] and therefore had to reflect, or at least not contradict, Diderot's own insistence on *morale universelle* in "Droit naturel." Thus, in the *Economie politique* Rousseau first says that "any body politic" is "a moral being that has a will," and that "this general will, which always tends toward the preservation and welfare of the whole and of each part, and which is the source of the law, is . . . the rule of what is just and unjust." But "this rule of justice," Rousseau immediately adds (perhaps with one eye on Diderot), while "infallible" for citizens within a particular polity, "can be defective with [respect to] foreigners." This is simply because "the will of the state, though general in relation to its [own] members, is no longer [such] in relation to other states and their members." At this early point, however, Rousseau was not yet ready to say (as he does in the *Lettres écrites de la montagne*) that humanity must yield to patriotism, that men matter less than citizens; thus, having begun by making the general will the will of some *particular* body politic, Rousseau falls back on the more or less Fénelonian

---

are very different. . . . The doctrine of Christ had only one object, that of calling and saving all men." Government, Rousseau suggests, saves only its own citizens.

[75] Ibid., p. 39.

[76] See Wokler, "Influence of Diderot," pp. 68ff.

thought that "the large town of the world becomes the body politic, of which the law of nature is always the general will, and the various states and peoples are merely individual members."[77] In his mature, fully confident works, that last echo of the *Chronologie universelle*, of a Dantean universal *respublica* under natural law,[78] finally vanishes altogether; after *Inequality*, there is usually no natural law with which *volonté générale* can be equated,[79] and after the *Lettres écrites de la montagne* and the *Gouvernement de Pologne*, "the various states" are no longer "members" of a world body politic. In the *Economie politique* there is still some vacillation between the polis and the cosmopolis, the general and the universal; that vacillation later gave way to a radical constancy.

The shared point of *Emile* and the *Première Version du contrat social* is that Malebranchian reason alone cannot create order and virtue (*Emile*), just as it cannot create a civic *volonté générale* (*Première Version*). This explains the weight Rousseau gives to education. For him, men do not naturally or originally think of themselves as parts of a greater whole;[80] they must therefore be brought to this non-natural belief. They must acquire a *kind* of faith, if no longer the faith of Pascal and Bayle. Viewed from one perspective, Rousseau's thought is Malebranchian rationalism tempered by Pascalian-Baylian fideism. It is a whole history of French moral thought—from the death of Pascal in 1662 to the publication of *Emile* and *Du contrat social* precisely a cen-

---

[77] Rousseau, *Economie politique*, in *On the Social Contract*, ed. Masters, p. 212.

[78] Dante, *De monarchia*, intro. D. Nicholl (London: Weidenfeld and Nicholson, 1954), passim.

[79] Rousseau, *Discours sur l'origine de l'inégalité*, in *Political Writings*, vol. 1, p. 137: Political writers "begin by looking for rules which it would be suitable for men to adopt for their common utility; and then they give the name *natural law* to the collection of these rules, without any other proof than the good which would result from their being universally practiced." This, Rousseau adds, is "une manière très commode de composer des définitions."

[80] Rousseau, *Du contrat social*, p. 52.

tury later—compressed into "Rousseaueanism." In the language of Hegel's *Phenomenology*, the particular individual must "go through the stages through which the general mind has passed";[81] in Rousseau's thought, the "stages" of French philosophy coexist in a timeless *nunc stans*.

The passages from *La Nouvelle Héloïse, Lettres écrites de la montagne*, and *Emile* that demonstrate Rousseau's wide and deep knowledge of seventeenth-century theological controversies mainly *reflect* those controversies, without transforming them. There are other passages, however, that engage in a great deal of transforming, particularly of works by Malebranche and Bayle. In *Nature et grâce* Malebranche had insisted not only on generality, simplicity, and uniformity but also on Christ as "architect" of the church viewed as a temple;[82] Bayle had recalled much of this when he complained, in the *Réponse aux questions d'un provincial*, that there is "nothing easier" for God as world architect than to "follow a simple, fecund and regular plan" that is "at the same time suitable for all creatures"—that God's "love for the public good" should outweigh a mere show of divine ability, just as a prince in commissioning a palace should insist that it be suitable for its inhabitants, even at the expense of regularity or magnificence.[83] Rousseau must have had Bayle's answer to Malebranche in mind when he wrote a portion of his *Jugement* (1756) of the Abbé de St. Pierre's *Polysynodie*; indeed, he had to inject only a little ex-

[81] Hegel, *Phenomenology of Mind*, trans. J. B. Baillie (New York: Harper and Row, 1967), p. 89.

[82] Malebranche, *Traité de la nature et de la grâce*, pp. 74-75: "Jesus Christ ayant besoin pour la construction de son Église des esprits d'un certain mérite . . . peut en général s'appliquer à eux, et par cette application répandre en eux la Grâce qui les sanctifie: de même que l'esprit d'un Architecte pense en général aux pierres quarrées, par exemple, lorsque ces sortes de pierres sont actuellement nécessaires à son batiment."

[83] Pierre Bayle, *Réponse aux questions d'un provincial*, in *Oeuvres Diverses de M. Pierre Bayle* (The Hague: Compagnie des Libraires, 1737), vol. 3, p. 825.

tra political content into inherited theological language. In the *Jugement* Rousseau urges that perfection "in a whole as complicated [*composé*] as the body politic" does not depend only on the perfection of each part," just as, by architectural analogy, "to design a palace it does not suffice to place each item well, but one must also consider the *rapports* of the whole, the most suitable connections, the most commodious order . . . the most regular symmetry." All of these "general objects" are so important that the able architect willingly sacrifices for the betterment of the whole "a thousand particular advantages"—particular advantages that he could have kept in a less perfect and less simple arrangement. In just the same way, politics "does not consider *en particulier* either finances, or war, or commerce," but relates all of these parts to a "common objective." The proportions most suitable to this common objective are the result of "general plans [*les plans généraux*]" that, "in seeking the greatest perfection of the whole," always look for "the simplest execution."[84] In this passage from the *Jugement* Rousseau is plainly siding with Malebranche against Bayle. After all, Rousseau insists on generality, simplicity, and the perfection of the whole. But, without a certain kind of tradition standing behind him, Rousseau would not have spoken in this language—an idiom addressed to those brought up on Malebranche and Bayle. By using a few "code" words, Rousseau is able to summon up the force of a century's argumentation over *généralité* and *simplicité*.

[84] Rousseau, *Jugement sur la polysynodie*, in *Political Writings*, vol. 1, p. 419. Rousseau then goes on to make two characteristic arguments against *particularisme*: against St. Pierre's lingering monarchism, Rousseau asks how the abbé has failed to see "dans le cours de sa vie et de ses écrits, combien c'est une vaine occupation de rechercher des formes durables pour un état de choses, qui dépend toujours de la volonté d'un seul homme"; against St. Pierre's retention of *corps intermediaires*, Rousseau declares that "les intérêts des sociétés partielles ne sont pas moins separées de ceux de l'État, ni moins pernicieux à la République, que ceux des particuliers." Clearly, the creation of a public *volonté générale* is the remedy for both of these defects. (The *Polysynodie* is a significant but utterly neglected work of Rousseau.)

Rousseau did not think, of course, that the Abbé de St. Pierre himself had succeeded in arriving at a *politique générale*; on the contrary, he complains in book 5 of *Emile* that "it was always the policy of the Abbé de St. Pierre to look for a little remedy for each particular evil [*chaque mal particulier*], instead of climbing to their common source and seeing that one cannot cure them except all at once." Falling back on the familiar body-members metaphor, he adds that "it is not a matter of treating separately each ulcer that appears on the body of a sick person, but of purifying the whole [*la masse*] of the blood that produces all of them." And Rousseau illustrates his political dictum that one must go to the root *causes générales*, not just toy with *chaque mal particulier*, by pointing out that Augustus's laws against celibacy neglected the general root in favor of a futile attack on particular manifestations: had the goodness of his general policies brought citizens to marry freely, he would not have had to make "vain" particular regulations.[85]

To be sure, the Malebranchian-Montesquieuean notion of *causes générales* that regularly produce all *effets particuliers* through the operation of general laws is not very prominent in most of Rousseau's moral and political writings; perhaps his great concern with freedom ordinarily led him to separate *généralité* from *causalité* and to stress "general will" sooner than "general cause." It may have been this that led him to complain, in an unpublished sentence intended for *Emile*, that "modern philosophy wants to explain all moral effects through physical causes; perhaps, on the contrary, there are more physical effects which depend on moral causes."[86] Nevertheless, in book 3, chapter 8 of *Du contrat social*, reflections of the thought and language of Montesquieu appear. First praising Montesquieu's notion that liberty is "not the fruit of every climate" ("the more one re-

[85] Rousseau, *Emile*, in *Oeuvres complètes*, Pléiade ed., p. 851. Indeed, according to Rousseau, Augustus's policies came too late: "Ces loix montroient déjà le déclin de l'empire Romain."
[86] Ibid., p. 1459.

flects on this principle established by Montesquieu, the more one feels its truth"), Rousseau goes on to insist that one must always distinguish between *les lois générales* and *des causes particulières*, and that "even if the Midi were covered with republics, and the whole North with despotic states, it would not be less true that, through the effect of climate, despotism is suitable to warm countries, and good polity to the intermediate regions." Those who think that a few exceptions disprove these general (Montesquieuean) laws "do not examine the thing in all of its *rapports*."[87] Rousseau was able, then, though rarely willing, to use Malebranchian-Montesquieuean analysis resting on *cause* and *rapport*.

The most striking instance of Rousseau's adoption of the Malebranchian-Montesquieuean notion of *rapport* while adding the distinction between physical and moral causes is to be found in book 4 of *Emile*, in which he urges that "the study suitable [*convenable*] to man is that of his relations [*rapports*]. So long as he knows himself only through his physical being, he ought to study himself only through his *rapports* with things; this is the occupation of his childhood. When he begins to feel his moral being, he ought to study himself through his *rapports* with men: this is the occupation of his whole life." In this passage Rousseau, while reflecting antecedents, remains wholly himself: he integrates Malebranchian and Montesquieuean terms into a developmental moral psychology and his general theory that human beings first understand physical necessity, then utility, and (finally) morality.[88] His notion that education cannot leap over the ideas and relations that are understood at different ages incorporates *rapport* and *physique-moral* while remaining entirely Rousseauean.

In *Rousseau juge de Jean-Jacques* Rousseau is, at least in one passage, even closer to the Malebranchian-Montes-

[87] Rousseau, *Du contrat social*, pp. 83-84.
[88] Rousseau, *Emile*, in *Oeuvres complètes*, Pléiade ed., pp. 493, 420, 426ff.

quieuean method of imagining moral *rapports* in the light of physical *rapports*, so that grace reflects nature, *la morale* echoes *la physique*:

Feeling [*sensibilité*] is the principle of all action. . . . There is a physical and organic feeling, purely passive, which seems to have for its end only the preservation of the body. . . . There is another feeling that I call active and moral, which is nothing else than the faculty of attaching our affections to those beings who are strangers to us. This [kind of feeling] . . . seems to offer, in minds, a sufficiently clear analogy to the attracting faculty of bodies. Its power is through relations [*en raison des rapports*] that we feel between ourselves and the other beings, and, according to the nature of these relations, it acts sometimes positively by attraction, sometimes negatively by repulsion, like a lover between two poles. . . .[89]

When one feels repulsed from others by a kind of moral Newtonianism, it is because an originally innocent and self-preserving *amour de soi* turns into an *amour-propre* that insists that all others "prefer us to all others," an *amour-propre* that has been "irritated" and made "discontented" by corrupting social *rapports* involving comparison and measuring.[90] This is simply radicalized *malebranchisme*, left-Oratorianism.

Transformed reflections and echoes of Malebranche (and Montesquieu) also appear throughout *Du contrat social*, but nowhere more clearly than in book 2, chapter 11 ("Des divers systèmes de legislation").[91] Rousseau begins with quasi-Malebranchian "general objects" of politics—above all equality—then modifies that *généralité* (or seems at first

---

[89] Rousseau, *Rousseau juge de Jean-Jacques*, in *Oeuvres complètes*, Pléiade ed., vol. 1, p. 805.
[90] Ibid., p. 806.
[91] Rousseau, *Du contrat social*, p. 61.

to modify it) in light of quasi-Montesquieuean *rapports particuliers*.

If, Rousseau begins, one starts his *recherche* into "what must be the end of all systems of legislation," one finds "two principal objects, *liberty* and *equality*: liberty, because all private dependence [*dépendance particulière*] is that much force subtracted from the body of the state; equality, because liberty cannot subsist without it." After insisting that by equality he does not mean exact sameness, but simply that "no citizen [must] be opulent enough to be able to buy another, and none so poor as to be constrained to sell himself," Rousseau admits that the abuse of equality is inevitable; nonetheless, "it is precisely because the force of circumstances constantly tends to destroy equality that the force of legislation should always tend to maintain it."[92] And law is, of necessity, *générale*.

Having begun with a *recherche* of *ces objets généraux*[93]—a liberty and an equality that cancel *toute dépendance particulière*—Rousseau turns from secularized Malebranchian terminology to the language of Montesquieu, that is, to another *side* of Malebranchism, the side stressing *rapports* and *causes particulières*. (As has been noted, Rousseau tends to bring out the voluntarist aspect of Malebranchism—above all *volonté générale*, now civic rather than heavenly—while Montesquieu gives greater weight to relations and causes; the moral *généralité* and scientific *généralité* that Malebranche had striven to keep precisely parallel drifted slightly apart after his death.) In turning toward Montesquieu, Rousseau urges that

> these general objects of all good institutions [liberty and equality] must be modified in each country by the relations [*rapports*] which arise as much from the local situation as from the character of the inhabitants; and it is in virtue of these *rapports* that one must assign to

[92] Ibid.
[93] Ibid., p. 62.

each people a particular system of legislation [*un sys-tème particulier d'institution*] which is the best, not per-haps in itself, but for the actual state for which it is des-tined. Is the soil, for example, ungrateful and barren, or the country too small for its inhabitants? Then turn to industry and the arts, whose products you will ex-change for the foodstuffs you lack. Do you, on the con-trary, occupy rich plains and fertile hillsides? In a good terrain do you need more inhabitants? Then devote your whole attention to agriculture, which causes men to multiply, and drive out the arts and crafts, which would serve merely to complete the depopulation of the country by concentrating in a limited number of places the few inhabitants it has. Do you occupy an ex-tensive and convenient seacoast? Then cover the sea with ships, cultivate commerce and navigation; your life will be brilliant and short. Does the sea at your shores lap only against cliffs that are virtually inacces-sible? Then remain barbarous and ichthyophagous; it will give you a more tranquil, perhaps a better, and cer-tainly a happier life. In short, in addition to the princi-ples which are common to all, each people has within itself something which requires those principles to be applied in a particular way, and which makes its legis-lation appropriate only to itself. Thus the Hebrews in former times, and the Arabs more recently, made reli-gion their main object, the Athenians literature, Tyre and Carthage commerce, Rhodes shipping, Sparta war, and Rome virtue. The author of *The Spirit of the Laws* has given innumerable examples of the skill with which the legislator directs his legislative system to each of these objects.[94]

Here Rousseau deviates from the *esprit de Montesquieu* even while seeming to paraphrase *De l'esprit des lois*; he can-

[94] Ibid. Translation based on that of F. Watkins, *Rousseau: Political Writ-ings* (Edinburgh: Nelson, 1953).

not bring himself to praise a commercial nation ("your life will be brilliant and short"), and he seems pleased that an agricultural nation will "drive out the arts and crafts"—the very arts and crafts he has grudgingly recommended to those who occupy "ungrateful or barren" soil. Montesquieu himself had said that the laws of each nation should only be the *cas particulier* of a more general *raison humaine*;[95] nonetheless, Rousseau is even less of a relativist than Montesquieu. For if one remembers the *Discourse on the Arts and Sciences*, one knows what Rousseau *really* thinks of Athens's obsession with literature;[96] and after seeming to have countenanced commerce and navigation where "invincible nature" necessitates it, he adds in a more characteristic footnote that "any branch of external commerce" brings only a "false utility" to "un royaume en général," enriching only *quelques particuliers*.[97] There is a terrific tension, then, in Rousseau's "Montesquieueanism": despite great effort, he simply cannot reconcile himself to the sovereignty of *causes physiques*, even while he *claims* that "the laws and natural circumstances" must "coincide at every point." His *recherche de la généralité* will not let him consistently accept so much particularism. This is not surprising, for if the *objet général* of "*all* systems of legislation" must be liberty and equality, then literature and commerce cannot be suitable social ends. According to Rousseau, in Athens there was not the liberty alleged in Pericles' Funeral Oration, but only the tyranny of orators;[98] a "republic of letters" is neither a possible Rousseauean idea nor ideal. Commerce, howsoever Montesquieu might have praised its English form in

[95] Montesquieu, *De l'esprit des lois*, in *Oeuvres complètes*, p. 532.

[96] Rousseau, *Discours sur les sciences et les arts*, in *Rousseau: Oeuvres complètes* (Paris: Editions du Seuil, 1971), vol. 2, pp. 52ff., esp. p. 56: "O Sparte, opprobre éternel d'une vaine doctrine: tandis que les vices conduits par les beaux-arts s'introduisaient ensemble dans Athènes . . . tu chassais de tes murs les arts et les artistes, les sciences et les savants."

[97] Rousseau, *Du contrat social*, p. 62n.

[98] Rousseau, *Sciences et arts*, p. 56: "Athènes devint le séjour de la politesse et du bon goût, le pays des orateurs et des philosophes."

book 11 of *De l'esprit des lois*,[99] destroys equality by enriching *quelques particuliers*. One must therefore read book 2, chapter 11 of *Du contrat social* slowly and with care, noticing that Montesquieu is openly praised and more quietly departed from. Liberty and equality cannot yield to literature and commerce; equality is not equal to anything else. As for literature, *liber libertatem non aequat*.

Rousseau's determination to avoid physical determinism, to avoid conceding very much to Montesquieuean *causes physiques* and historically contingent *rapports particuliers*—to keep generality more closely related to *will* than to *cause*—is evident even in those passages that seem to treat Montesquieu with admiration. In the Preface to *Emile*, Rousseau begins with an echo of Malebranchian *simplicité* before turning to Montesquieuean topics:

> In every kind of project there are two things to consider: first the absolute goodness of the project; in the second place, ease of execution.
>
> In the first respect it suffices, in order for the project to be admissible and practicable in itself, that the goodness be in the nature of the thing; here, for example, that the education proposed be suitable to man, and well-adapted to the human heart.[100]

Since by offering the finished *Emile* Rousseau is tacitly saying that his scheme of education is indeed "suitable to man" in general and "well-adapted to the human heart" as such, one should not expect that he will concede much to the *circonstances particulières* that might detract from this general suitability. He begins by allowing that education "depends on certain relations [*rapports*] given in certain situations: relations accidental to [particular] things and which, in consequence, are not at all necessary, and can vary infinitely." Thus he says, at his most Montesquieuean,

---

[99] Montesquieu, *De l'esprit des lois*, pp. 585ff.
[100] Rousseau, *Emile*, in *Oeuvres complètes*, Pléiade ed., p. 243.

"some education may be practicable in Switzerland and not be in France; some other may be for the middle class [*chez les bourgeois*] and another among the great [*chez les grands*]." These things depend on "a thousand circumstances, which it is impossible to determine other than through a particular application of the method to this or that country, or this or that [social] condition."[101]

Suddenly, however, Rousseau's view of a general education suitable to man *en soi* rises up, effacing all of these Montesquieuean *rapports accidentels*: "Now all of these *applications particulières*, not being essential to my subject, do not enter into my plan. Others can occupy themselves with them, if they like, each for the country or condition that he will have in view." So much for Montesquieu! As for himself, Rousseau concludes, it suffices that "wherever men are born, one can achieve what I propose"—that is, for the "human heart" as such. This in turn leads him to say, in book 1 of *Emile*, that "our true study is that of the human condition . . . thus we must generalize our views, and consider in our pupil man in the abstract."[102] By this point, *rapports* that are merely *accidentels* and *particuliers* vanish altogether.

In very late works such as *Rousseau juge de Jean-Jacques* and the *Rêveries du promeneur solitaire*, in which Rousseau feels that he no longer has any *rapports* at all with other human beings, language inherited from Malebranche, Montesquieu, and Pascal is neither simply reflected nor merely transformed but actually *inverted*, transmogrified. In the "Première Promenade" of the *Rêveries du promeneur solitaire*—the one that begins with the arresting and affecting words, "me voici donc seul sur la terre, n'ayant plus de frère, de prochain, d'ami, de société que moi-même"—Rousseau turns the Pascalian language of a "body" and its "members," as well as the language of *particularité* and

[101] Ibid.
[102] Ibid., pp. 243, 252.

amour-propre, against the Oratorians, against those who, in Rousseau's case, had forgotten Malebranchian charitable principles. Recalling that his former Oratorian friends could not forgive the appearance of *Emile*, Rousseau says bitterly that "individuals [*les particuliers*] die," but collective bodies do not. Thanks to the immortality of groups, the same passions are perpetuated. Even if all of Rousseau's individual enemies [*ennemis particuliers*] should die, the Oratorians *en masse* will live forever, and will give his memory no more peace than they gave him while he lived. The Oratorians, "whom I loved, whom I esteemed, in whom I had all confidence and never offended," will be "forever implacable" out of wounded *amour-propre*.[103] Thus, by an irony that must have been intentional, Rousseau turns Malebranchian phrases on the very religious order that Malebranche had done the most to make famous but that was now helping to destroy Rousseau's social "relations." In *Rousseau juge de Jean-Jacques* he adds that the Oratorians are "the most dangerous enemies that ever were, not only because of the body [*corps*] that they compose and the colleges that they govern; but because they know, even better than the philosophers, how to hide their cruel animosity under a sanctimonious and mealy-mouthed manner."[104]

In this bitter attack on immortal and self-loving collectivities, Rousseau finally abandons his own love for general "greater wholes" from which one derives his "life and being." In the sixth "Promenade" he says flatly that he is not sociable, that he has "never been suited to civil society, where all is annoyance, obligation, duty," that as soon as he "feels the yoke" of either necessity or men he becomes rebellious or, rather, becomes "nothing." Nonetheless, he

---

[103] Rousseau, *Rêveries du promeneur solitaire*, in *Oeuvres complètes*, Pléiade ed., vol. 1, pp. 995, 998-999. On Rousseau's *rapport* with the Oratorian order, see Gilbert Py, "Jean-Jacques Rousseau et la congrégation des prêtres de l'oratoire de Jesus," in *Annales de la Société Jean-Jacques Rousseau*, vol. 38, pp. 127ff.

[104] Rousseau, *Rousseau juge de Jean-Jacques*, p. 906n.

adds, reviving the language of body and members, the fault of his detractors and persecutors "has not been to exclude me from society as a useless member, but to proscribe me from it as a pernicious member." And that is a mistake, for Rousseau insists that, while he has done "very little good," there is also "no man in the world" who has done less evil.[105]

Rousseau's characteristic penchant for *généralité* is inextinguishable even in the *Rêveries*—though membership in a body is now ruled out, partly by Rousseau's own independence and partly by the machinations of enemies, both real and imagined. Generality as something *morally* valuable reappears in a different and nonpolitical guise in the fourth "Promenade," in which Rousseau is trying to decide whether lying is ever justifiable.

> General and abstract truth [e.g., concerning the permissible occasions of withholding the truth] is the most precious of all goods. Without it, man is blind; it is the eye of reason. By it, man learns to direct himself, to be what he ought to be, to do what he ought to do, to head toward his true end. Particular and individual truth is not always a good; it is sometimes an evil, very often an indifferent thing.[106]

The "general and abstract truth" concerning the permissibility of lying turns out to be the notion that "to make a lie innocent it is not enough that there be no express *intent* to harm." Malebranche had said in his letter of 1706 to André that a "little" lie is permitted, provided one does not will to undercut order,[107] but that is not enough for Rousseau, for whom "there must in addition be certainty that the error into which those spoken to are thrown [by one's well-meaning deceit] can harm neither them nor anyone in any

---

[105] Rousseau, *Promeneur solitaire*, p. 1059.
[106] Ibid., p. 1026.
[107] Malebranche, letter to Y. M. André, in *Oeuvres complètes*, vol. 19, pp. 742-743.

way whatever. It is rare and difficult to come by such certainty; thus it is difficult and rare for a lie to be perfectly innocent."[108]

In this passage Rousseau still clings to *généralité*—no longer the general will of the citizen, however, but the general devotion to not harming others ("do good to yourself with as little harm as possible to others") on the part of a moral person who is neither a Spartan nor a Roman nor a Genevan. There is always some tension in his thought between universalism and mere generality within some particular republic; when he speaks of "general" moral truth in the fourth "Promenade," he really means universally valuable moral truth valid for all persons *as such*, not as "Caius" or "Lucius."[109]

Even in the very late *Rousseau juge de Jean-Jacques*, in which the former *citoyen de Génève* describes himself again and again as "alone" and as cruelly persecuted by a league of malignant enemies, *généralité* is not really abandoned. In trying to distinguish between legal punishment and mere persecution, Rousseau contrasts "the judicial formalities which must be general and without exception" (even if "the whole city should have seen one man assassinate another in the public square") with the unjust proceedings of those who have condemned others (including Rousseau himself) without a real hearing. In this connection he imagines some highly particular principles that "overturn . . . all those of justice and morality":

Picture to yourself men who begin by putting on each a good and well-attached mask, who arm themselves to the teeth with iron, who then surprise their enemy, seize him from behind, strip him naked, tie up his body, his arms, his hands, his feet, his head so that he cannot move, stuff a gag in his mouth, put out his eyes, throw him to the ground, and finally spend their noble

---

[108] Rousseau, *Promeneur solitaire*, p. 1029.
[109] Rousseau, *Emile*, Pléiade ed., p. 249.

lives in massacring him gently, for fear that, dying of his wounds, he will cease to feel them too soon.[110]

This, Rousseau urges, is the "equity" and the "righteousness" of persecutors who trample the law's *généralité*.

In some other passages of *Rousseau juge de Jean-Jacques* Rousseau uses the received vocabulary of *causes générales* and *particulières*, as well as that of occasionalism, to throw light on his own case (the main one that interested him during his final fifteen years); the search after truth becomes the search after persecutors. Asking how an "envenomed hatred" for himself was fanned into flames by the shadowy *marches souterraines* of his adversaries, Rousseau says that he has uncovered the *cause secrète* that drove the authors of the "conspiracy" to a fury:

> The path that J.-J. had taken was too contrary to their own for them to be able to pardon him for giving an example which they did not want to follow, and for occasioning [*d'occasioner*] comparisons which it did not suit them to suffer. Besides these general causes [*ces causes générales*] . . . this primitive and radical hatred of these ladies and gentlemen had other [causes that are] *particulières* and relative to each individual, which it is neither suitable to state nor easy to believe, and so I will refrain from speaking of them; but the force of their effects are too much felt for one to be able to doubt their reality.[111]

Remembering politics in the midst of paranoia, Rousseau makes it clear that it was precisely his own search after *le bien général* that excited a "violent animosity" against him: the "authors of the plot" saw Rousseau "will and follow neither party nor sect, [saw him] say only what seemed to him true, good, useful to men, without consulting therein his own advantage or that of anyone *en particulier*." Rous-

[110] Rousseau, *Rousseau juge de Jean-Jacques*, pp. 731, 756.
[111] Ibid., p. 883.

seau's taking the high road was "the great source of their hatred"; they could not forgive him for failing to "ply his morality for his profit, like themselves," for "clinging so little to his [own] interest and to theirs." Rousseau had advanced "general truths [*des vérités générales*]" that had proven intolerable to "these people so eaten up by self-love," particularly men of letters.[112]

In order to make Rousseau as hateful to the public as he already was to themselves, his literary enemies "began by denaturing all his principles, by transmogrifying a severe republican into a seditious muddle-head, his love of lawful liberty into an unbridled license, and his respect for the laws into an aversion to princes." These enemies, "vulgar men incapable of noble and elevated feelings," could never imagine disinterested sentiments in anyone else: "not being able to believe that the love of justice and of the public good could excite such zeal," Rousseau's detractors "always searched for personal motives, like those which they themselves hid." Since Rousseau had revealed to all "this pretended social order which actually covers the cruelest disorders" (here a trace of left-Malebranchism briefly reappears), his persecutors had stirred up against him an *animosité générale* through their malignant *soin particulier*. This animosity, "so lively and so general," which aimed *particulièrement* at his defamation, arose from resentment of "the reproaches that he had levelled against his contemporaries": "the public knaves, the intriguers, the ambitious whose manoeuvres he uncovers, the passionate destroyers of all religion, of all conscience, of all liberty, of all morality, stung to the quick by his censures, must hate him."[113]

While Rousseau has begun by searching for the *causes générales* and *particulières* of his own miseries, for the "occasions" of real and imagined persecutions, his love of moral-political *généralité* always reemerges: his own particular

[112] Ibid., p. 886.
[113] Ibid., p. 887–889.

sufferings lead him to more general reflections on the wretchedness of all social victims. Since he was actually chased out of both France and Switzerland for his views,[114] who is to say that his *recherche de le généralité* was not perhaps the *cause occasionnelle* of his misfortunes, particularly of his being stateless—a man without a country—after 1763?

It is no small irony that the Republic of Letters, which Rousseau maligned directly in *Arts and Sciences* and tacitly in *Du contrat social*, was the only social body of which he was really capable of being a "citizen." But Rousseau could scarcely have relished being told this before 1763, when he still styled himself *citoyen de Génève*;[115] least of all could he have enjoyed being told it (as he actually was) by Voltaire, who had removed to Geneva in 1755—though as mere *habitant*, not as *citoyen*. To make the irony more barbed, Voltaire could not resist referring to the Malebranche whose language reappeared not just in Rousseau (in a *volonté générale* no longer God's but still divine), but also in Voltaire's own thoroughly Malebranchian notions of nature and grace. It did *not* reappear in Voltaire's politics, where *lumière*, anticlericalism, and the overcoming of superstition left no room for mere *généralité.*

Voltaire could sometimes make jokes about the Republic of Letters at Rousseau's expense by reminding him of the Malebranchism that they shared (at least up to a point). Reacting to the appearance of the *Discourse on Inequality* ("one wants to walk on all fours when he reads your work"), Voltaire tells Rousseau that "letters nourish the soul, rectify it, console it; they will even make your glory while you are writing against them. You are like Achilles, who lost his temper with glory, and like Père Malebranche, whose bril-

---

[114] Rousseau, *Les Confessions*, Pléiade ed., pp. 576ff. See also the appended notes by Gagnebin and Raymond, pp. 1557ff.

[115] On the title page of *Inégalité*, for example; see Rousseau, *Inégalité*, p. 125.

liant imagination wrote against the imagination."[116] An ancient and a modern: Voltaire calculated nicely to pique the Rousseau who could call himself "a modern who has an ancient soul."[117]

In a sense, Voltaire was entitled to make Malebranchian jokes against Rousseau, for much of Voltaire's thought strongly reflects—sometimes almost transcribes—the Oratorian's ideas. To be sure, Voltaire doubted that anyone could *prove* that "we see all things in God"—though he added that there is *quelque chose de sublime* in this "daring" notion (*Le Philosophe ignorant*, chapter 21)[118]—but what he says about "grace" and "miracles" could almost pass for additional "additions" to the *Traité de la nature et de la grâce*. In the *Dictionnaire philosophique* Voltaire urges that all theologians (Malebranche evidently excepted) have been mistaken about grace, thanks to having reasoned "following a principle [that is] evidently false."

> They have supposed that God acts in particular ways [*par des voies particulières*]. Now an eternal God without general, immutable and eternal laws, is a being of reason, a phantom, a fabulous God. . . .
>
> The universal theologian, that is to say the true philosopher, sees that it is contradictory that nature not act by the simplest means. . . .
>
> Why would the absolute Master of all have been more concerned to direct the interior of a single man than to conduct the rest of entire nature? Through what *bizarrerie* would he change something in the heart of a Courlander or a Biscayan, while he changes nothing in the laws that he has imposed on the stars?
>
> How pitiful to suppose that he continually makes,

---

[116] Voltaire, letter to Rousseau (August 1755), cited in *Rousseau: Oeuvres complètes*, du Seuil ed., vol. 2, pp. 268–269.

[117] In the *Polysynodie* (p. 421) Rousseau speaks of "quelques modernes qui avaient des âmes anciennes"; he himself is almost certainly the principal *moderne* of whom this is true.

[118] Cited in Alquié, *Malebranche* (Paris: Seghers, 1977), p. 82.

unmakes, remakes feelings in us! And what audacity to believe ourselves exceptional among all beings![119]

If this passage could almost serve as an addition to *Nature et grâce*, this is because Voltaire calls divinely made natural laws not merely "general" and "simple" (simple *malebranchisme*) but also "immutable" and "eternal." For Malebranche himself, that confuses the arbitrary laws of nature and grace with eternal and immutable *rapports de grandeur* and *rapports de perfection*;[120] for him it is Spinozism to call laws governing nature "eternal," since it destroys Creation—even if Creation, for Malebranche, is embarrassingly particularistic.

Voltaire's view of miracles is again shaped by a demi-Malebranchism. "Is it not the most absurd of follies," he asks, "to imagine that the infinite Being should, in favor of three or four hundred ants . . . transpose the eternal working of these immense springs which make the universe move?" Supposing that God "had willed to single out a small number of men by particular favors [*par des faveurs particulières*]," would it be necessary that he change "what he has established for all times and for all places? He certainly has no need of this change, of this inconstancy, to favor his creatures; his favors are in the laws themselves. He foresaw all and arranged all for them."[121] These last phrases depart from Malebranche, who will not say that useless grace and useless rain favor humanity particularly. For Voltaire, nature itself is a kind of "grace," so that one might say *nature est grâce* sooner than *nature et grâce*.

While Voltaire insists on general lawfulness in nature, uninterrupted by miracles or *des faveurs particulières*, he seems not to carry this over into politics. If one stresses *loi* and *généralité* and fulminates against "particular favors" in political theory, one becomes a Rousseauean, which is just

[119] Ibid., p. 84.
[120] Malebranche, in *Oeuvres complètes*, vol. 5, p. 18.
[121] Cited in Alquié, *Malebranche*, p. 83.

what Voltaire never became. (Might Voltaire have thought or feared that Rousseau was wrong in viewing the law's generality as a sufficient guarantee against the barbarism and cruelty that he so eloquently denounces in *Prix de la justice*?[122] *Généralité* is a formal standard, and, as Hegel observed in attacking Kant, anything can be generalized if one is willing to endure the consequences.)[123] Voltaire preserves the Malebranchian *généralité* that governs nature and grace; the equally Malebranchian *moral* notion of *volonté générale* seems to have been as unimportant to him as it was central to Rousseau.

It is not just Rousseau's political writings that reflect seventeenth-century philosophy, Malebranchism in particular. It is true that one does not usually think of Rousseau as a science writer, notwithstanding his late botanical studies. Nevertheless, when he does write on a scientific subject, as in the *Institutions chymiques* (c. 1747), he uses the notions of *généralité* and *particularité* as much as in the realm of nature as in that of grace; as in Malebranche, generality and simplicity have equal weight for Rousseau in *la physique* and in *la morale*.[124]

This is especially clear in the fine set piece called "Of the Mechanism of Nature," with which Rousseau opens book 2 of the *Institutions chymiques*. Beginning with an analogy between nature and the opera ("in our opera-theaters . . . each gives his attention to a particular object; rarely is there someone who appreciates the whole"), he goes on to complain that even scientists become so obsessed with particu-

---

[122] Voltaire, *Prix de la justice et de l'humanité*, in *Oeuvres complètes de Voltaire* (Brussels: Ode et Wodon, 1828), vol. 34, pp. 1ff.

[123] Hegel, *Philosophy of Right*, T. M. trans. Knox (Oxford: Clarendon Press, 1942), pp. 89-90.

[124] Rousseau, *Institutions chymiques*, in *Annales de la Société Jean-Jacques Rousseau*, vol. 13, pp. 44ff. For a good appreciation of this important early work, see Pierre Burgelin, *La Philosophie de l'éxistence de J.-J. Rousseau* (Paris: Presses Universitaires de France, 1952), pp. 412-413.

larities ("des Papillons, des Mouches") that nature in its totality escapes them altogether: "But if each part, which has only a particular function [*une fonction particulière*] and a relative perfection, is capable of delighting with astonishment and admiration those who take the trouble to consider it correctly, how [much finer] must it be for those who know the relations of all the parts and who thereby judge the general harmony [*l'harmonie générale*] and the operation of the whole mechanism[?]"[125] Here, inverting Pascal, one must imagine a body full of nonthinking "members." Plainly, it is a fault to let *particularité* obscure one's view of the *rapports* of the parts in an *harmonie générale* (a perfectly Malebranchian thought that also informs the *Jugement* of St. Pierre's *Polysynodie*).

Malebranchism is even more evident in Rousseau's remarks about the God who must have produced this *harmonie générale*. Setting out with the thought that "an intelligent Being is the active principle of all things," Rousseau goes on to urge that, while it is true that such a being "could no doubt have produced and preserved the universe by the immediate concourse of his power and will alone" (that is, through a multiplicity of *volontés particulières*), it was nonetheless "more worthy of his wisdom to establish general laws [*des loix générales*] . . . whose effect is alone sufficient for the preservation of the world and all that it contains."[126] This is simply Malebranche's *Nature et grâce* recapitulated; moreover, the notion that general laws are "worthy" of God's "wisdom" anticipates St. Preux's defense of Malebranchian *généralité* in *La Nouvelle Héloïse*.[127]

When it comes to *knowing* (adequately) the general laws of nature, Rousseau is instantly more cautious—as he was to be, later, in *Lettres écrites de la montagne*, in which he insists that miracle-recognizers must know what is natural and what supernatural. "It would be necessary to know the

<hr/>

[125] Rousseau, *Institutions chymiques*, p. 45.
[126] Ibid., p. 46.
[127] Rousseau, *La Nouvelle Héloïse*, p. 671.

structure of the universe better than we do," he admits, "in order to determine which are the first and most general of these laws [of nature]; perhaps they are all reducible to a single one." But if general natural laws are reducible to one only, it is hard to see how that can be simple Cartesian motion: "we see well enough that movement is the universal agent . . . but when Descartes claimed to draw from this one principle the generation of the universe, he built a system singular for its ridiculousness" that "armed" doctrinaire materialists with absurd ideas of self-moved matter. Movement alone, Rousseau complains, will never be able to produce "the least of all the plants, nor the most vile insect"; anticipating the argument of Kant's *Critique of Judgment*, he insists that "the construction of an organized body through laws of movement [alone] is a chimera that one is forced to leave to those who content themselves with words."[128] Despite these fascinating intimations of Kant, the crucial point of the *Institutions chymiques* remains that *harmonie générale* is the *vérité* to be *recherché*, even if one does not yet know that general harmony perfectly. Malebranche would never have countenanced Rousseau's harsh words about Descartes. Nevertheless, he would have recognized the rest of the opening of book 2 of the *Institutions chymiques*, for Malebranche and Rousseau both search after generality in nature and in grace.

This is nowhere more evident than in Rousseau's *Lettre à Voltaire sur la Providence* (1756), in which *particularité* is subordinated to *généralité* in understanding both nature and human affairs.[129] In his *Poème* on the disastrous 1755 Lisbon earthquake, Voltaire had ridiculed the Leibnizian notion of a *Providence générale* in which "all is well," complaining that

[128] Rousseau, *Institutions chymiques*, p. 47. For a comparison of Rousseau's and Kant's use of teleology in biology, see the author's *Kant's Political Philosophy* (Totowa, N.J.: Rowman and Littlefield, 1983), pp. 72-73.

[129] For a superb study of this *Lettre*—including the text actually sent to Voltaire, as well as all important manuscript variations—see R. A. Leigh, "Letter to Voltaire," pp. 247ff. The author is indebted to George A. Kelly for insisting on the importance of this *Lettre*.

la mort met le comble aux maux que j'ai soufferts,
Le beau soulagement d'être mangé de vers.[130]

In his response, Rousseau taxes the poet with forgetting the Malebranchian *généralité* that Voltaire himself had insisted on:

That the body of a man should nourish worms, wolves or plants is not, I grant, a compensation for the death of this man; but if in the system of the universe it is necessary to the conservation of the human race that there be a circulation of substance between men, animals and vegetables, then the particular ill [*mal particulier*] of an individual contributes to the general good [*le bien général*]. I die, I am eaten by worms, but my children, my brothers will live as I have lived; my cadaver will enrich the earth whose products they will eat.[131]

Rousseau immediately and characteristically gives this consoling generality a political turn, saying that a man's earth-enriching death will produce, "by the order of nature and for all men," that which was done voluntarily by the legendary ancient heroes—Codrus, Curtius, the Decii, the Spartan Leonidas—who sacrificed themselves for the good of "une petite partie des hommes."[132] (Since those ancient patriots sacrificed themselves *volontairement* for *le bien général*, they obviously had a *volonté générale*—the will that one has "as a citizen.")[133]

The same *bien général* that Rousseau sees as the object of the will of ancient citizens he also sees writ large in the universe itself, much as Plato had seen the harmonious *psyche*

---

[130] Voltaire, *Poèmes sur le désastre de Lisbonne et sur la loi naturelle* (1756), vv. 99-100, cited in Rousseau, *Religious Writings*, p. 42 n. 1.

[131] Rousseau, *Letter to Voltaire on Providence*, in *Religious Writings*, p. 42.

[132] Ibid. As Grimsley points out in his notes, Marcus Curtius threw himself into a chasm that opened in the Roman Forum (362 B.C.) after the seers had said that it would never close until Rome's most valuable treasure (a brave citizen) was cast into it. Leonidas, King of Sparta, was killed at the battle of Thermopylae (480 B.C.).

[133] Rousseau, *Du contrat social*, p. 35.

of the polis member writ large in the "harmony of the spheres":[134]

> [One must] distinguish with care between *le mal particulier*, whose existence no philosopher has ever denied, and the general evil that optimism denies. It is not a question of knowing whether each of us suffers or not, but whether it is good that the universe be, and whether our ills [*maux*] were inevitable in its constitution. . . . Instead of *all is well* [*tout est bien*], it would perhaps be better to say, *the whole is well* [*le tout est bien*], or *all is well for the whole* [*tout est bien pour le tout*].[135]

Rousseau believes that the soul's immortality helps us to resign ourselves to worms and wolves in the *économie universelle*: "If my soul is immortal, thirty years of life are nothing for me and are perhaps necessary to maintain the universe." "I hope," he says finally, "and hope embellishes everything."[136] His central point is still clear: whether one gives oneself up to worms in the realm of *la physique* or, emulating Curtius, throws oneself into a chasm in the Roman Forum in the realm of *la morale*,[137] the *bien général* of the whole outweighs every *mal particulier*. At least one can believe in a *Providence bienfaisante* if mortals are immortal: "I feel it, I believe it, I want it, I hope for it, I shall defend it til my last breath."[138]

That felt, hoped-for immortality also helps Rousseau to resolve a Malebranchian dilemma that he had stated in an earlier treatment of optimism and divine *Providence générale*, his letter of 1742 on Pope's *Essay on Man*. In that letter Rousseau, echoing Malebranche's obsession with *rapports*, had said that "there is no relation at all between the finite and

---

[134] See R. L. Nettleship, *Lectures on the Republic of Plato*, ed. Charnwood (London: Macmillan, 1929), pp. 355ff.

[135] Rousseau, *Letter to Voltaire on Providence*, pp. 42-43.

[136] Ibid., p. 50.

[137] See note 132.

[138] Rousseau, *Letter to Voltaire on Providence*, p. 51.

the infinite [*il n'y a point de rapport du fini à l'infini*]";[139] in the *Traité de la nature et de la grâce* Malebranche had urged that, since "there is no relation between the infinite and the finite," God cannot produce a finite world unless it is redeemed by Christ.[140] Since Rousseau viewed Christ sooner as an *homme de bonne société* than as Savior, he could hardly use him to fill the gap between finitude and infinity. In the *Letter to Voltaire on Providence*, what justifies a finite world is not Jesus but the feeling of finite, mortal beings that their existence is worthwhile *provided* that their immortal souls escape the operations of worms and wolves: "For him who feels his existence it must be better to be than not to be. But one must apply this rule to the total duration of each sensible being, and not to some particular moment of his duration, such as human life; which shows how much the question of Providence depends on that of the soul's immortality."[141] If one sees beyond particular moments, if one can believe in immortality, then one can "save" *Providence générale* and a finite world in a non-Malebranchian, Christ-free redemption. Yet Malebranche himself supplies some of the questions that Rousseau will answer in a non-Malebranchian way.

Rousseau's *recherche de la généralité*, particularly in politics, is not without its difficulties, and his reflection and trans-

---

[139] Rousseau, *A Letter about Pope's Essay on Man*, in *Religious Writings*, p. 20. Rousseau wholly approved these lines from Pope's *Essay on Man I*:

> But errs not Nature from this gracious end,
> From burning suns when livid deaths descend,
> When earthquakes swallow, or when tempests sweep
> Towns to one grave, whole nations to the deep?
> "No" ('tis replied) "the first Almighty Cause
> Acts not by partial, but by general laws. . . ."

Cited in Alexander Pope, *Selected Poetry and Prose*, ed. W. K. Wimsatt, Jr. (New York: Holt, Rinehart and Winston, 1965), p. 133.

[140] Malebranche, *Nature et grâce*, in *Oeuvres complètes*, vol. 5, pp. 11-13.

[141] Rousseau, *Letter to Voltaire on Providence*, p. 45.

formation of seventeenth-century theological notions is perhaps not always advantageous. No one has seen this more clearly than the Italian scholar Alberto Postigliola in a fine essay entitled "De Malebranche à Rousseau: Les Apories de la volonté générale et la revanche du 'raisonneur violent.' "[142]

Postigliola begins by uncovering Malebranchian themes "of a philosophical and epistemological character" that he later finds echoed in Rousseau. He especially stresses Malebranche's "important depreciation of that which is limited, finite, particular" accompanied by the magnification of "that which is universal, constant, general"—particularly of a general order ordained by a God whose rational, non-arbitrary authority operates through "the principle of the simplicity of means." Without claiming that Rousseau's account of a just human society "reflects à la lettre" Malebranche's model of a just universe, Postigliola still finds striking parallels: in Malebranche "we have . . . the universal and sovereign divine reason, which acts through general wills . . . that conform to general laws which it establishes itself"; in Rousseau "we have the sovereignty of the *moi commun* which is exercised through general wills . . . which yield a [system of] legislation."[143] In Postigliola's view, sometimes Rousseau's reflection of Malebranchian themes leads to an unfortunate if interesting result: Rousseau, having appropriated Malebranche's notion of justice ("understood as a rationalist and 'geometrizing' generality") committed the "unforgivable" error of forgetting that the general will of a people lacks the divine attribute of infinity. "The error of Rousseau," Postigliola concludes, "consisted precisely in using the epistemological categories of Malebranche . . . while continuing to speak of a generality of the will which could not exist in reality as 'unalterable and pure' unless it were the will of an infinite being.

[142] Postigliola, "De Malebranche à Rousseau," passim.
[143] Ibid., pp. 132, 135.

. . . In the Rousseauean city, generality cannot fail to be finite, since it can be no more than a sort of finite whole, if not a heterogeneous sum."[144]

Postigliola's historical inquiries into the *provenance* of *volonté générale* cast valuable new light on the still-obscure history of the general will before Rousseau. They serve to remind that the argument that generality is good and particularism bad—an argument that gives shape to most of Rousseau, some of Kant,[145] and even part of Hegel—really has its origins in the late seventeenth century in the arguments between Malebranche, Pascal, Fénelon, Bossuet, Arnauld, Leibniz, and Bayle. Without knowing this, how could one make sense of Hegel's claim, in section 140 of the *Philosophy of Right*, that hypocrisy is "knowledge of the true general [or universal]" coupled with "volition of the particular which conflicts with this generality"—a particular willing that is "evil in character"? (Hegel immediately goes on to cite Pascal's *Lettres provinciales*, then relates the struggle

---

[144] Postigliola's article has the great merit of proving that the history of *volonté générale* is of philosophical importance—that one may be able to understand some of Rousseau's arguments better if one knows the provenance of "general will." See "De Malebranche à Rousseau," p. 137.

[145] Particularly the Kant of *Critique of Judgment*, part 1 ("Aesthetic Judgment"), 40: "[It] indicates a man of enlarged mind if he detaches himself from the subjective personal conditions of his [aesthetic] judgment . . . and reflects upon his own judgment from a general standpoint [*aus einem allgemeinen Standpunkte*] (which he can only determine by shifting his ground to the standpoint of others)." Immanuel Kant, *Kritik der Urteilskraft*, in *Immanuel Kants Werke*, ed. Ernst Cassirer (Berlin: Bruno Cassirer Verlag, 1922), vol. 5, p. 369. Ingenious but misguided is the attempt of Hannah Arendt, *Lectures on Kant's Political Philosophy* (Chicago: University of Chicago Press, 1983), to "find" Kant's "unwritten" political philosophy in "Aesthetic Judgment" 's notion of an intersubjective "general standpoint"; mere generality is not sufficient for the Kant who could say that "true politics cannot take a single step without first paying homage to morals"—to the categorical imperative enjoining respect for persons as ends-in-themselves. Since, however, Arendt cannot share Kant's belief in "apodictic" moral certainty, she wants to reconstruct a quasi-Kantian politics based on the intersubjectivity and generality of aesthetic judgment. This will not do as a reading of Kant *an sich*, whatever merits it might have.

between the general and the particular to "the old questions about efficacious grace.")[146]

A mere citation of Pascal, of course, does not necessarily indicate a perfectly sympathetic understanding of the whole of French philosophy, and one can wonder whether Hegel does not occasionally place more distance between his own political thought and that of Rousseau than is warranted. After all, Rousseau would agree with Hegel's assertion, in the Preface to the *Philosophy of Right*, that human thought is "perverted into wrong" if it "knows itself to be free only when it diverges from what is generally recognized and valid [*Allgemein-Anerkannten*], and when it has discovered how to invent for itself some particular character." This sounds like, and is, a Teutonic echo of the *Economie politique*. Moreover, Rousseau would find little to reject—though much to reword—in Hegel's further claim that in the "ethical substantial order . . . the self-will of the individual has vanished together with his private conscience which had claimed independence and opposed itself to the ethical substance," so that there is finally an "identity of the general [or universal] will with the particular will [*Identität des allgemeinen und besonderen Willens*]."[147]

If Hegel praises Rousseau for correctly "adducing the will as the principle of the state" (rather than falling back on "gregarious instinct" or "divine authority"), if he congratulates him for seeing that "the will's activity consists in annulling the contradiction between subjectivity and objectivity and giving its aims an objective instead of a subjective character, while at the same time remaining by itself even in objectivity," he also, rather surprisingly, accuses Rousseau of deifying "the will of a single person in his own private self-will, not the absolute or rational will."[148] This

---

[146] Hegel, *Grundlinien der Philosophie des Rechts*, in *Sämtliche Werke*, ed. H. Glockner (Stuttgart: Frommanns Verlag, 1952), vol. 7, pp. 205–206.

[147] Hegel, *Philosophy of Right*, pp. 4, 142.

[148] Ibid., pp. 156, 32-33.

seems unjust, even perverse, if it is true that Rousseauean *volonté générale* is neither merely private nor simply rational—that it is general rather than universal, Lycurgus-shaped rather than reason-ordained. Hegel speaks as if there were nothing *between* the private and capricious on the one hand, and the rational and universal on the other; that simply rules out Rousseau's distinctive mediation between subjective egoism and objective "higher" will. Thus when Hegel says in section 258 of the *Philosophy of Right* that Rousseau's " 'general will' . . . reduces the union of individuals in the state to a contract and therefore to something based on their arbitrary wills," he neglects (generally, willfully) Rousseau's heroic effort to transform traditional Lockean contractarianism into a notion of educated, no-longer-fraudulent consent at the end of civic time, after the general will is finally as "enlightened" as it was always "right." He does injustice to Rousseau's valiant striving to transcend arbitrariness by bringing each denatured citizen to think of himself, *à la* Pascal, as part of a greater whole. Hegel thought he saw in Rousseau the embryo of Robespierre, the germ of the Terror: "The phenomena which [Rousseaueanism] has produced both in men's heads and in the world are of a frightfulness parallel only to the superficiality of the thoughts on which they are based."[149] This reading of Rousseau is itself (arguably) superficial; Rousseau, not unlike Hegel, wanted citizens to embrace a concrete universal—the polity—not mere Kantian universalizing of maxims through apolitical "good will."[150] The gap between Hegel and Rousseau is much exaggerated by Hegel himself, who, in Shklar's words, "refused to honor his debt to Rousseau."[151]

[149] Ibid., pp. 157, 33.
[150] See George A. Kelly, *Hegel's Retreat from Eleusis* (Princeton: Princeton University Press, 1978), pp. 55ff., for a fine account of Hegel's critique of Kant.
[151] Judith N. Shklar, *Freedom and Independence: A Study of the Political Ideas of Hegel's 'Phenomenology of Mind'* (Cambridge: Cambridge University

If Hegel knew that *généralité* had been launched by Pascal and deepened by Rousseau, and if he also used the notion of generality in a wholly favorable sense (the "deep insight" of Hegel's general class of enlightened civil servants springs to mind), then one cannot stop inquiry with the general will *before* Rousseau, for there is plainly a general will *after* Rousseau, not least in Hegel. But that is a question for another day.

———

At least Hegel was clear that the idea of *volonté générale* constitutes the heart of Rousseau's social theory. Indeed, it is scarcely open to doubt that the notions of "will" and "generality" are central to Rousseau's moral and political philosophy. Without will there is no self-determination, no moral causality, no obligation; without generality the will may be capricious, egoistic, self-loving, "willful."

Rousseau shared with modern individualist thinkers the conviction that all political life is conventional, and that it can be made obligatory only through voluntary, individual consent. Despite the fact that he sometimes treats moral ideas as if they simply "arise" in a developmental process, in the course of "socialization,"[152] he often, particularly when speaking of contract and obligation, falls back on the view that the wills of free men are the "causes" of duties and of legitimate authorities. Thus, in an argument against obligations based on slavery in *Du contrat social*, Rousseau urges that "to deprive your will of all freedom is to deprive your actions of all morality," that the reason one can derive no notion of right or morality from mere force is that "to

---

Press, 1976), p. 207. Invaluable for its treatment of Hegel's views on Rousseau and Kant.

[152] See particularly Rousseau's *Lettre à Monseigneur de Beaumont*, in *Oeuvres complètes*, du Seuil ed., vol. 3, pp. 340ff., esp. p. 348: "My feeling is, then, that the human mind, without progress, without instruction, without cultivation, and such as it is when it leaves the hands of nature, is not in a condition to elevate itself to sublime ideas by itself . . . ; but that these ideas are presented to us in proportion as our mind is cultivated."

yield to force is an act of necessity, not of will."[153] In *Inéga-lité*, in a passage that almost prefigures Kant, he insists on the importance of free agency, arguing that, while physics or natural science might explain the "mechanism of the senses," it could never make intelligible "the power of will-ing or rather of choosing"—a power in which "nothing is to be found but acts which are purely spiritual and wholly in-explicable by the laws of mechanism." It is this power of willing, rather than reason, that distinguishes men from beasts.[154] In the unpublished *Première Version* of *Du contrat social* he had even said that "every free action has two causes which concur to produce it: the first a moral cause, namely the will which determines the act; the other physi-cal, namely the power which executes it."[155] Rousseau, then, not only requires the idea of will as "moral causality"; he actually *uses* that term. If it is a term that prefigures Kant, it is also one that is reminiscent of Malebranche's distinc-tion between power and a moral will.

All of this is confirmed by what Rousseau says about will in *Emile*, in which he argues (through a speech put into the mouth of the Savoyard vicar) that "the motive power of all action is in the will of a free creature," that "it is not the word freedom that is meaningless, but the word neces-sity." The will is "independent of my senses": I "consent or resist, I yield or I win the victory, and I know very well in myself when I have done what I wanted and when I have merely given way to my passions." Man, he concludes, is "free to act," and he "acts of his own accord." Moreover, human free will does not derogate from Providence, but magnifies it, since God has "made man of so excellent a na-ture, that he has endowed his actions with that morality by which they are enobled." Rousseau cannot agree with those theologians (Hobbes, for example) who argue that

---

[153] Rousseau, *Du contrat social*, p. 26.

[154] Rousseau, *Discourse on Inequality*, in *The Social Contract and Discourses*, trans. G.D.H. Cole (New York: Everyman, 1950), p. 208.

[155] Rousseau, *Première Version*, in *Political Writings*, vol. 1, p. 499.

human freedom would diminish God by robbing him of his omnipotence: "Providence has made man free that he may choose the good and refuse the evil . . . what more could divine power itself have done on our behalf? Could it have made our nature a contradiction and have given the prize of well-doing to one who was incapable of evil? To prevent a man from wickedness, should Providence have restricted him to instinct and made him a fool?"[156]

For Rousseau, then, a determined human will—supposedly necessitated by a Hobbesian divine omnipotence—is not a theological requisite (any more than it had been for Malebranche); so much for the supposed "Calvinism" of one who is closer to being a Pelagian, as Pascal would have pointed out.[157] Hence Rousseau can understand "will" as an independent moral causality with the power to produce moral effects. He definitely thought that he had derived political obligation and rightful political authority from this power of willing: "Civil association is the most voluntary act in the world; since every individual is born free and his own master, no one is able, on any pretext whatsoever, to subject him without his consent." Indeed, the first four chapters of *Du contrat social* are devoted to refutations of erroneous theories of obligation and right—paternal authority, the "right of the strongest," and obligations derived from slavery. "Since no man," Rousseau concludes, "has natural authority over his fellow men, and since might in no sense makes right, convention remains as the basis of legitimate authority among men."[158]

Even if "will" is a central moral, political, and theological notion in Rousseau, this does not mean that he was willing to settle for just any will, such as a particular will or a "willful" will. Indeed, his constant aim is to generalize will,[159]

---

[156] Rousseau, *Emile*, trans. B. Foxley (London: Dent, 1911), pp. 243–244.

[157] Rousseau's argument about the efficacy of free will is rather close to the "Molinism" that Pascal rejects in the *Ecrits sur la grâce*, p. 134.

[158] Rousseau, *Du contrat social*, pp. 105, 27.

[159] On this point see the important passage in Rousseau's *Première Ver-*

either through civic education, as in the *Gouvernement de Pologne*, or through private education, as in *Emile*. In his view, ancient societies such as Sparta and republican Rome had been particularly adept at generalizing human will; through their simplicity, their morality of the common good, their civic religion, their moral use of fine and military arts, and their lack of extreme individualism and private interest, the city-states of antiquity had been political societies in the proper sense. In them man had been part of a larger whole from which he "in a sense receives his life and being";[160] on the other hand, modern prejudices, "base philosophy," and "passions of petty self-interest" assure that "we moderns can no longer find in ourselves anything of that spiritual vigor which was inspired in the ancients by everything they did."[161] This "spiritual vigor" may be taken to mean the avoidance through identity with a greater whole of that "dangerous disposition which gives rise to all our vices," self-love. Political education in an extremely unified state will "lead us out of ourselves" and provide us with a general will before the human ego "has acquired that contemptible activity which absorbs all virtue and constitutes the life and being of little minds."[162] It follows that the best social institutions "are those best able to denature man, to take away his absolute existence and give him a relative one, and to carry the self into the common unity."[163]

If these reflections on the pernicious character of self-love and particularism are reminiscent of Malebranche, and

---

sion: "That which generalizes the public will is not the quantity of voters, but the common interest which unites them." Furthermore, every authentic "act of sovereignty" involves an "agreement between the body politic and each of its members," which is "equitable because it is voluntary and general." This passage makes it clear that Rousseau attached great weight to both *will* and *generality*. In *Political Writings*, vol. 1, pp. 472-473.

[160] Rousseau, *Du contrat social*, p. 52.
[161] Rousseau, *Gouvernement de Pologne*, p. 430.
[162] Rousseau, *Economie politique*, in *The Social Contract and Discourses*, p. 308.
[163] Rousseau, *Emile*, excerpt in *Political Writings*, vol. 2, p. 145.

more distantly of Pascal,[164] it is in comparing Rousseau with Malebranche that an important difficulty arises. In Malebranche, God's will is essentially and naturally general; in Rousseau, men's will must be *made* general—a problem he more than once likens to the problem of squaring the circle. Yet one can reasonably ask: Is will still "will" (qua moral cause) if it must be transformed? Do Rousseau's notions of education—private and civic—leave will as the autonomous producer of moral effects that he originally defines it as?

To retain the moral attributes of will while doing away with will's particularity and selfishness and "willfulness"— to generalize this moral cause without destroying it—is one of the central problems of Rousseau's political and moral thought, and one that reflects the difficulty Rousseau found in making free will and rational, educative authority coexist in his political and moral thinking. Freedom of the will is as important to the morality of actions for Rousseau as for any traditional voluntarist, but he was suspicious of the very "faculty"—the only faculty—that could moralize. Thus he urges in the *Economie politique* that "the most absolute authority is that which penetrates into a man's inmost being, and concerns itself no less with his will than with his actions."[165] Can the will be both an autonomous moral cause *and* subject to the rationalizing influence of educative authority? Rousseau never settled this point altogether. Even Emile, the best educated of men, chooses to continue to accept the guidance of his teacher: "Advise and control us; we shall be easily led; as long as I live I shall need you."[166] How much more, then, do ordinary men need the guidance of a "great legislator"—the Numa, or the Moses, or the Lycurgus of whom Rousseau speaks so often[167]—when they em-

---

[164] Pascal goes well beyond Rousseau in calling the self "hateful"; see *Pensées*, in *Oeuvres*, vol. 2, passim.

[165] Rousseau, *Economie politique*, in *The Social Contract and Discourses*, p. 297.

[166] Rousseau, *Emile*, trans. Foxley, p. 444.

[167] Rousseau, *Gouvernement de Pologne*, pp. 427-430. See also Rousseau's

bark on the setting up of a system that will not only aid and defend but also moralize them! The relation of will to authority is one of the most difficult and inscrutable problems in Rousseau. The general will is dependent on "a union of understanding and will within the social body,"[168] but that understanding, which is provided by authority, weakens the idea of will as an autonomous "authorizing" faculty.

This notion of the relation of educative authority to will appears not just in Rousseau's theories of public or civic education, particularly in the *Economie politique* and the *Gouvernement de Pologne*,[169] but also in his theory of private education in *Emile*. In educating a child, Rousseau advises the tutor, "let him think he is master while you are really master." Then, "there is no subjection so complete as that which preserves the forms of freedom; it is thus that the will itself is taken captive."[170] One can hardly help asking what has become of will when it has been "taken captive," and whether it is enough to preserve the mere forms of freedom. On this point Rousseau appears to have been of two minds: the poor who agree to a social contract that merely legitimizes the holdings of the rich "preserve the forms of freedom," yet Rousseau dismisses this contract (in *Inégalité*) as a fraud.[171] Thus it cannot be the case—as John Charvet argues—that Rousseau simply was not "worried by the gap which opens up between the appearance and the reality of freedom."[172] At the same time, Charvet seems to have a point, since will is "taken captive" in *Emile* and "penetrated" by authority in the *Economie politique*; and neither notion is criticized by Rousseau, despite the Rousseauean dictum about depriving one's actions of morality if one deprives one's will of freedom. So one sees again why a gen-

early prize essay, *Discours sur la vertu du héros*, in *Oeuvres complètes*, du Seuil ed., vol. 2, pp. 118-120.

[168] Rousseau, *Du contrat social*, p. 51.

[169] See particularly Rousseau, *Gouvernement de Pologne*, pp. 437-443.

[170] Rousseau, *Emile*, trans. Foxley, p. 84; cf. p. 290.

[171] Rousseau, *Inégalité*, pp. 180-182.

[172] John Charvet, *The Social Problem in the Philosophy of Rousseau* (Cambridge: Cambridge University Press, 1974), p. 58.

eral will would appeal to him: capricious willfulness would be "canceled," will rationalized by authority, "preserved."[173]

If will in Rousseau is generalized primarily through an educative authority, so that will qua moral cause is not quite so free as he would sometimes prefer, it is at least arguable that any tension between will and the authority that generalizes it is only a provisional problem. Rousseau seems to have hoped that at the end of political time (so to speak) men would finally be citizens and would will only the common good in virtue of what they had learned *over* time; at the end of political time, they might actually be free, and not just "forced to be free."[174] At the end of its political education, political society would finally be in a position to say what Emile says at the end of his "domestic" education: "I have decided to be what you made me."[175] At this point of decision there would be a "union of understanding and will" in politics, but one in which "understanding" is not just the possession of a Numa or a Lycurgus. At this point, too, "agreement" and "contract" would have meanings; the general will, which is "always right," would be enlightened as well, and "contract" would go beyond being the mere rich man's confidence trick (legalizing unequal property) that it is in *Inégalité*. At the end of political time, the general will one has as a citizen would have become a kind of second nature, approaching the true naturalness of *volonté générale* in Malebranche's divine *modus operandi*. "Approaching," however, is the strongest term one can use, and the relation of will to the educative authority that generalizes it remains a central problem in Rousseau—the more so because he ordinarily denied that there is any natural authority on earth.[176]

---

[173] This, of course, is Hegel's language in the *Phenomenology of Mind*, p. 234: "The negation characteristic of consciousness . . . cancels in such a way that it preserves and maintains what is sublated, and therefore survives its being sublated."

[174] Rousseau, *Du contrat social*, p. 36.

[175] Rousseau, *Emile*, trans. Foxley, p. 435.

[176] Above all in *Du contrat social*, pp. 27ff.: "Since no man has natural au-

One may still ask: How can one reconcile Rousseau's insistence on an all-shaping educative authority with his equal insistence on choice and personal autonomy ("civil association is the most voluntary act in the world")? The answer is, precisely *through* his theory of education, which is the heart of his thought. At the end of civic time, when men have been denatured and transformed into citizens, they will finally have civic knowledge and a general will, just as adults finally have the moral knowledge and the independence that they (necessarily) lacked as children. For Rousseau there are unavoidable stages in all education, whether private or public: the child, he says in *Emile*, must first be taught necessity, then utility, and finally morality, in that inescapable order; and if one says "ought" to an infant he simply reveals his own ignorance and folly. This notion of necessary educational time, and of becoming what one was not, is revealed perfectly in Emile's utterance, "I have decided to be what you made me."[177] The statement is deliberately paradoxical, but it shows that the capacity to decide is indeed "made." (It is education that "forces" one to be free.) Similarly, Rousseau's "nations" are at first ignorant: "There is with nations, as with men, a time of youth, or, if you prefer, of maturity, for which we must wait before subjecting them to laws."[178] Waiting, however, requires time; autonomy arrives at the end of a process, and the general will is *at last* as enlightened as it was always right. On a close reading, Rousseau does not, as some of his critics allege, vibrate incoherently between Platonic education and Lockean voluntary agreement;[179] the *généralité* of antiquity and the *volonté* of modernity are fused by this "modern who has an ancient soul."

---

thority over his fellow-man, conventions alone remain as the basis of all legitimate authority among men."

[177] Rousseau, *Emile*, trans. Foxley, p. 435.

[178] Rousseau, *Du contrat social*, p. 56.

[179] Particularly Vaughan, in his Introduction to Rousseau's *Political Writings*, vol. 1, pp. 35ff.

Rousseau, then, uses the notion of general will precisely because it "conveys everything he most wanted to say"— though how one goes about "generalizing" will remains a problem; and he was able to use the Malebranchian term *volonté générale* because it was ready-made for his philosophical purposes.

One could, of course, arrive at a partial understanding of *volonté générale* and *volonté particulière* without knowing the entire history of those notions in Pascal, Malebranche, Leibniz, and Montesquieu. Yet it seems clear that, if one knows this history, one may avoid making certain claims about Rousseau that would not be made by one more fully informed. Thus, a contemporary interpreter of Rousseau holds that "as a term Rousseau's *general will* can obscure his non-individualist meaning, for the word will suggests the natural ego of a deliberative individual";[180] one would be less likely to make this claim if one saw that Rousseau belongs firmly to a moral tradition in which will is essential ("to deprive your will of all freedom is to deprive your actions of all morality"), and in which generalizing will does not necessarily produce non-individualism. Generality rules out *particularism*, not individualism; in Rousseau, an individual can and should have a general will. Thus Rousseau, following in a Malebranchian-Montesquieuean tradition, speaks against *volonté particulière*, not against *volonté individuelle*. The will of an individual can be either general or particular; if a general will were *not* the will of an individual, that individual qua citizen would have no obligations, since, according to Rousseau, "civil association is the most voluntary act in the world."[181] If one sees "general will" as obscuring Rousseau's meaning, then, one is likely to leave his notion of will out of account and to read an attack on particularism as if it were an attack on individuality. But if one sees that *volonté générale* is a certain kind of individual will—"the will one has as a citizen"—one will not oneself

---

[180] Stephen Ellenburg, *Rousseau's Political Philosophy: An Interpretation from Within* (Ithaca: Cornell University Press, 1976), p. 103n.
[181] Rousseau, *Du contrat social*, pp. 105, 28.

generate obscurities; if one knows that in Rousseau, as in Pascal, Malebranche, Leibniz, and Montesquieu, generality is the enemy of *particularisme*, not of individuality, one will be clear about Rousseau by remembering that he fits into a tradition that was hostile to *amour-propre*, not to "deliberative individuals."[182]

This is only a particular instance of a general point, namely, that knowledge of the history of philosophy may occasionally keep one from making purely analytical and nonhistorical mistakes—such as thinking that generality excludes individuality because it excludes particularity. It was not mere chance that led Rousseau to use the terminology of Pascal, Malebranche, Leibniz, and Montesquieu; the terminology that he used permitted him to draw distinctions—such as that between individuality and particularity—that he needed to draw. Since it was Malebranche, even more than Montesquieu, who most fully treated the relations between generality, particularity, individuality, and will, there is a sense in which he was Rousseau's nearest predecessor. If the notion of generality as the motive of divine will led Malebranche (to cite Fontenelle's elegant jest) to "des vues particulières sur la grâce,"[183] it was *grâce à* Malebranche that a ready-made notion of non-particular, non-willful will was available to Rousseau, who completed Montesquieu's conversion of the general will of God into the general will of the citizen.

[182] See Rousseau's perfectly clear argument in *Du contrat social* (p. 35): "Each individual may, as a man, have a *volonté particulière* contrary to or unlike the *volonté générale* which he has as a citizen." Here an individual can have either a particular or a general will.

[183] Fontenelle, "Eloge du Père Malebranche," in *Oeuvres complètes* (Paris, 1818), vol. 1, p. 205.

S I X

A BRIEF CONCLUSION

By now it should be clear that what holds together the tradition of French moral and political thought from Pascal to Rousseau, unifies it, and distinguishes it from either English or German practical thought, is the notion that *généralité* is good, *particularité* bad—that, if one is just, one will embrace the general good of the body, to which one will subordinate egoism and self-love. In the first instance this is traceable to 1 Corinthians 12, a passage much admired by the French Augustinians of the *grand siècle*, which insists that the foot and the eye must "realize" (in a double sense) their "membership"; this Pauline generality then received strong reinforcement from Descartes, who stressed the constant operation of simple, general laws in the governance of the universe, so that *scientific* generality came to the aid of *moral* generality. This comes out most clearly in Malebranche, who praises God's wisdom in operating simply and generally but also condemns the *morale particulière* and *raison particulière* of those who allow their individual passions to override *le bien général*.[1] For Malebranche, moral generality and scientific generality—St. Paul and Descartes—seem to belong together, as revealed by his characteristic assertion that, thanks to the generality of the universe's operation, we should not complain of divine injustice or incompetence if useless grace falls on hardened

---

[1] N. Malebranche, *Traité de morale*, in *Oeuvres complètes de Malebranche*, ed. André Robinet (Paris: Vrin, 1966), vol. 11, passim.

hearts as useless rain falls in the sea.[2] Pascal could not see things in this way; since, according to *pensée* no. 792 (Brunschvicg), "charity" is even further separated from mind (knowledge, science) than mind is from body, one cannot use Cartesian physics in the way that Malebranche does.

> The infinite distance between body and mind is a symbol of the infinitely more infinite distance between mind and charity; for charity is supernatural. . . .
>
> All bodies, the firmament, the stars, the earth and its kingdoms, are not equal to the lowest mind; for mind knows all these and itself; and these bodies nothing.
>
> All bodies together, and all minds together, and all their products, are not equal to the least feeling of charity. This is of an order infinitely more exalted.
>
> From all bodies together, we cannot obtain one little thought; this is impossible, and of another order. From all bodies and minds, we cannot produce a feeling of true charity; this is impossible, and of another and supernatural order.[3]

In Malebranche, by contrast, charity is finally equivalent to order (in which, *à la Phaedo*, mathematical and moral relations are timeless and changeless). This cannot be Pascal's view, though he speaks of "love" using the sublimated erotism of the *Phaedrus*—another side of Plato altogether.[4] Nonetheless, Pascal is as devoted to *généralité* in moral conduct as Malebranche; *pensées* nos. 472-483 make that wholly clear.

[2] Malebranche, *Traité de la nature et de la grâce*, in *Oeuvres complètes*, vol. 5, pp. 50-51.
[3] Blaise Pascal, *Pensées*, trans. W. F. Trotter, intro. T. S. Eliot (New York: Dutton, 1958), pp. 234-235. For a definitive commentary on this passage, see Nannerl O. Keohane, *Philosophy and the State in France* (Princeton: Princeton University Press, 1980), pp. 266-267.
[4] Plato, *Phaedrus*, in *Plato: The Collected Dialogues*, ed. E. Hamilton and H. Cairns, (Princeton: Princeton University Press, 1961), pp. 500-502. Certainly one can speak of "sublimated erotism" in both Pascal and Plato.

Soon enough one finds Rousseau saying that the general will—the will one has as a citizen, when one thinks of the common good and of civic membership—is "always right" (even if natural men lack a general will at the beginning of political time and must acquire such a will *over* time through a denaturing, antiparticularistic civic education supplied by a great legislator). In insisting on general will, of course, Rousseau is insisting on a kind of will that everyone *ought* to have—unless he is to be a self-sufficient, Stoic independent (in the manner of the opening books of *Emile*) or a hermit who loves men better when he is at a distance from them (in the manner of Rousseau himself). For all his links to Pascal and Malebranche, Rousseau would have said that neither of his predecessors had an adequate notion of human will, even if they did have some idea of the will of God (to save all men, for example). From a Rousseauean perspective, Pascal cannot really hope that all men (as body-members) will have the general will that they ought to have, because Pascal's own Augustinian theory of grace does not leave men sufficiently independent and self-determining to have a will. In the *First Writing on Grace* Pascal is clear that, while all men receive "sufficient" grace, that gift is rather inaptly named, since the elect need an "efficacious" grace—the gift of perseverance—that alone will really save them. Mere willing is not enough, for that is Pelagianism.[5] In Pascal one cannot say, *in magnis et voluisse sat est.*[6] From Rousseau's perspective, Pascal does not leave a voluntary embracing of *généralité* "in our power" (to recall

[5] Pascal, *Ecrits sur la grâce,* in *Oeuvres de Blaise Pascal,* ed. L. Brunschvicg (Paris: Librairie Hachette, 1914), vol. 11, pp. 146ff.

[6] A line cited by Hegel: "In great things it is enough to have willed." See *Philosophy of Right,* trans. T. M. Knox (Oxford: Clarendon Press, 1942), p. 252. (The original line is from Propertius—whose thought has been illuminated for the author by his friend and colleague Randall Colaizzi.) For a full treatment of Hegel's voluntarism, see the author's *Will and Political Legitimacy: A Critical Exposition of Social Contract Theory in Hobbes, Locke, Rousseau, Kant and Hegel* (Cambridge, Mass.: Harvard University Press, 1982), chapter 6.

Epictetus's phrase). Malebranchism suffers from a similar problem: if Malebranche's human beings are only the occasional causes of their own actions, while God acts as sole veritable *cause générale*—if a person cannot really will anything (such as *le bien général*), since for Cartesianism mind as thinking substance cannot modify body as extended substance—then one cannot have a general will (in particular) because one cannot have any will at all, except as a Malebranchian "immanent" power to suspend consent to a delectation.[7]

Rousseau, then, not only wants to secularize the general will, to turn it away from theology and from God's supposed wish to save all men; he wants to endow human beings with a will, a really efficacious power, that can then be subjected to the generalizing influence of civic education—a republican education that Montesquieu eloquently described but took to have vanished from the modern monarchical world. First *real* will, then *general* will; that is what Rousseau would say to his great predecessors.

This is not to say that Rousseau thought he knew perfectly what *la volonté* is; on the contrary, some of Malebranche's worries about the operation of "will" color even Rousseau's most extensive and important treatment of volition, in book 4 of *Emile*. But Rousseau never allowed the unavoidably incomplete knowledge of will to cast doubt on either the real existence or the moral necessity of this faculty; thus, he has the Savoyard vicar ask:

> How does a will produce a physical and corporeal action? I know nothing about that, but I experience in myself [the fact] that it produces it. I will to act, and I act; I will to move my body, and it moves; but that an inanimate body at rest should begin to move itself by itself, or produce movement—that is incomprehensible and unexampled. The will is known to me by its

---

[7] Malebranche, *Réflexions sur la prémotion physique*, in *Oeuvres complètes*, vol. 16, pp. 47-48.

acts, not by its nature. I know this will as motor cause, but to conceive matter as the producer of movement is clearly to conceive an effect without a cause, which is to conceive absolutely nothing.[8]

This doctrine, Rousseau has the vicar say, is admittedly obscure; but it "makes sense" and contains nothing repugnant to either reason or observation. (Malebranchian occasionalism is apparently repugnant to both, since Rousseau does not mention this alternative, with which he was surely acquainted.) "Can one say as much of materialism?" the vicar finally asks.[9]

The answer is clearly "No." That answer remained constant, seven years after *Emile*, when Rousseau wrote his magnificent *Lettre à M. de Franquières*, in which he urges his correspondent to abandon a materialism and a determinism that are fatal to morals.

Why do you not appreciate that the same law of necessity which, according to you, rules the working of the world, and all events, also rules all the actions of men, every thought in their heads, all the feelings of their hearts, that nothing is free, that all is forced, necessary, inevitable, that all the movements of man which are directed by blind matter, depend on his will only because his will itself depends on necessity; that there are in consequence neither virtues, nor vices, nor merit, nor demerit, nor morality in human actions, and that the words 'honorable man' or 'villain' must be, for you, totally devoid of sense. . . . Your honest heart, despite your arguments, declaims against your sad philosophy. The feeling of liberty, the charm of virtue, are felt in you despite you.[10]

Here, more than anywhere else in Rousseau, *le coeur a ses*

---

[8] Jean-Jacques Rousseau, *Emile* (Paris: Pléiade, 1959), p. 576.

[9] Ibid., pp. 576-577.

[10] Rousseau, *Lettre à M. de Franquières*, in *Lettres philosophiques*, ed. Henri Gouhier (Paris: Vrin, 1974), pp. 180-181.

raisons que la raison ne connaît point. But this Pascalian "heart" is used to defend a freedom of willing that Pascal himself might have called "Pelagian." And if that will can be generalized by a nonauthoritarian educative authority, the final product will be the realization of Rousseau's highest civic ideal: the *volonté générale* that one has as a citizen.

One can approach Rousseau along several spacious avenues, each one laden with real fruit. One can (and somewhere should) approach Rousseau as the high point of the social contract tradition—as the greatest successor to Hobbes and Locke—though here one would have to counterbalance Rousseau's pure contractarian claim that "civil association is the most voluntary act in the world"[11] with his idea that, at the beginning of political time, natural men do not yet have a civic general will and must therefore be denatured through a quasi-Platonic civic education that will bring them to choose the non-natural common good. On this view Rousseau will stand at the end of a particular path, even if Kant added some refinements to contractarianism.[12]

One can (and somewhere should) approach Rousseau not so much as the end of a developed tradition but as the beginning of those radical critiques of existing society that flower fully in Marx's hands, especially in the *Critique of the Gotha Program.*[13] Not that Rousseau, even in *Inégalité,* was a kind of pre-Marxist; he characteristically combined radical analysis (*Arts and Sciences* and *Inequality*) with cautious, con-

---

[11] Rousseau, *Du contrat social,* in *Political Writings,* ed. C. E. Vaughan (Oxford: Basil Blackwell, 1962), vol. 2, p. 105.
[12] For a fuller treatment of this point see the author's *Will and Political Legitimacy,* passim.
[13] Karl Marx, *Critique of the Gotha Program,* in *Karl Marx: Selected Writings,* ed. D. McLellan (Oxford: Oxford University Press, 1977), pp. 564ff. See the author's "Marx and Morality," in *Marxism,* ed. J. R. Pennock and John Chapman (New York: New York University Press, 1983), for a fuller treatment of *Gotha Program.*

servative prescription (*Gouvernement de Pologne*). But left-Rousseaueanism has authentic roots in the citizen of Geneva himself, even if Robespierre grew from those roots a plant that Rousseau would never have recognized.

One can (and somewhere should) approach Rousseau not so much as the terminator of a largely English contractarian tradition, or as the initiator of a largely German critical tradition, but as the outgrowth of a distinctively French tradition bequeathed to him by Pascal, Malebranche, Bayle, Bossuet, Fénelon, and Montesquieu. There are many good studies of Rousseau as the last contractarian, and as the first radical;[14] Rousseau the heir of France is little-known outside France. Clearly, though, the French theological and scientific tradition that had viewed *généralité* as the chief characteristic of God's will (in a general will to save all men) as well as the chief characteristic of a nature ruled by simple, constant, uniform general laws regularly producing all *effets particuliers* was inherited and transformed by Rousseau. For Rousseau cherished *généralité* in theology (where God ought to distribute graces equally, not by particular favors), in science (where miracles ought not to disturb the generality and simplicity of natural laws), in politics (where the general will of the sovereign people is always right), and even in the individual mind (where love of generally valuable truth should override one's mere *intérêt particulier*). Platonism had been held together by a mathematics-based *kosmos* or harmony, writ small in the individual psyche, larger in the well-ordered, consonant polis, largest in the harmony of the spheres that crowns the final book of *The Republic*;[15] Rousseaueanism derives its unity from generality, seen as a theological-scientific fact and as a moral-

[14] The most subtle reading of Rousseau as a (limited) pre-Marxist is that of Lionel Gossman, "Time and History in Rousseau," in *Studies on Voltaire and the 18th Century* (Banbury: Voltaire Foundation, 1975), vol. 30, pp. 311ff.

[15] See R. L. Nettleship, *Lectures on the Republic of Plato*, ed. Charnwood (London: Macmillan, 1929), pp. 308ff.

political imperative. To show that generality is not merely a civic ideal in Rousseau—that he also found lawful generality in nature and in God's operation, so that the cosmos is as generally lawful as the polis—would illustrate the overall coherence and unity of Rousseau's thought, which is frequently accused of unrigorous sentimentality. It is "the grandeur of generality" (in Samuel Johnson's phrase) that Rousseau cherishes—the same *généralité* that Dr. Johnson had found in Homer's epic poems: "His positions are general, and his representations natural, with very little dependence on local or temporary customs, on those changeable scenes of artificial life, which, by mingling original with accidental notions, and crowding the mind with images which time effaces, produce ambiguity . . . and obscurity."[16] For Johnson, time could not efface Homeric general nature; for Rousseau, it could not tarnish the efforts of Lycurgus and Moses to draw out a latent civic *volonté générale* that echoes an orderly nature.

What occasioned the transformation of divine *volonté générale* into civic *volonté générale* between 1662 and 1762? That depends, evidently, on a more general theory of the genesis and metamorphosis of ideas. If one is a Hegelian, one will perhaps speak of ideas realizing themselves (in both senses) over time as they "cancel" the discordant and "preserve" the real;[17] a Marxist who stands Hegelianism "right side up" might speak of changed ideas as superstructural, epiphenomenal reflections or echoes of changes in the causing (or at least conditioning) material substructure.[18] If one finds neither a Hegelian idealist nor a Marxian ideological "explanation" very explanatory, he may prefer to say

[16] Samuel Johnson, *Life of Pope*, cited in Jean H. Hagstrum, *Samuel Johnson's Literary Criticism* (Chicago: University of Chicago Press, 1967), p. 86.
[17] Hegel, *Philosophy of Right*, pp. 10-12.
[18] Marx, *Preface to a Critique of Political Economy*, in *Marx and Engels: Basic Writings*, ed. L. Feuer (New York: Anchor, 1959), pp. 42-43.

simply that between the seventeenth and eighteenth centuries there was a rising consciousness that ideas once imputed or ascribed to God, such as justice, goodness, wisdom, generality, and constancy, are merely moral ideals made yet more attractive by being translated to heaven. If one brings back to earth, back to the human world, moral ideas that really never left it at all, then one will perhaps say, with Kant, that "so far . . . as practical reason has the right to serve as our guide, we shall not look upon actions as obligatory because they are the commands of God, but shall regard them as divine commands because we have an inward obligation to them"—that we will be acting divinely only "insofar as we hold sacred the moral law" enjoining respect for persons as "objective ends" that "reason teaches us," and only by "furthering what is best *in the world*, alike in ourselves and in others."[19]

One cannot honestly say that this sort of Kantian consciousness manifests itself fully in Rousseau—though he did, like Malebranche, put the *idea* of divinity above mere Scripture. Rousseau was assuredly a more orthodox believer than Kant, and the deepest part of his consciousness was *self*-consciousness. (Who can even imagine Kant's *Confessions?*) Moreover, Rousseau's rejection of a reason-ordained *morale universelle* in the *Première Version du contrat social* rules out Kantianism in advance, since the categorical imperative is both rational and universal. Perhaps, then, the following explanation of Rousseau's civicization of *volonté générale*—an explanation neither Kantian nor Hegelian nor Marxian—will have to serve.

The mere venerability of *volonté générale* could by no means have induced Rousseau to make that notion the core of his thought; mere respect for Pascal, Malebranche, Bayle, and Montesquieu would not have been sufficient. In fact, Rousseau did not want to keep his whole "inherit-

---

[19] Immanuel Kant, *Critique of Pure Reason*, trans. Kemp Smith (London: Macmillan, 1963), A819/B847, p. 644.

ance." He had doubts about the rationalism of Malebranchian order, about the adequacy of Pascal's notion of human will, about Montesquieu's seemingly greater concern with *causes générales* than with *volontés générales*. But the fact that inherited general will could conjure up, simultaneously, a divine way of acting and the willing of Spartan *généralité*; that it could filter a century of French moral and political thought through many centuries of ancient thought, letting one stand on the shoulders of Pascal and Cato, Malebranche and Lycurgus, Montesquieu and Moses; that the *généralité* of no-longer-fraudulent, more-than-Lockean contract and the *généralité* of ancient Rome could help Rousseau to be a "modern who has an ancient soul"—all of this *together* was too much to be resisted, especially in view of the advantage of acceptance. The general will expresses so much for Rousseau—divinity, voluntariness, generality, Sparta, citizenship, equality, lawfulness, the common good, antiquity, modernity, Plato, Locke, Machiavellian civic *virtù*—that it is too resonant not to be heard. This is why Shklar is so profoundly right when she says that "the general will . . . conveys everything he most wanted to say."[20]

---

[20] Judith N. Shklar, *Men and Citizens: A Study of Rousseau's Social Theory* (Cambridge: Cambridge University Press, 1969), p. 184.

INDEX

Augustine, St. (*cont.*)
Augustine's defense of
Abraham, 15, 17 n. 44;
Enchiridion, 11, 17; God wills to
save all *kinds* of men
(*Enchiridion*), 11; interpretation
of Paul's "God wills that all men
be saved," 11–12; Jansenius'
interpretation of, 11–12;
Malebranche's interpretation of,
121, 124 and n. 70, 125; Pascal's
reading of, 14–17; struggle with
Pelagians, 5, 78
Augustinians, 251
Augustinus, see Jansenius,
Cornelius
Augustus (Roman Emperor), 215
Averroes, 125
Ayer, A. J., *Part of my Life*, xii n. 6

Baird, A.W.S., on Pascal's ethics,
24 n. 64
Barbeyrac, Jean, made Pufendorf
seem to be early theorist of
general will, 178–80; translator
of Leibniz' *Opinion on Principles
of Pufendorf*, 107
Barrière, Pierre, 139 n. 4
Bauni (Bauny), Étienne, 92
Bayle, Pierre, against
particularism, 83; compared to
Hobbes, 83–85; compared to
Montesquieu, 147; compared to
Rousseau, 82–85; converts
general will and particular will
into political ideas, 97–98;
critique of Jaquelot's
Malebranchism, 93–98; defends
Malebranche's *Nature et grâce*,
25, 80; doubts about general
will, 5, 89–91 (*Réponse aux
questions*); general will as good,
particular will as bad in
Commentaire philosophique, 87–89;
his Malebranchism in *Pensées
diverses*, 80–83; influence of
Arnauld, 90; on Louis XIV's
particularism in *La France toute
catholique*, 85–87; on revocation

of Edict of Nantes, 85–86;
politics should be governed by
general laws, 82–83; rejection of
Malebranchian general will in
Entretiens, 93–98; secularizes
theological ideas, 98, 138;
treated by Rousseau in *Émile*,
199–202; treatment of Abraham,
Sarah, and King David in
Dictionnaire, 91–93
Beaumont, Christophe de,
Archbishop of Paris, 196, 241n
Beitzinger, A. J., 18 n. 45
Bentham, Jeremy, 107 and n. 28
Berkeley, George, 127
Berlin, Isaiah, 140 and n. 8, 175–76
n. 102
Beyer, C. J., 163 n. 66
Blake, William, xii n. 6
Blanchard, Pierre, 100 n. 5
Bodin, Jean, 177
body and members, used as
political-moral concept in I
Corinthians, 19–20; in
Descartes, 138 n. 2; in Locke,
20–21; in Malebranche, 26–27; in
Montesquieu's *Persian Letters*
and *Romans*, 149–54; in Pascal's
Pensées, 18–22; in Rousseau's
"Bonheur Public," 21–22; in
Rousseau's "Chronologie
universelle," 206–207
Borgia, Cesare, treated by
Descartes, 138
Bossuet, Jacques Benigne, accuses
Malebranche of "naturalizing"
grace, 71–73; accuses
Malebranche of mis-using
Cartesianism, 72–73;
commissions Fénelon to write
against Malebranche, 74–77;
compared to Pascal, 67;
compared to Rousseau, 72, 191;
criticizes Malebranche's *Nature
et grâce*, 25, 45; critique of
Jansenism, 67–68; critique of
Richard Simon, 77; *Histoire
universelle* favors idea of
Providence générale, 73–74;

de Mairan, Dortous (*cont.*)
Malebranche's self-defense
against, 158 n. 55
Demolets, Nicolas, introduces
Montesquieu to Parisian society,
139; publishes several *pensées* of
Pascal, 139–40; puts together
Spicilège for Montesquieu, 152
de Montcheuil, Yves, *Malebranche
et le quiétisme,* 100 n. 5
Derathe, Robert, 141 n. 9, 176 n.
103
Desautels, A. R., 140 n. 6
Descartes, René, Cartesian
constancy in nature (for
Malebranche), 28; Cartesianism,
44–46, 58, 62, 72, 102, 116,
120–22, 138, 146, 147, 164, 168,
170, 189, 196, 233; letter to
Elisabeth on social duties, 138 n.
2; letter to Mersenne on grace
and Pelagianism, 123 n. 68;
Malebranche's reading of
Descartes as "Augustinian,"
121, 123 and n. 68; occasionalism
in Cartesianism, 120–22; on
Cesare Borgia, 138; treated by
Leibniz, 62; treated by
Montesquieu, 146–47; treated by
Rousseau in *Institutions
chymiques,* 233; and in
Confessions, 196
Desgraves, L., *Bibliothèque de
Montesquieu,* 157 n. 51
Diderot, Denis, compared to
Malebranche, 52–54; "Droit
Naturel" (*Encyclopédie*), 202–206;
general will "never errs," is "tie
of all societies" ("Droit
Naturel"), 4; general will as
morale universelle for entire *genre
humain,* 202–206; particular wills
are "suspect," 203; Rousseau's
critique of in *Première Version,*
202–211; Wokler on Rousseau's
debt to, ix, 203 n. 57
Dreyfus, Ginette, on general will
in Malebranche, xi n. 3, 25–26,
27 n. 74, 40 n. 103, 43, 71 n. 17;

La Volonté selon Malebranche, 100
n. 5, 119 nn. 56 and 58, 128 n.
81, 130 n. 90
Durkheim, Émile, 140 and n. 8
DuTertre, Rodolphe, 41–42

Edict of Nantes, 85
Ellenburg, Stephen, 249 n.
180.
Encyclopédie (ed. Diderot), Diderot,
"Droit Naturel," 3–4, 202–206;
Montesquieu, "Essai sur le
Goût," 160–61; Rousseau,
Économie politique, 210–12
Epictetus, 254
equality, as "general object" of
good politics in Rousseau's *Du
contrat social,* 217–21; Fénelon's
linking of equality, generality
and justice, 185–87;
Malebranche's theory of natural
equality in *Traité de morale,*
53–54; Rousseau, *Discourse on
Inequality,* 242–43
Escobar y Mendoza, Antonio, 92
Esquirol, L., 134 n. 98

Faydit, Pierre-Valentine, 70, 71 n.
16, 99–100
Fénelon, François de Salignac de la
Mothe de, admired by
Rousseau, 206–207; critic of
Malebranche as destroyer of
Providence particulière, 74–77;
critic of Malebranche's theory of
general will, 74–77; linking of
equality, generality and justice,
185–87; Malebranche's letter to
(1713), 125–26; on defects of
Malebranche's theory of grace,
117; Rousseau on Fénelon's
rejection of general will, 185–87;
treatment of Bossuet's *Histoire
universelle,* 77; treatment of grace
and predestination in letters to
Lami, 185–87
Five Propositions, *see* Jansenius,
Cornelius

Library of Congress Cataloging-in-Publication Data
Riley, Patrick, 1941-
  The general will before Rousseau.

  (Studies in moral, political, and legal philosophy)
  Includes index.
  1. General will—History. 2. Political science—
France—History. I. Title. II. Series.
JC328.2.R55 1986   320'.01'1   86-4859
ISBN 0-691-07720-7 (alk. paper)